# HOMO SEXU ALITY

## THE STRAIGHT AGENDA

Editor: Brian Edwards

Series Editor: Andrew Anderson

D1425231

© Day One Publications 1998
First printed 1998

Most scripture quotations are from The New International Version © 1973, 1978,
1984, International Bible Society. Published by Hodder and Stoughton.

British Library Cataloguing in Publication Data available
ISBN 0 902548 81 6

Day One Publications
3 Epsom Business Park
Kiln Lane
Epsom
Surrey  KT17 1JF
☎ 01372 728 300   **FAX** 01372 722 400
e-mail address: ldos.dayone@ukonline.co.uk

Designed by Steve Devane and printed by Clifford Frost Ltd, Wimbledon SW19 2SE

# Contents

# Foreword

FACING THE ISSUE is a series of books designed to help Christians to think biblically on a variety of pressing issues that confront evangelicals at the present time. The themes are primarily theological but, as the Bible never teaches doctrine in isolation, all have a keen practical edge to them.

The series began its life in the cut and thrust of discussion in the Theological Committee of the Fellowship of Independent Evangelical Churches whose brief is to monitor and respond to challenges and changes in the world of evangelical theology. The Committee commissions the writers, discusses their approach with them, and is available for consultation. Though united in our understanding of the gospel, we do not always come to exactly the same conclusions on every detail. So the views put forward by the authors do not necessarily reflect in every respect those of the Committee or, for that matter, those of the FIEC or the Publisher.

The series is written with the general reader in mind and the books do not assume a background training in theology. They are, however, written by people of proven ability in grappling with important theological trends. We hope that each book will stimulate thought and action—both controlled by the Bible.

**Andrew Anderson**
**Series Editor**

HOMOSEXUALITY: THE STRAIGHT AGENDA touches one of the most pressing issues for society and for the church—the issue of homosexual practice. The writers of this symposium believe that the teaching of the Bible is decisive on all matters of morality and they are convinced that, on this matter, its teaching is unequivocally straightforward.

The scheme of this book addresses itself to the male homosexual side of the debate. In biblical terms we do not believe there is any moral difference between gay and lesbian relationships, but there are significant differences which need to be recognised by those who seek to understand and help. Insufficient attention has been given to this area; it is our hope that some of the excellent organizations at work in this field will rectify this in the near future.

**Brian Edwards**
**Editor**

# Setting the Scene

Some denominations in Britain are facing the possibility of major schism between the politically correct and the biblically correct. General Secretary of the British Evangelical Council, **Alan Gibson,** presents a survey of the current scene

Albert Square may not be a real place but it does have real clout. Three times a week the goings on among its fictional East End residents are avidly followed by 18 million viewers. During 1996, BBC's Eastenders finally overtook Coronation Street in the ratings war, so ITV hit back with an additional Sunday episode. The pundits looked for the explanation, however, not in the scheduling but in the content of these old rivals. Eastenders had become so much spicier than the veteran Granada soap opera. A prominent storyline at the time featured Tony dumping his live-in girl friend in favour of her brother, Simon. The programme covered his wrestling with his sexuality, his 'coming-out', and the way his father eventually came to terms with the real Simon. The Rovers Return just could not compete with it.

The powerful influence of media images must not be underestimated. By bringing Tony and Simon's homosexual kiss into the nation's living rooms at peak viewing time the programme's producers were pursuing a deliberate policy. Media portrayal of homosexuality is mainly designed to underline its essential normality. If Brookside, Neighbours and even the once gentle Emmerdale are to reflect society and grapple with its issues then, it is argued, they must portray lesbians and gays as no more unusual than the red-haired and the left-handed. In fact, they must go further. They must redress the generations of misunderstanding and repression these folk have endured by portraying them positively, sensitively and courageously. So this is the diet on which our young people are fed. The propaganda must be driven home not only in the late afternoon studio audience discussions imported from the USA and in the minority interest Channel 4 'Dyke TV' series, but in the mass audience soaps.

A whirlwind has swept our generation. Our fathers found it hard to look us in the eye and speak the word 'homosexual'. For them, gay still meant 'cheerful' or 'brightly-coloured'. Now our children have become as street-wise as their peers. They are the first generation to be taught in school about Aids and to be de-sensitised by the 'safe-sex' education experts. They now know precisely which politically correct answers will not offend the Equal Opportunities policy of their job application forms. Where race discrimination began, sex discrimination has not been slow to follow. A vocal minority in society ensures that the subject is never far from their impressionable minds.

## College life

A review of the student scene will be instructive at this point. College life is a focused microcosm where the future attitudes and actions of society at large are already being worked out. While a generation of Christian students has deliberately stood aloof from student politics, the gay lobby has been active in pushing their agenda. Gay students have become involved in the democratic processes of the local Students' Union branch through many channels, the university newspaper and radio, the elected posts on the various representative councils and the Students' Union executive. Once in post they have often been successful in passing 'anti-discriminatory' policies against what they now call 'heterosexism'. They have become extremely powerful, not least at the level of the National Union of Students, in which it is now very hard to get elected unless you are actively promoting gay rights. They know that today's students are tomorrow's leaders and see their role not only in 'educating' the whole student body but also in deliberately challenging first-years to examine their own sexuality. All this is going on in an atmosphere where individual 'rights' are beyond challenge and every person has the right to express his or her own sexuality in whichever way they may choose.

In the last ten years there has been a significant switch in the universities from the title 'Gay Soc' to the more generic 'Lesbian, Gay and Bisexual' group, LGB for short. There has also been growing acceptance of bisexuality as a valid alternative life-style. This has several implications. It affects the standard defence, 'well I was just made that way, it is as natural for me to be attracted to people of the same sex as it is for you to be attracted to the opposite sex'. The essentially bi-sexual cannot claim either attraction to be 'natural' for him or her, it is merely a matter of choice. By the same token then, anyone choosing only opposite sex partners is merely exercising the same choice. But even more is at stake. Granting moral approval to the active bisexual is an implicit sanctioning of promiscuity. A person can, theoretically at least, be faithful to a partner of the opposite sex or to a partner of the same sex. To be bisexual is, by definition however, to be sexually active with more than one sex, which means involving at the very least more than one partner. Any concept of faithfulness goes out of the window.

With characteristic vigour the LGBs have often challenged the Christian presence in the universities in a determined manner. Some have argued that no society open to students should have a 'closed membership' which is restricted to those with particular doctrinal views. Others have attempted to label all Christians as bigots, unworthy of being elected to any student committee. Christian Union meetings advertised to handle sexual topics have been heckled and even closed down. Regrettably, the Christian response to these pressures in recent years has not always been wise. Adopting a confrontational approach has proved counter-productive and Christian Unions are having to learn that quoting passages from Leviticus, however well intentioned, is simply not an adequate response.

This book is about precisely that question. What does represent a proper evangelical response to the enormous social pressures of the homosexual lobby today? What are the moral and social issues which our generation is now facing? Some of these are intensely pastoral and practical but behind them we now find there is debate about the basic biblical teaching. Even within the churches, attitudes are changing and long-held assumptions are being questioned. How are we to cope with these new challenges?

## Twentieth century culture

Why has the twentieth century seen such an explosion of interest in homosexuality? The apparent increase in bisexuality may throw some light on this question of great interest in contemporary society. If a percentage of the population is born with a congenital disposition of sexual attraction to the same sex then we would expect that proportion to be more or less equal in every generation and in every culture. Those who adopt this view suggest that nineteenth century Victorian prudery repressed the expression of these desires in the Western world until a more liberal atmosphere permitted them to surface again. And surface they most certainly did! Almost fifty years ago the Kinsey Report astonished us in claiming that 37% of American males engaged in some homosexual experience[1]. Subsequent re-appraisal of Kinsey has shown that its findings were greatly exaggerated, being based on an unrepresentative sample but even revised claims are still being made for proportions between 4 and 10 percent. There are others who suggest, however, that homosexual orientation is largely a product of cultural factors, whether the influence of the individual's childhood experience or the effect of the moral environment in wider society. This 'nature-nurture' debate is well documented by the American evangelical Thomas Schmidt[2] and we shall give it fuller consideration in Chapter 3.

What are we to make then of the bisexuals? Kinsey did at least throw some light on this issue by showing that the development of personal sexual identity does go through various stages. He introduced a rating scale between 0 [exclusively heterosexual with no homosexual tendencies] to 6 [exclusively homosexual]. It is also well established that in closed communities, like single sex schools or prisons, a number of individuals use those of the same sex as a substitute for partners of the opposite sex. Apart from anything else, this does warn us all against the simplistic identification of an individual as 'a homosexual', as if this fixes their personality and behaviour pattern for the whole of their life. It has been further suggested that at least some homosexual activity is a deliberate rejection of the family structure within society. The libertarianism of the so-called 'swinging sixties' gave rein to a moral anarchy from which Western civilisation has never fully recovered. A tape recording of an early Nationwide Festival of Light meeting in 1971 picks up the heckling from the crowd and includes someone from a homosexual movement shouting 'Death to the family'[3]. For whatever reasons, subsequent decades have seen a steady erosion of the role of the nuclear family in the fabric of community life.

While the majority of homosexuals enjoying a higher profile in public life may not be politically motivated, there can be little doubt that their numbers and influence are contributing to this decline. They are now to be found among the highest earners in the entertainment industry, with people like George Melly in the jazz scene, Julian Clary prominent in what is known as 'alternative comedy' and Elton John an elder statesman of pop music. Millions who have never read a line of Michel Foucault's post-modernist depravity or Jeanette Winterson's lesbian fantasies witness show-biz personalities promoting the same life-style in the public arena. After all, it is only one of the pick-'n-mix sexualities on offer today. But what kind of role-models are being provided for the rising generation?

To keep all this in perspective, however, we must remember that it is only a vocal minority who are pursuing this moral revolution. The great majority of men in Britain (70%) still think that sex between men is always or mostly wrong, well over half (58%) of women agreed and an American survey in 1989 found that three-quarters of respondents said the same [4]. As with some other moral issues, those pressing for social change have got into the driving seat. A supposed intellectual elite, it is they who command attention from the mass media ever hungry for a bit of drama. Patient pastors tending their flocks do not make the headlines. If a celibate bishop runs off with a widow or a prominent MP is 'outed'—that really does sell newspapers! By the same token, confrontation between traditionalists and liberalisers always makes good copy, even in the church.

## Church controversies

It is to be expected that attitudes in the churches change more slowly than those in society at large. Yet if this change is slower it is no less marked and it is perhaps more painful. Some denominations in Britain are currently facing the possibility of major schism between the politically correct and the biblically correct.

In 1991 the Church of England bishops produced a discussion document, Issues in Human Sexuality, which has never been approved by General Synod and, formally at least, has not replaced the earlier Synod decision on this subject. That was passed in 1987 with a 98% majority and it insisted that all homosexual practice is sinful and 'is to be met by a call to repentance'. By a strange compromise, the bishops' report insists that nobody can be ordained who engages in genital homosexual activity but accepts that such acts should not debar anyone from church membership. In order to clarify their own theological principles, the Church of England Evangelical Council issued The St. Andrew's Day Statement in 1995 in which they insisted that 'the church ... assists all its members to a life of faithful witness in chastity and holiness, recognising two forms of vocation in which that life can be lived: marriage and singleness. There is no place for the church to confer legitimacy upon alternatives to these'.

'Reform', an evangelical grouping in the Church of England, conducted a survey of bishops in 1996 asking them to affirm the traditional view, to discipline those who dissent from it and to ordain only those who teach and model it in their own lives. Only 11 bishops were prepared to subscribe to these statements, 27 replied that they were not willing to subscribe and over 50 refused to respond at all. Unsurprisingly, Reform is deeply troubled that bishops with a responsibility 'to banish and drive away all erroneous and strange opinions'[5] should be perceived as moving away from the clear teaching of the Bible. In March 1996 Reform appointed two 'Regional Advisers' to exercise oversight on behalf of those looking for an alternative to the existing episcopate. Many see this as a step towards their seeking to appoint their own bishops and the Archbishop of Canterbury warned that 'it is certain to bring them into renewed collision with ... the church hierarchy'[6].

Further controversy was inevitable when Southwark Cathedral was used in November 1996 for the celebration of the 20th anniversary of the Lesbian and Gay Christian Movement. The Bishop of Guildford, John Gladwin, used his sermon to defend both heterosexual marriage and the validity of a gay presence within the unity of the church. Even before this historic event the fires had been stoked by Anne Atkins, an evangelical novelist and wife of an Anglican vicar in London, whose 'Thought for the Day' radio broadcast criticised the Church authorities for its soft line on homosexual activity. What seemed to cause most offence was her insistence that, 'It is the Church's duty to condemn sin'[7]. Such plain speaking brought her considerable grass roots support but incurred the wrath of the Church of England communications director, who demanded an apology from the BBC for allowing her to say such things on the air! Shortly afterwards Dr George Carey tried to be even-handed in commenting on the Southwark controversy[8] but his denouncing opponents of gay rights as 'bullying, loud-mouthed controversialists' was welcomed by the LGCM and did nothing to cool the temperature of the evangelicals, who objected to being treated as the equivalent of the gay pressure groups.

The 1997 General Synod was heavily lobbied by the LGCM and heard of plans for the Lambeth Conference, the ten-yearly meeting of heads of the world-wide Anglican communion, to set up an international commission on the issue. This was the system which led to the ordination of women and it provoked one traditional spokesman to say that, 'The floodgates have just been opened. The debate will be seen as an amber light here and as a green light in America. The commission will be an interim stage to an inevitable end'.[9]

The whole debate is set to become the next major flash point for dissent within the national church in England as it focuses the centuries-old issue of whether Scripture, church teaching or human reason is to have the final voice. The crunch issue will be whether the Church formalises in statute what some bishops have openly acknowledged they have done in the past, that is, the ordaining of practising homosexuals into the ministry. Some in the Reform grouping have already complained of the 'creeping institutionalisation of homosexual relationships' in the Church and suggested that this would be the catalyst for their reluctant secession from the Church of England.

An international conference of evangelical Anglicans from the southern hemisphere met in Malaysia during 1997 and issued a significant declaration of the conservative position on Scripture and a range of moral issues. The 'Kuala Lumpur Statement' pointedly rebuts, among other topics, the revisionist case on homosexuality and has already become a banner to rally those maintaining traditional concerns. The Reform conference that year affirmed its support for this Statement. Jesmond Parish Church also allied itself to the Statement, when its parochial church council refused to accept the oversight of the newly appointed Bishop of Newcastle, Martin Wharton, who said on his appointment that 'homosexuality within a loving permanent relationship is no sin'.

It is becoming clear that conservative Anglicans see more hope for a traditional consensus at the international level in the Lambeth Conference of the Anglican Communion than in the national discussions of the General Synod in England. The Southern Cone, as it is known, contains a raft of conservative delegates from Australia and Africa, in contrast to the northern hemisphere representatives, among whom the more liberal Anglicans of North America have a strong financial and numerical influence.

A distinct polarisation has been taking place among British Methodists since a denominational Conference in 1993 agreed a group of statements, which are now being interpreted in opposite ways. The evangelicals assumed that commitment to 'chastity' meant 'no sex outside marriage' but others are claiming that it means no more than 'faithfulness within a relationship', whatever form that relationship might take. In America, 40% of United Methodist representatives at a 1996 meeting voted that homosexuality is not 'incompatible with Christian teaching' and 15 bishops called for them to ordain homosexuals[10].

Here in the UK, a United Reformed Church Working Party Report prompted a robust response from GEAR [The Group for Evangelism and Renewal] in 1993, fearful that, 'the biblical witness to God's condemnation of homosexual activity was being set aside by other Christians' and calling for a debate and a resolution upholding the traditional Christian view.[11] The Assembly voted in July 1997 'to arrange for further work to be done ecumenically ... on the nature of Biblical authority for the life of the church; [and on] the implications of ordaining ministers in committed homosexual relationships'.[12] They also agreed that while this further work is done, the Assembly would 'uphold a call to such an ordinand or minister issued by a local church'[13] and recognised that the fact of a homosexual relationship shall not be the ground for rejecting a candidate for ministry. It is at local church level, then, that the door is now open and it is not surprising that the URC is setting up a Working Group to enable sensitive care of all those who feel pain and distress as a result of these measures.

Pressure on Bible-believing churches in the USA is much farther advanced than in Britain and at this stage it is not easy to say how much effect the Righter case will have here. In 1990 Bishop Walter C Righter ordained a professing homosexual to the diaconate of the Episcopal Church, which is itself in communion with Canterbury. For this he was accused of heresy, that is of action which violated church doctrine; his opponents cited the Church's 1979 General Convention resolution deeming it 'inappropriate for this Church to ordain a practicing homosexual or any person who is engaged in heterosexual relationships outside of marriage'. Despite that ruling, 25 of the 100 dioceses already do so and four of his judges had 'done the same thing as the accused has done'. In May 1996, however, these charges were dismissed by 7 out of 8 bishops sitting in a church court, claiming that ordaining homosexuals is not contrary to doctrine, which they defined as 'the essence of Christianity ... that which is necessary for salvation'. Only one dissenting Bishop, James M Stanton, held that the doctrine of God is in fact violated by Righter's action since, 'It takes maleness and femaleness, masculinity and femininity, coming together to reflect the image of God'[14]. If Stanton is correct, as we are convinced he is, then the homosexual issue is significantly broadened. Those committed to overthrowing the traditional Christian view are not only pushing out the boundaries of Christian morality, they also constitute a threat to consistently Christian doctrine.

David Monteath of St Helen's Church, Bishopsgate, does not go too far in portraying the 1996 LCGM Celebration not as Christianity at all but as '... a lie. What we were witnessing in Southwark was not simply the broadening of the Church of England to accommodate practising homosexuals but rather the emergence of a new religion altogether, in which the gay community becomes the people of God, in which conversion to Christ is replaced by 'coming out', in which sin (homophobia excepted) is not repented of but celebrated. Like a virus invading a cell, the new religion appropriates the language of Christianity and hijacks the infrastructure of the Church of England for the purpose of its own self-replication, while well-meaning bishops beam on benignly.'[15]

## Evangelical attitudes

One serious feature calling for more immediate comment, however, is how the former consensus about homosexual issues among those professing to be evangelical Christians has been breaking down. As long ago as 1984, the Evangelical Fellowship within the Gay Christian Movement produced a booklet in which Jeremy Ridgway, a former student of the London Bible College, protests that he holds an orthodox doctrine of Scripture but he applies it with a situational ethic which rules out nothing except sex that hurts another. One reviewer pointed out, however, that the writers Joseph Fletcher and James Barr, whom Ridgway recommends for further reading 'are no more evangelical than Ian Paisley is a papist'![16] At that time the evangelical apologists for homosexuality did not have any arguments of their own, they were simply recycling those of the liberal authors who condoned their way of life. They accepted that the Bible does condemn homosexual behaviour but denied that this is proscriptive for our own generation. Any Old Testament rule-based ethic was condemned as 'legalism' and inconsistent with the gospel of love. The New Testament writers were dismissed as children of their age whose teaching is not normative for us today.

But things have been changing. In 1979 an evangelical academic David Atkinson, then teaching ethics at Wycliffe Hall, wrote a scholarly reply[17] to the liberal D Sherwin Bailey's seminal 1955 work which purported to question the western Christian tradition on biblical grounds. Although not 'popular' in style Atkinson's booklet was highly thought of and at the time many regarded it as the best serious evangelical treatment of the topic. In December 1995, however, Atkinson wrote an extended article in a professedly evangelical publication qualifying his earlier views in the light of his subsequent experience. 'I mostly hold to the biblical work I did then and to the moral theology I developed then. But I would now want to put all of this in a much larger context—to say much more about social justice and the evils of discrimination against people on the grounds of their sexual orientation. And I want to listen much more now to the testimony of the prayerful, godly, Christ-centred, gospel-motivated Christian people who do not believe that their same-sex orientation is for them a calling to a life of celibacy, and who can thank God for their homosexual orientation, and sometimes celebrate the gift of a partner in a stable, faithful, loving and permanent relationship.' Atkinson goes so far as to say that a stable same-sex relationship 'can be understood as a responsible way to make moral sense of life in an imperfect situation.'[18] It is surely significant that what brought about this change of view was not further light from careful exegetical study; it was the testimony of people he has been listening to. In other words, his previous evangelical position has been modified by factors entirely outside Scripture itself.

We shall need to develop this point later but its importance cannot be exaggerated. Recent years have seen marked growth in the evangelical constituency in Britain. Those professing to accept the Bible as their authority are on the increase. But how are they using the Bible? If it is being interpreted in ways inconsistent with Scripture then we are drifting near treacherous rocks. Already we hear young men justifying their unchaste behaviour by the arguments of Michael Vasey's 'new exploration of homosexuality and the Bible'.[19]

This area of concern goes beyond personal morality to raise important issues about the nature of biblical authority and what is essential to authentic evangelical identity. That is why we shall have to give special attention to a discussion of hermeneutics, the science of biblical interpretation. This is where the action is. It has already proved crucial for issues as diverse as those of feminism and eternal punishment. The loss of evangelical consensus over homosexuality is a marker for far wider issues as well.

And that is not all. Loss of confidence in the Bible will do enormous damage to our public witness. If the Bible is not considered adequate to expose the roots of the current same-sex phenomena then neither will our society look to the Bible for answers to the problems these issues pose. Tragically, our generation will turn away from the only message which can bring it real hope. How we use the Bible is never merely an academic issue; in the long run, the gospel itself is at stake.

The New Testament predicted this process with frightening accuracy. In Romans 1 the Apostle Paul shows that a society's moral and social behaviour is a reflection of its spiritual orientation. He traces a downward spiral from men suppressing the truth, to increasing degradation, which itself results in idolatry and reaps futility of life in every sphere of human conduct. This is not some abstract principle of cause and effect but the judgement of a righteous God, giving men up to the fateful consequences of their evil choices. While other forms of wickedness are mentioned, it is the shameful lusts of homosexuality to which Paul gives greatest prominence.[20]

## People matter

The whole scene may be viewed then, from a range of perspectives. It has social, doctrinal, exegetical and ethical dimensions. It affects how we think about the morality of sex, how we understand the Bible, how we use it and how we cope with change in our community life. But above all, most discussion of homosexuality is about people, real people, otherwise ordinary people. That is where Thomas Schmidt begins his invaluable book [see Appendix B], not with doctrine but with people. 'I sit staring at a computer screen looking for words to introduce a moral issue, an issue so important that it increasingly appears to be the battleground for all the forces seeking to give shape to the world of the next century. What appear before me, however, are not words but faces.'[21] Before he introduces his discussion of Scripture teaching and his salutary exposure of the physical and psychological pain associated with homosexuality he introduces us to people he has known, people who love and want to be loved, some of them wanting to love those of the same sex and some of these being Christians.

What saves Schmidt from the cold abstraction of doctrine divorced from life must also warn us of the same danger. Even labelling someone 'a homosexual' can be misleading and even a hindrance to our helping them. A person may feel attractions of a sexual nature toward someone of the opposite sex and, recognising the biblical prohibitions on sex outside marriage, neither indulge fantasies nor act out those desires. Temptation is not sin; it is yielding to temptation which is sin. To illustrate this point, an evangelical preacher once described himself as a 'celibate adulterer'. He admits to being tempted to heterosexual adultery but knowing it is wrong, he resists the temptation and has never committed the sin. There is no shame in that.

Unfortunately in the discussion of this moral issue we have no unambiguous term to use for those who feel but do not give in to homosexual temptation. Some have spoken of individuals having an 'orientation' to same-sex desire and others of the 'celibate homosexual'. The gay lobby has a vested interest in promoting the concept of sexual identity, as if this is the one feature which determines every person's life-style. Once that is admitted, then the inviolable human right to self expression is invoked in their claims for civic funds and community support for their interests. In the USA, the State of Hawaii has taken the first steps towards the recognition of 'gay marriage' by granting state benefits to homosexual partners. In Britain gay lobbying succeeded in reducing the age of consent for homosexual intercourse from 21 to 18 years and the election of a Labour government in 1997 made more likely a further move to 16 years and parity with heterosexuality. In most Western countries any questioning of this political correctness is pilloried as 'homophobia' or condemned as bigotry.

The Church of England Evangelical Council's 1995 contribution to the controversy within its own denomination is worthy of wider usefulness. It contains a warning against allowing others to define the terms on which the debate is fought. 'Our sexual affections can no more define who we are than can our class, race or nationality. At the deepest ontological level, therefore, there is no such thing as 'a' homosexual or 'a' heterosexual; there are human beings, male and female, called to redeemed humanity in Christ, endowed with a complex variety of emotional potentialities and threatened by a complex variety of forms of alienation.'[22] In this way they are seeking to answer the argument that young people can be dubbed 'gay' and that's that. Once labelled, they no longer see themselves as persons created in God's image and called by the gospel to a holy life in Christ consistent with that image. But what is crucial to our identity is our relationship with God, not our relationship with any other person, nor even with our own sexuality.

It may well be that, for some who read this book, the subject is not just theoretical, it is intensely personal. They are among the small proportion of people who are physically and emotionally attracted not to those of the opposite sex but to those of their own. Some attend evangelical churches; the conversion of people from the world around makes this inevitable. A society where unstable marriages are the rule, not the exception, is bound to lead to confusion over gender identity. Sexual desire is driven by the problem of aloneness, something all too common in our fractured society. Peer pressure and media exploitation are bringing to the surface problems which may have been repressed in former generations. Those working in this field speak of Christians feeling battered by both sides of the Church debate and afraid to share their true feelings with those nearest to them. So however uncomfortable some may find these issues, they can no longer be avoided by responsible Christians. That is why this book has been written.

The subject is complex. It will involve us in discussion of the social, biblical, and personal aspects of homosexuality. This is a topic in which few would profess to be 'experts'; hence the book is a symposium. The writers are from different backgrounds but they all share the same gospel convictions. We are convinced that love should hallmark all our words and actions and that means that we are strongly opposed to the victimisation of homosexuals. 'There is absolutely no biblical basis for 'gay-bashing'—verbal as well as physical, abuse of homosexuals—of any description'.[23] Such love for them constrains us to listen carefully to those who may differ from us. But our love for them also compels us to bring them face to face with the absolute wisdom and authority of the word of God, the Maker and Judge to whom we must all answer.

If the gospel saves from sin then it saves from all sin. How then does the good news of Jesus Christ relate to these issues? What do we have to say to the brazen and unashamed campaigner? And to the sensitive and confused struggler? We shall be looking at the pastoral and the evange-listic implications of this subject in a biblical and sensitive manner [chapter 11]. Our aim is to bring the Bible's light into an area some find dark, and Christ's love into an area with which many find it hard to sympathise.

### About the author

**Alan Gibson** spent 24 years in pastoral ministry in independent evangelical churches before becoming General Secretary of the British Evangelical council in 1982. He obtained a theology degree from London University while at the London Bible College. Alan has worked with the FIEC Citizenship Committee—formerly the Public Questions Committee—for over 25 years. A founder member of the Evangelical Coalition on Sexuality, he served on that body for eight years. He and his wife, Jacqueline, are involved in the life of Spicer Street Chapel, St Albans. They would enjoy having more time to visit their three married children and seven grand-children

## Chapter 1 notes

1   **A C Kinsey, W B Pomeroy** & **C E Martin**, *Sexual Behaviour in the Human Male*, Philadelphia, 1948.

2   **Thomas E Schmidt**, *Straight and Narrow?*, Inter Varsity Press, 1995, chapter 7.

3   **D J Atkinson**, *Homosexuals in the Christian Fellowship*, Latimer Studies, 1979, p 7.

4   *Sexual Attitudes and Lifestyles*, Blackwell, Oxford, 1994, p 241.

5   Canon C18.

6   quoted in *Fulcrum*, magazine of Action for Biblical Witness to our Nation, Summer 96, p 7.

7   *Thought For The Day*, BBC Today Programme, 10 November 1996.

8   *Daily Mail*, report of sermon at Great St Mary's, Cambridge, 24 November 1996.

9   **Rev Stephen Trott,** *The Times*, 15 July 1997.

10  *Christianity Today*, 17 June 1996, p 58.

11  *Homosexuality & the Gospel*, 1995.

12  Resolution 18, Assembly of the United Reformed Church, July 1997.

13  Resolution 19, b) 2.

14  *Christianity Today*, 17 June 1996, p 57.

15  *Evangelicals Now*, January 1997, p 1.

16  **David Field,** *Third Way*, March 1985, p 28.

17  **D J Atkinson,** *Homosexuals in the Christian Fellowship*, Latimer Studies.

18  *Third Way*, December 1995.

19  **M Vasey,** *Strangers and Friends*, Hodder & Stoughton, 1995.

20  Romans 1:18-32.

21  See ref 19, p 11.

22  *The St Andrew's Day Statement*, 30 November 1995, Church of England Evangelical Council.

23  CARE *Briefing Paper* No 28, February 1992.

# Learning from history

In order to understand how so many denominations are in turmoil over homosexuality today, we need to turn to history, argues **Kenneth Brownell** pastor and editor of the theological magazine *Foundations*

On Saturday, 15 November, 1996 a service was held in Southwark Cathedral in London celebrating the 20th anniversary of the Lesbian and Gay Christian Movement. That such a movement exists at all is distressing for many Christians, but sadly not all that surprising. That a service celebrating its founding was held in a cathedral of the Church of England is still more distressing. But most distressing and surprising of all is that the preacher at the service was a bishop who calls himself an evangelical. How have we arrived at this point? The purpose of this chapter is simply to trace the path that led to that service in Southwark Cathedral. Of course in itself the service was a relatively minor event, but it did symbolise a major shift of outlook within society in general and the Christian church in particular. For evangelical Christians who want to remain faithful to Scripture and to the historic teaching of the church this presents a great challenge. It is important for us to know how Christians of previous generations looked at this matter, and to learn from them as we try to obey God in very different circumstances today.

Of course there are some people for whom the service in Southwark was neither distressing nor surprising. For them it indicated that the church was at long last returning to the attitude it originally had concerning homosexual behaviour. Until relatively recently it was generally assumed that the church had always been opposed to sexual activity between people of the same gender and it was also assumed that this position was firmly based on the teaching of the Bible. Today there is an increasing number of people who question this assumption. The first significant dissent from the prevailing view came in 1955 with the publication of D. Sherwin Bailey's book, *Homosexuality and the Western Christian Tradition*[1]. Bailey's thesis is that the traditional Christian hostility to homosexual activity is built on a misunderstanding of Genesis 19 and the sin of Sodom. Rather than being guilty of wanting to homosexually rape Lot's visitors the men of Sodom were guilty of inhospitality[2]. Others have followed the path Bailey pioneered, the most significant to date being Professor John Boswell of Yale University. In two remarkable books—*Christianity, Social Tolerance and Homosexuality: Gay Christians in Western Europe from the Beginning of the Christian Era to the Fourteenth Century* (1989) and *The Marriage of Likeness: Same Sex Unions in pre-Modern Europe* (1994)[3]—Professor Boswell has sought completely to revise the way in which we understand homosexuality historically. Boswell contends that since the 14th century the church has misunderstood the New Testament teaching and has turned away from an earlier, more tolerant view of homosexuality. While Boswell's conclusions, and indeed his handling of the historical material, have been challenged by fellow academics, his views have been widely accepted in many church circles. For many, Boswell has proved the case that the church must return to a more open and tolerant attitude to homosexuality and even recognise same sex marriages[4]. A recent example is Michael Vasey's *Strangers and Friends* (1995) which is the first book in Great Britain written by a professing evangelical to advocate the recognition of same sex relationships.[5]

In surveying the history of Christian attitudes to homosexuality I will have to take into account this revisionist thinking. Given the limits of space I will of necessity have to be somewhat selective and perhaps superficial in my treatment. Nevertheless I will show that there is no need to revise our understanding of the church's historic position on the practice of homosexuality, but rather every reason to maintain it in spite of the strong cultural pressure to the contrary.

## The Early Church (100-600)

Christianity was born into a social context in which male homosexuality was tolerated and widely practised. The homosexuality or bisexuality of many of the emperors is well-known, but the evidence for male prostitution shows that homosexuality was not confined to the higher reaches of society. In Roman society it was permitted for men freely to engage in sexual activity with inferiors, especially with slaves.[6] There were limits, however, and homosexuality involving children (pederasty) was not tolerated legally or socially. Although there were relatively few laws relating to homosexuality before the fourth century AD, those that did exist were concerned primarily with pederasty. This was the background against which Paul wrote his letters and the early fathers taught. Subsequent chapters will deal with the biblical teaching on homosexuality, but at this point it is important to see that there is a clear continuity between the teaching of the New Testament and that of the early church. The early church fathers condemned the practice of homosexuality just as roundly as did the apostle Paul. The social historian Eva Cantarella, a leading authority in this area, writes: 'The fact that Christian teaching condemned homosexuality from the beginning is a fact (although sometimes denied) that emerges with absolute clarity from the sources'. She goes on to write that 'Paul's preaching ... lays the foundation for a new sexual ethic, which Christian writers in the following centuries were to repeat with decisive certainty, without any concession or hesitation'.[7]

What is the evidence for this? There are a number of references to homosexuality in some of the earliest Christian writings. In the *Didache* or the Teaching of the Apostles (second to third centuries) there is a household code similar to that in the New Testament letters. Here homosexual activity involving young boys is prohibited: 'Do not murder; do not commit adultery; do not corrupt boys; do not fornicate; do not practice magic ...'.[8] Later in the fourth century the *Apostolical Constitutions* of the Syrian Church incorporated and expanded the *Didache*: 'You shall not corrupt boys; for this wickedness is contrary to nature, and arose from Sodom, which was therefore entirely consumed with fire sent from God. Let such a one be accursed and all the people shall say "Amen"'.[9] In his *Apology* (c.155 AD) **Justin Martyr** (d.165) mentions how Christians did not give away their children as pagans often did 'for the purpose of sodomy'.[10] The Latin lawyer and theologian **Tertullian** (c.160-c.220) writes in *Against Marcion* of how God 'punishes with death both sacrilegious incest and the portentous madness of lust against male persons and cattle'. In his later Montanist period Tertullian was even more forthright in his condemnation: '... all other frenzies of the lusts that exceed the laws of nature and are impious towards both [human] bodies and the sexes, we banish, not only from the threshold but also from all shelter of the Church, for they are not sins so much as monstrosities'.[11] **Lactantius** (c.240-c.320) wrote in his *Divine Institutes* that when God created two sexes he 'placed in them the desire of each other and joy in union. So he put in bodies the most ardent desire of all living things, so that they might rush most avidly into those emotions and be able by this means to propagate and increase their kind'. This was the divine order and the devil opposes it by tempting people into sexual immorality. 'The [devil] has even joined males and has contrived abominable intercourse against nature and against the institution of God'. [12]

Slowly the cultural environment around the church began to change. In the later Roman empire homosexual practice was tolerated less and less, especially among the urban middle classes. New laws proscribing homosexuality appeared from the third century onwards. Why did this change occur? Historians attribute the change in part to the dominance of Christianity by the fourth century. Eva Cantarella writes that '[by] Justinian's time, the patristic writers had worked out a theology of sexuality which condemned relationships between persons of the same sex as "against nature"'. She notes that there was also a profound change in pagan morality in this period 'from bisexuality, based on aggressive gratification into heterosexuality based on reproduction'. In short, chastity became a virtue. There are a number of reasons for this, but one is the formative influence of Christianity on the culture as it sought 'to introduce a different sexual ethic'.[13]

Among the most influential theologians in this later period were the three great Cappadocian fathers—Basil of Caesarea, his brother

Gregory of Nyssa and their friend Gregory of Nazianzus—who dealt with the issue of homosexuality in their teaching. Around 375 **Basil** (c.330-379) wrote that 'he who is guilty of unseemliness with males will be under discipline for the same time as adulterers'.[14] One of the greatest preachers of the early church was **John Chrysostom** (c.345-407), given that name,'the golden mouthed', because of his eloquence.

Chrysostom was forthright in his opposition to homosexuality. When he was the principal preacher of Antioch he faced the pastoral problem of homosexual activity among the children of Christians that even their parents tolerated. In the following quotation there may be an element of rhetorical exaggeration, but it indicates something of the problems of maintaining biblical standards in a sexually permissive culture.

'Those very people who have been nourished by godly doctrine, who instruct others in what they ought and ought not to do, who have heard the Scriptures brought down from heaven, these do not consort with prostitutes as fearlessly as they do with men. The fathers of the young men take this in silence: they do not try to sequester their sons, nor do they seek any remedy for this evil. None is ashamed, no one blushes, they take pride in their little game; the chaste seem to be the odd ones, and the disapproving the ones in error. If these disapprovers are insignificant, they are intimidated; if they are powerful, they are mocked and laughed at, refuted with a thousand arguments. The courts are powerless, the laws, instructions, parents, friends, teachers—all helpless.'[15]

After Chrysostom became bishop of Constantinople, the imperial capital, in 398 he continued to be uncompromising in upholding biblical teaching. In his sermon on Romans 1:26-27 he calls sexual lust vile, but especially 'lust after males' and, referring to Sodom, sees the greatness of the sin in the fact that it 'forced hell to appear even before its time'. For Chrysostom homosexual activity was unnatural and destructive of human society. The sermon deals with the whole issue of homosexuality very thoroughly and at great length.[16]

Chrysostom's contemporary Augustine (354-430), bishop of Hippo in north Africa was equally strong in his opposition. Augustine is one of the towering theological figures of the Christian church and one of the most formative intellectual influences on western culture. In his *Confessions* he comments on homosexuality in the context of discussing his own struggle with heterosexual lust as a young man.

'Can it be wrong for any of us at any time or in any place to love God with his whole heart, and with his whole soul, and with his whole mind, and to love his neighbour as himself? Therefore, vicious deeds that are contrary to nature, are everywhere and always detested and punished, such as were those of the men of Sodom. Even if all nations should do these deeds, they would all be held in equal guilt under the divine law, for it has not made men in such fashion that they should use one another in this way. For in truth society itself, which must obtain between God and us, is violated, when the nature of which he is author is perverted by a polluted lust.'[17]

In his greatest work, *The City of God,* Augustine returns to this theme. Speaking of Sodom he says that:

'It was a place where sexual promiscuity among males had grown into a custom so prevalent that it received the kind of sanction generally afforded by law to other activities. But the punishment of the men of Sodom was a foretaste of the divine judgment to come. And there is a special significance that those who were being rescued by the angels were forbidden to look back. Does it not tell us that we must not return in thought to the old life, which is sloughed off when a man is reborn by grace, if we look to escape the final judgment?'[18]

The teaching of the early fathers was reflected in official enactments of church councils. The Council of Elvira in Spain in 305-6 forbade practising homosexuals to take communion. A few years later in 314 the Council of Ancyra (Ankara) addressed the issue of those who 'commit defilement with animals or males'. Much later the second Council of Tours in 567 sought more rigorously to enforce the Rule of St. Benedict which among other things forbade monks from sleeping in the same bed. [19] Apparently there was a problem with homosexuality in the monasteries that had begun to spread throughout Christendom from the fourth century onwards. Basil of Caesarea had to counsel monks under his supervision to avoid situations in which they might be tempted in this area.[20]

It is clear from this brief survey that the early church was opposed to the practice of homosexuality for four reasons: it was harmful to young boys; it was against nature; it was the sin for which Sodom was punished by fire, and it was contrary to the divine order as revealed in Scripture. This would remain the church's basic position until the present day.

Recently some historians have challenged this interpretation of the early church's attitude towards homosexuality. In particular, John Boswell has tried to show that the early church was far more tolerant than has been commonly thought. Boswell's stated intention is to show that the church has not always been opposed to homosexual behaviour. He claims, for example, that there were some well-known practising homosexual Christians such as Paulinus of Nola and his friend Arsonius. His evidence for this is the affectionate way in which they addressed each other in their letters. He claims that early Christians practised homosexual acts, based largely on the evidence of accusations brought against Christians by their opponents. He also subjects the relevant passages from the early fathers to intense critical scrutiny in an attempt to relativise their force.[21] In his book *The Marriage of Likeness,* Boswell argues that the early church sanctioned same-sex 'marriages' for which there were appropriate liturgies.[22]

Boswell's argument is very sophisticated, but also very questionable. Fellow historians have challenged his methods and questioned his conclusions. He has been accused of 'advocacy scholarship' in trying to use history to support a contemporary cause, in this case homosexual rights. The Roman Catholic theologian and cultural commentator John Richard Neuhaus describes Boswell's method in this way:

'Boswell's reading of early Christian and medieval history [like his interpretation of the biblical texts] turns up what he wants to find. Christian history is a multifarious affair, and it does not take much sniffing around to discover frequent instances of what is best described as hanky-panky. The discovery process is facilitated if one goes through history with what is aptly described as narrow-eyed prurience, interpreting every expression of intense affection between men as proof that they were 'gay'.... Boswell rummages through Christian history and triumphantly comes up with the conclusion, 'They were everywhere'. Probably at all times in Christian history one can find instances of homosexual behaviour. And it is probably true that at some times more than others such behaviour was viewed with 'tolerance', in that it was treated with a wink and a nudge.... Despite his assiduous efforts, what Boswell's historical scavenger hunt does not produce is any evidence whatever that authoritative Christian teaching ever departed from the recognition that homosexual acts were morally wrong.' [23]

Historians in the field concur. The distinguished evangelical church historian David Wright has written extensively on this matter and concludes that, while influential, Boswell's book is 'highly misleading'. [24] In an important article, 'Early Christian Attitudes to Homosexuality', Wright says, 'Boswell's edifice is certainly impressive, but closer acquaintance ...exposes ever widening cracks' and concludes after examining his case that, 'Boswell's book provides in the end of the day *not one firm piece of evidence* that the teaching mind of the early church countenanced homosexual activity'. Contrary to what some think the early fathers were not obsessed with the subject or with singling out active homosexuals, 'But what they do say leaves little room for debate: homosexual behaviour was contrary to the will of God as expressed in Scripture and nature'. [25] The American Episcopalian historian J.R. Wright questions, among other things, Boswell's treatment of the patristic material. In particular he points out that Boswell neglected to consult 'a large body of critical writing that would not lend support to his cause', by which he means the *Biblia Patristica,* a large computerised index of the commentaries of the early fathers on the New Testament. He concludes that Boswell's case is 'undemonstrated' and therefore a shaky foundation from which to change the historic teaching and practice of the church. [26]

### The Medieval Period (600-1500)

The doctrinal consensus of the early church concerning homosexuality was maintained throughout the medieval period. During this period Christianity dominated everything in most of Europe, and Christian standards became the norm of acceptable moral behaviour. There was relatively little legislation relating to homosexuality. Sherwin Bailey says that over a period of 1,000 years there were only 100 or so items of legislation in the whole of Europe which would seem to indicate that by and large the authorities in church and state were not overly concerned with homosexuality. Bailey writes:

'[The homosexual] is certainly denounced as one guilty of very grave sin, but he is not singled out for sadistic persecution; he is offered reconciliation with God and man through the Church's penitential discipline, but if he refuses the means of grace, he has to take the eternal consequences and the temporal consequences of his crime ...' [27]

The **synods** of the church were somewhat more concerned about homosexuality. The sixteenth Council of Toledo in 693 condemned homosexual practice. In his opening address to the assembled clergy, the Visogothic ruler Egica said, 'Among other matters, see that you determine to extirpate that obscene crime committed by those who lie with males'. And so the council tried to do. In its third decree it said: '... if any one of those males who commit this vile practice against nature with other males is a bishop, a priest or a deacon, he shall be degraded from the dignity of his order, and shall remain in perpetual exile, struck down by damnation'. In a supplementary edict the council said, 'Certainly we strive to abolish the detestable outrage of that lust by the filthy uncleanness of which men do not fear to defile other men in the unlawful act of sodomy ...' Other enactments against homosexuality include the Ordinance of Aix-en-Chapelle of 789, the decrees of the Council of London of 1102 and a canon of the Third Lateran Council of 1179 which became a benchmark for subsequent ecclesiastical legislation. The most severe ecclesiastical legislation is to be found in the canons of the Council of Naplouse of 1120 which demanded execution by burning for practising homosexuals. [28]

Far more significant for understanding the attitude of the church towards homosexuality in the medieval period are the **penitentials.** Originating in the Celtic church of Ireland and Wales and eventually spreading to the continent, penitentials were handbooks for confessors that provided schedules of penances for various sins. Almost every conceivable sin known to man is covered, including homosexuality. Some have seen the detailed treatment of homosexual offences as evidence that homosexuality was widespread, particularly within monastic communities. This is a mistake. The penitentials simply try to cover all contingencies that a priest might face in the confessional. Homosexuality is invariably seen as a sin, but not one qualitatively worse than many others. Penances were applied according to the type of homosexual sin which ranged from kissing to sodomy. The penances were also more severe for clergy than for laymen (the higher the office the more severe the penalty), and for men than for women. The concern of the penitentials is always pastoral and aims at restoration rather than punishment. A good example is the penitential regulation of **Pope Gregory III** (731-741) which, as Bailey points out, 'well expresses ... the general Christian attitude at the time towards such acts'.

'If any ordained person has been defiled with the crime of sodomy, which is described as a vice so abominable in the sight of God that the cities in which its practitioners dwelt were appointed for destruction by fire and brimstone, let him do penance for ten years, according to the ancient rule. Some, however, being more humanely disposed, have fixed the term at seven years. Those also who are ignorant of the gravity of the offence are assigned three years in which to do penance. As for boys who know that they are indulging in this practice, it behoves them to hasten to amend; let them do penance for fifty days, and in addition let them be beaten with rods; for it is necessary that the crop which has brought forth bad fruit be cut down.'[29]

The area where considerable attention has been focused in the contemporary debate on homosexuality is in the medieval phenomenon known as 'spiritual' or **'passionate' friendships**. Boswell puts great weight on this in making his case that the church had a more tolerant attitude towards homosexuality before the fourteenth century. He cites, for example, the circle of friends around **Alcuin** (735?-804) in the court of Charlemagne in the 8th century. Apparently they used affectionate pet names among themselves and wrote love poems for one another. Alcuin himself, one of the most learned and devout men of his age, could write to a bishop in these terms, 'I think of your love and friendship with such sweet memories ... that I long for that lovely time when I may be able to clutch the neck of your sweetness with the fingers of my desires'.[30] **Anselm** (1093-1109), one of the church's greatest theologians and the author of the classic on the atonement *Cur deus homo?*, would customarily address his correspondents, 'Beloved Lover', and could write to one correspondent, 'Wherever you go my love follows you, and wherever I remain my desire embraces you .... How can I forget you? He who is imprinted on my heart like a seal on wax—how could he be removed from my memory?'[31] But the most significant writer in this strain was **Aelred** of Rievaulx who wrote the classic work *On Spiritual Friendship*. Aelred was a highly respected abbot whose monastery at Rievaulx in England was known for its high standard of monastic discipline. He wrote his book in response to a question about nurturing friendships among monks, but it is well worth reading by anyone wanting to reflect on the character of genuine friendship within a Christian framework. Among other things Aelred warned his readers of the danger of carnality in friendship, although it is difficult to know if he is referring here to sexual attraction or more broadly to other passions. He speaks of how passing 'into the other, as it were, coming into close contact with the sweetness of Christ himself, the friend begins to taste his sweetness and to experience his charm. Thus ascending from the holy love with which he embraces a friend to that which he embraces Christ, he will joyfully partake in abundance of the spiritual fruit of friendship awaiting the fullness of all things in the life to come'.[32] Aelred mentions his own experience of friendship as a young monk in such a way that some, such as Boswell, have claimed that he was a homosexual, albeit a celibate one. He wrote that their friendship grew 'until we attained that stage at which we had one mind and one soul, to will and not to will alike .... For I deemed my heart in a fashion his, and his mine, and he felt in like manner towards me.... He was the refuge of my spirit, the sweet solace of my griefs, whose heart of love received me when fatigued with labours, whose counsel refreshed me when plunged in sadness and grief.... What more is there, then, that I can say? Was it not a foretaste of blessedness thus to love and thus to be loved?' Clearly for Aelred friendships between men could be deeply emotional and could involve passionate affections. 'Feelings are not ours to command', he wrote. 'We are attracted to some against our will, while towards others we can never experience a spontaneous affection'. 33

What then are we to make of these passionate friendships? Are they evidence of a more tolerant attitude towards homosexuality in the early Middle Ages? It is not difficult to see why Boswell and others have tried to build their case on these friendships. Certainly to our ears the almost erotic language used is very strange indeed. But such language was a common form of address in this period. Speaking of the alleged homosexual relationship of Edward II and Piers Galveston, Caroline Bingham writes that Edward II:

'lived in a period when an intimate friendship between two men was a formal relationship governed by a code of rules like that of courtly love. Such a relationship was the subject of the Anglo-Norman romance, *Amis and Amilou*. Two friends could be described as *'leals amants'* (loyal lovers) and their relationship as *'fyne amor'*, but homosexuality was completely outside the convention.' 34

It is not coincidental that Bernard of Clairvaux wrote his long allegorical commentary on the Song of Solomon in the same period in which he expounds the Christian's relationship to Christ through the metaphor of the courtship and marriage of the lover and his beloved. Is it surprising that a similar idiom was used by Aelred and others to speak of male friendships without any suggestion of sexual passion? Christopher Brooke speaks of the 'shifting attitudes to human love' in 12th century Europe and writes, 'One tradition stemming from the ancient world saw human affection issuing in real comradeship, as chiefly to be found in the relationship of man to man'. He goes on to mention Bernard and how he could 'use a language of affection which might be supposed homosexual—but one has only to contemplate the use he makes of erotic imagery in his *Sermon on the Song of Songs* to realise that metaphor was to him a wholly abstract thing—as to many writers of the 11th and 12th centuries, a fact which renders their full meaning peculiarly difficult to grasp'.35 Confirmation of this is seen in the numerous references in this period to the friendships of David and Jonathan and Jesus and the 'beloved disciple', which were highly emotional and even physical without the remotest suggestion of homosexuality. Perhaps the difficulty is not so much with the language of friendship in the 12th century, but the shallowness of friendship in the 20th century. Today many cannot think of intimate same-sex relationships without thinking about sex.

No doubt there were instances of homosexual behaviour among the clergy in the medieval period. Boswell cites several cases that may well have been true, but these tell us nothing more about the church's official attitude towards homosexuality than do moral lapses or even aberrant teaching by church leaders today.36 There were certainly periods when Christian leaders felt that homosexuality was a widespread problem. Earlier in the period Boniface (c.680-754), the great missionary to the Germans, complained in a letter to the King of Mercia that '... the people of England have been living a shameful life, despising lawful marriages, committing adultery, and lusting after the people of Sodom'.37 Though disputed by Boswell, the last reference was probably to homosexuality. In the 12th century Anselm wrote to a colleague after the Council of London had decreed against homosexuality that 'this sin has hitherto been so public that hardly anyone is embarrassed by it, and many have therefore fallen into it because they are unaware of its seriousness'.38 The French social historian Henri Bresc points out that the 13th century was obsessed with sexual vice in general and homosexuality in particular and that during the century there seems to have been an increase in prosecutions of homosexuals.39 As with many things there may have been periods when homosexuality was fashionable, especially among the elite classes to which the higher clergy belonged. With the revival of classical learning in the Renaissance there seems to have also been a revival of what the Romans called 'Greek love'. Homosexuality in the academies of Rome and other Italian universities was alleged to be rife in the late 15th century. John D'Amico writes that for 'some [priests] the imposed celibacy of the clerical state may have exacerbated individual tendencies' and that the name Socrates ' was a byword for more than wisdom in the Renaissance'.[40] Visitors to Italy noted the number of male prostitutes. Not surprisingly **Bernardino** of Siena and **Savanarola** (1452-1498) preached against this vice in their campaigns for ecclesiastical and social reform. Between 1348 and 1461 there were some fifty court cases related to homosexuality in Florence, but there is little evidence that homosexuals in any large numbers were ever put to death there or elsewhere and most historians do not think that homosexuality was very widespread.[41]

But, whatever lapses there were, the church maintained her teaching on homosexuality. In addition to the penitentials and canon law the church's theologians consistently taught that homosexual activity was sinful. The most extreme example of this was a book entitled *Liber Gomorrhianus* by **Peter Damiani** (1007-1072). Peter considered the penitentials far too lenient in relation to homosexuality and in violent language recommended that offenders be punished without mitigation.[42] The book was not well received; the authorities, while not favourably disposed towards homosexuality, preferred to deal with the problem more dispassionately and pastorally. Such was the approach of **Albertus Magnus** (c.1193-1280) and his even greater protégé **Thomas Aquinas** (1225-1274), the foremost of all medieval theologians. In several places in his *Summa Theologicae* Thomas deals with homosexuality. His principal objection was that homosexuality is against Scripture, reason and nature.

Thomas's understanding of nature and natural law was a synthesis of biblical teaching and Aristotelian philosophy. As Arthur Holmes explains, 'Natural law is inherent in the essence of created things, in the good ends that are natural for all humans to pursue, the potential that humans generically share'.[43] So Thomas opposed homosexuality both by citing texts such as Leviticus 19:16 and by showing that there are some sins contrary to nature such 'as ... those that run counter to the intercourse of males and females natural to animals, and so are peculiarly qualified as unnatural vices'. He wrote that a 'lustful man intends sex for pleasure, not human fruitfulness, and he can experience this without a generative act; this is what he seeks in unnatural vice'; in other words homosexuality was by definition unfruitful and therefore unnatural. Against the argument that freely consented homosexual coitus was not as serious as other sins since it harmed no one other than the participants, Thomas argued that it was an injury done to God since it contravened his natural order.44 The thinking of Thomas was reflected in the literature of the period. **Alain de Lille's** book *De Plancto Naturae* (The Complaint of Nature) excoriated the homosexuality he felt was so prevalent in the late 13th century. His theme was 'the complaint of Nature against all who deviate from the natural modes of conduct and intercourse, by the observance of which Man glorifies his Creator and attains true happiness and fulfilment in life'.45 All this Boswell interprets as great intellectual change that turned the church away from its previously more open attitude to homosexuality to a more hostile and repressive one.46 I suggest that although the position was more refined and sophisticated it was nevertheless fundamentally the same as the church had always held.

**The Reformation Period to the Victorian Era (1500-1900).**
We have had to spend considerable time looking at the attitude towards homosexuality of the early and medieval church since this is the point where Boswell and others have challenged the traditional position of the church. From now on we can move much faster. In the early 16th century the western church experienced the upheaval of the Reformation as many people rediscovered the gospel. But whatever the differences between Roman Catholics and Protestants over doctrine, all were agreed that homosexuality was sinful and socially destructive. For our purposes I will concentrate on the thinking of Protestant theologians, but the position of the Roman church should not be forgotten.

Homosexuality was not a major concern of the reformers. Contrary to modern images of ranting preachers seeking to intrude into every corner of people's private lives the Protestant leaders of the 16th and 17th centuries were rather sparing in their references to homosexuality and, when they had to deal with it, did so with some distaste. When lecturing on Genesis at Wittenburg **Martin Luther** (1483-1546) came to chapter 19 and the account of Sodom and Gomorrah with a very heavy heart. It gave him no pleasure to speak of God's wrath or of such an unseemly sin. He says that:

'Moses proceeds with a description of a terrible sin. I for my part do not enjoy dealing with this passage, because so far the ears of Germans are innocent and uncontaminated by this monstrous depravity; for even though this disgrace, like other sins, has crept in through an ungodly soldier and a lewd merchant, still the rest of the people are unaware of what is being done in secret.... [Nevertheless] this passage contains a necessary and profitable doctrine. We see that when sins become the fashion and human beings smugly indulge in them, the punishment of God follows immediately....The heinous conduct of the people of Sodom is extraordinary inasmuch as they departed from the natural passion and longing of the male for the female, which was implanted into nature by God, and desired what is altogether contrary to nature. Whence comes the perversity? Undoubtedly from Satan, who, after people have turned away from the fear of God, so powerfully suppresses nature that he blots out the natural desire and stirs up a desire that is contrary to nature.'

Luther was shocked by the openness and shamelessness of this sin and mentions his own experience of visiting Rome where he saw 'cardinals who were esteemed highly as saints because they were content to associate with women'. Luther was always fearful of social anarchy and sought to apply to his hearers the lesson of Sodom's destruction.

'Therefore if the Lord had not brought on the punishment which they deserved, the government would gradually have collapsed and could not have continued to exist. For if you do away with the marriage bond and permit promiscuous passions, the laws and all decency go to ruin together with discipline. But when these are destroyed, no government remains; only beastliness and savagery are left. Therefore as an example for others the Lord was compelled to inflict punishment and to check the madness that was raging beyond measure.' [47]

In commenting on Romans 1:24, Luther related the sin of homosexuality to the spiritual and moral decay of society: 'From this text we may therefore deduce that if someone surrenders to these passions, it is a sure sign that he has left the worship of God and has worshipped an idol, or he has turned the truth of God into a lie'. [48] Luther's views need to be seen against the background of a desire on the one hand to redress lax discipline of sexual sins in the Catholic Church and on the other to re-establish the divine calling of marriage and family life. The Lutheran theologian Andreas Musculus wrote of how the devil hates marriage and uses homosexuality to destroy it. [49]

The Genevan reformer **John Calvin** (1509-1564) adopted the same attitude as Luther. In his commentary on Genesis 19 he calls homosexuality 'an abominable sin' and exclaims 'How blind and impetuous is their lust; since without shame they rush together like brute animals! How great their ferocity and cruelty; since they reproachfully threaten the holy man and proceed to all extremities.... But when the sense of shame is overcome, and the reins are given to lust, a vile and outrageous barbarism succeeds and many kinds of sins are blended together so that a most confused chaos is the result.' [50]

Interestingly Calvin does not interpret the word 'know' in verse 5 to mean sexual knowledge, but rather social acquaintance as many of the revisionists would prefer to understand it. Nevertheless it is clear that Calvin believes that homosexuality was the primary sin for which Sodom was punished. In his commentary on Romans 1:26 Calvin speaks of '...the dreadful crime of unnatural lust' and how 'it appears that they not only abandoned themselves to beastly lusts, became degraded beyond the beasts, since they reversed the natural order'. [51] In his commentary on 1 Corinthians 6:9 he writes of homosexuality as 'the most abominable of all the monstrous pollution which was but too prevalent in Greece'. [52] Calvin's colleague **Heinrich Bullinger** (1504-1575), the successor to Zwingli in Zurich, was equally forthright. Bullinger is significant because of the great influence of his doctrinal sermons, *The Decades,* in England where they were recommended reading for the clergy of the newly reformed Church of England. Bullinger writes 'The abominable sin of sodomy, and meddling with beasts, also is plainly forbidden, against which we have most evident and express laws set down in the 18th and 19th chapters of Leviticus. We have also a very severe, but yet a most just, punishment laid by God himself upon the pates of the detestable Sodomites; for with fire and stinking brimstone sent down from heaven, he consumed those filthy men to dust and ashes.' 53

It is clear then from these examples that the reformers maintained the ancient teaching of the church on homosexuality. It is surprising, therefore, to discover that the great Protestant confessions of the 16th and 17th centuries do not, with one exception, mention homosexuality. Why is this? In part it is because, for the reformers and their successors, the issue was so clear that it did not need to be mentioned, but it is also because they were not particularly obsessed with the issue. The one exception is the **Heidelberg Catechism** which in Question and Answer 87 says:

'*Question:* Can those who do not turn to God from their ungrateful, impenitent life be saved?

*Answer:* Most certainly not! Scripture says, Surely you know that the unjust never come into possession of the kingdom of God. Make no mistake: no fornicator or idolater, none who are guilty either of adultery or homosexual perversion, no thieves or grabbers or drunkards or slanderers or swindlers, will possess the kingdom of God.'

The teaching and emphasis of the reformers was maintained in succeeding generations. The Puritan **Thomas Goodwin** called homosexuality or sodomy an 'unnatural uncleanness'.54 Later **David Clarkson** sought to illustrate the baleful effects of Roman Catholic teaching in his *Practical Divinity of the Papists discovered to be destructive of Christianity and Men's Souls* by mentioning how prevalent sodomy was in Italy where unmarried priests were so thick on the ground.55 In his great compendium of Christian ethics, The Christian Directory, **Richard Baxter** spoke of the 'filthy lusts' of the Sodomites and put homosexual sin in the same category as fornication.56 The great Puritan commentator **Matthew Henry** leaves us in no doubt in his comment on Genesis 19:4:

'It was the most unnatural and abominable wickedness that they were now set upon, a sin that still bears their name, and is called *Sodomy.* They were carried headlong by those vile affections (Romans 1:26,27) which are worse than brutish, and the eternal reproach of the human nature, and which cannot be thought of without horror by those who have the least spark of virtue, and any remains of natural light and conscience. Note, those that allow themselves in unnatural uncleanness, are marked for the vengeance of eternal fire.'

He wrote that by force 'they proclaim their war with virtue and bid open defiance to it'. [57] He makes a similar comment on Judges 19:22-30 when he says that the men of the town sought 'the gratification of that unnatural and brutish lust, that was expressly forbidden in the Law of Moses and called an abomination'.[58] In his very influential work, *Holy Living and Dying* Bishop **Jeremy Taylor** considered all 'Who are adulterous, incestuous, *sodomitical,* or commit fornication' as violators of the seventh commandment.[59] Later in the 18th century the Baptist pastor and theologian **Andrew Fuller** wrote that men of Sodom sought not only to rob and insult Lot's guests 'but to perpetuate a crime too shocking and detestable to name'. [60]

The teaching of the reformers and Puritans on homosexuality needs to be seen in its social context. From the 16th to the 18th centuries homosexuality was at times believed to be rampant and considered destructive to the social order, not least because it might provoke God's judgement. Periodically it came to be considered fashionable in aristocratic circles and was known to exist in the courts of Elizabeth I and James I/VI and later of Charles II. The period after the Restoration in 1660 was morally very relaxed and therefore a play such as John Wilmot's *The Quintessence of Debauchery,* which had sodomy as its theme, would not have been too shocking in polite London society. The Duchess of Orleans could comment in 1698 that 'nothing is more ordinary in England than this unnatural vice' and Thomas Bray could lament in *For God or Satan* that 'the sodomites are invading the land'. In the late 18th century homosexuality was again fashionable among the upper classes. That acute social observer Mrs Thrale commented in 1781 that it was 'now so modish' and in 1790 that 'there is a strange propensity in England for these unspeakable crimes'. The papers of the day carried detailed reports of sodomy trials. Not surprisingly laws were introduced in England and elsewhere proscribing homosexuality. Henry VIII removed jurisdiction for homosexual offences from the church to the state and thereby made it a criminal act. In New England, where Puritanism shaped society in a biblical mould, homosexuality became a capital offence.[61] But this was not unique to New England or even to Protestant nations. During this period there were a number of campaigns against homosexuality in both Protestant and Catholic countries. For example, in the 1730s there was a particularly well documented campaign in the Netherlands where people were shocked by revelations of the extent of the homosexual underworld and felt that the republic was in danger of being overwhelmed by immorality of the grossest kind. Sodom was the theme of much Dutch Calvinist preaching during this period.[62] There were similar campaigns in Venice, Spain and France. Yet in all this it must be said that in Britain and America homosexuality does not seem to have been widespread enough to have made it an issue of great concern for Christian leaders. They maintained the orthodox tradition when the issue arose, but otherwise tended not to discuss it.

During the 19th century in Britain and America there was a renewed emphasis in society on marriage and family life largely because of the profound influence of evangelical Christianity in the wake of the revivals of the 18th and early 19th centuries. Homosexuality was considered deviant and homosexuals were socially ostracised. The trial of Oscar Wilde in 1895 was a great scandal in late Victorian England, but it was also an exposure of a measure of hypocrisy and a revelation of a homosexual subculture. Homosexuality was not unknown in English public schools and in cities like London homosexual prostitutes were common, many of whom were boys or young men. Some Christians were concerned about this and in 1883 established the White Cross Society which became the **White Cross League** in 1891. The New Testament scholar Bishop Lightfoot and Bishop Randall Davidson (who later became Archbishop of Canterbury) and his wife, were very involved in this work.[63]

## The Twentieth Century

The consensus of Christian teaching in the early 20th century remained opposed to homosexual activity. Sometimes this could be little more than prudish as seen in the comment of the *Interpreter's Bible* in 1954 on Romans 1:27: 'The subject is one which in honesty must be faced, but on which no man of fine feeling would care to linger'.[64] Linger the commentator doesn't; he moves quickly on to more edifying matters. More robust was **Karl Barth's** treatment of homosexuality in his monumental *Church Dogmatics*. Speaking of homosexuality he says:

'This is the physical, psychological and social sickness, the phenomenon of perversion, decadence and decay, which can emerge when men refuse to admit the validity of the divine command.... In Romans 1 Paul connected it with idolatry, with changing the truth of God into a lie, with the adoration of the creature instead of the Creator (v.25).... From the refusal to recognise God there follows the failure to appreciate man, and thus humanity without the fellow man. And since humanity as fellow-humanity is to be understood in its root as the togetherness of man and woman, at the root of this inhumanity there follows the ideal of a masculinity free from woman and a femininity free from man. And because nature and the Creator of nature will not be trifled with, because the despised fellow-man is still there, because the natural orientation on him is still in force, there follows the corrupt emotional and finally physical desire in which—in a sexual union which is not and cannot be genuine—man thinks that he must seek and can find in man, and woman in woman, a substitute for the despised partner.... The command of God shows him irrefutably—in clear contradiction of his own theories— that as a man he can only be genuinely human with woman, or as a woman with man. In proportion as he accepts this insight, homosexuality can have no place in his life, whether in its more refined or cruder forms.' [65]

As Richard Lovelace points out 'Barth is not here affirming that true humanity is impossible outside the married state; ... but is simply saying that all human beings realise their humanity as they open themselves in humility to the complementary excellencies of the opposing sex...' [66] The German Lutheran theologian Helmut Thielicke thinks Barth's view somewhat superficial and insensitive. While believing homosexual activity to be contrary to God's will and therefore sinful, Thielicke nevertheless thinks that homosexuality can be a genuinely human encounter between two people and that the church must be more pastorally sensitive than it has been in dealing with it. Thielicke's understanding of the biblical material incorporates much of the revisionist interpretation favoured by those who do not see homosexual activity as sinful, but Thielicke himself does not come to that conclusion. He considers homosexuality in the light of creation and the Fall and concludes that it is a perversion in the same way that disease, suffering and pain is. No moral stigma is attached to being a homosexual as such and the church's responsibility is to help the homosexual to struggle with his or her condition and to live a celibate life if necessary. [67]

While Barth and Thielicke were writing, others were beginning to challenge the traditional Christian approach to homosexuality. This needs to be seen against a backdrop of profound cultural changes after the Second World War and changing attitudes towards homosexuality. In 1948 Alfred Kinsey published his *Sexual Behaviour in the Human Male* in which he estimated that 4% of American men were confirmed homosexuals and that 37% had had homosexual experience. These findings have been subsequently questioned but they were at the time very influential. In Britain the recommendation of the Wolfenden Report of 1957 recommending the decriminalisation of homosexuality was enacted in 1967 as part of Roy Jenkins' programme of liberal reforms. The Gay Liberation movement effectively began in 1969 in the aftermath of the Christopher Street riots in New York with its motto 'Gay is Good' and has been gaining in strength ever since. It was only a matter of time before the American Psychiatric Association removed homosexuality from the category of mental illness in 1973. Meanwhile pressure has been mounting to lower the age of consent from 18 and to allow open homosexuals to serve in the armed forces. In the United States—and to a lesser extent Britain—the issues surrounding homosexual rights has become a key battleground in the culture wars between social conservatives and progressives. Alan Shead of Moore College in Sydney helpfully sums up these social changes in this way:

'Following the questioning of traditional values represented by the Kinsey report, the 1950s were a time of legal debate and of the beginning of a supportive homosexual community. The 1960's saw legal debate progress to legislation, and homosexual support progress to gay liberation. The movement was out of the closet. In the 1970's the gay movement worked to change society's social and moral perceptions of homosexuality. Its major breakthrough was the 1973 victory of the American Psychiatric Association: homosexuality was now officially a normal and thus morally neutral condition.' [68]

It was in this social context that the church in the west began to wrestle with the question of homosexuality. This was at a time when liberal theology was ascendant in the mainline Protestant denominations after the Second World War and when the Roman Catholic Church would experience theological upheaval after Vatican II. For many Protestants what Scripture taught was no longer the primary theological criterion in discerning the mind of God on ethical issues. An example of this is the influential book, published in 1967 by the process theologian **Norman Pittenger** entitled *Time for Consent—a Christian's Approach to Homosexuality,* in which he reinterprets the key texts and refers to medical and psychological studies to make his case for a more open attitude towards homosexual behaviour. For Pittenger a homosexual relationship is justified so long as it is faithful and loving; an ethical standpoint developed more fully in the situation ethics of Joseph Fletcher.[69] In 1970 the Jesuit theologian **J.J. McNeill** became the first Roman Catholic advocate of acceptance of homosexual activity as morally acceptable.[70] As already noted John Boswell published *Christianity, Social Tolerance and Homosexuality* in 1980 in which he radically reinterpreted the key biblical passages and church history prior to the 14th century.

By and large evangelicals have stood against the tide, but recently some have broken ranks. In the United States **Letha Scanzoni** and **Virginia Ramey Mollenkott,** two of the early evangelical feminists, argued the case for acceptance of loving homosexual relationships within the church in their 1978 book *Is the Homosexual My Neighbour?* Mollenkott has herself published in 1992 a book entitled

*Sensuous Spirituality* in which she speaks of her own lesbianism and acceptance of what can only be described as a New Age version of Christianity.[71] In Britain Michael Vasey, a tutor at the historically evangelical St. John's College in Durham, has advocated the acceptance of faithful same-sex relationships within the church in his controversial book *Strangers and Friends*. Perhaps the most sophisticated treatment of the issue from this standpoint is the book by the Dutch Protestant philosopher Pim Pronk entitled *Against Nature—Types of Moral Argumentation Regarding Homosexuality* (1993). Pronk questions the notion maintained consistently by Christian theologians through the centuries that homosexuality is against nature and subjects this claim to very detailed philosophical examination. He admits that the biblical authors view homosexuality as a sin and nowhere see it positively, but that for him is not the point because the 'issue is not decided for any Christian by exegesis alone. The understanding of the texts is always mediated by interpretative frameworks'. Everyone, says Pronk, comes to Scripture with prior moral commitments and he concludes, 'The Bible is not ... a necessary condition for knowing what good and evil is'. Ethical decisions must be decided on the basis of general revelation and not special revelation.[72]

Through much of the 1970's and 80's most of the larger mainstream denominations were in turmoil over homosexuality. The primary issue was whether or not to ordain practising homosexuals. In 1972 the first openly practising homosexual was ordained in the United Church of Christ in America. Three years later a practising lesbian was ordained by the Episcopal bishop of New York in contravention of canon law. The activities and writings of Bishop **Jack Spong** of Newark, New Jersey, were especially notorious in encouraging homosexuals to enter the ordained ministry. In 1979 the General Convention allowed homosexuals to be ordained so long as they were 'able and willing to conform to that which the church affirms as wholesome'. In spite, or perhaps because of this somewhat ambiguous statement, a number of bishops and clergy continued to ordain and bless the relationships of openly practising homosexuals. Similar controversies wracked other denominations such as the United Methodist Church, the Lutheran Church of America, the

United Church of Christ and the United Presbyterian Church. In 1991 the General Assembly of the latter body rejected a report that recommended full acceptance of ordained homosexuals so long as relationships were characterised by 'mutuality, honesty, consent and fidelity'. Even so the General Assembly refused to declare homosexual activity sinful or heterosexual marriage as 'the only God-ordained relationship for the expression of sexual intercourse'. That same year the journal *Christianity Today* noted that homosexuality was one of the top religious news stories.[73] That was certainly true in Britain in the following years, as the introductory chapter of this volume has shown. Yet with all this debating the main denominations have not yet positively sanctioned same-sex relationships. There is much fudge, ambiguity and inconsistency, but the historic position is still officially the position of all the main churches in the English-speaking world. In part this is due to the moral conservatism of the laity, but how long that will last in the present moral climate is impossible to say. Where there has been a significant shift has been in the Netherlands where Gereformeerde Kerken (the GKN or Reformed Churches in the Netherlands), the traditionally conservative denomination of Abraham Kuyper and Herman Bavinck, has officially approved of same-sex relationships and agreed to allow people in such relationships to enter the ministry. This issue is causing considerable distress within GKN's sister body in the United States, the Christian Reformed Church (the denomination of Louis Berkof and William Hendricksen), where the issue of homosexuality is being hotly debated.

All of which brings us back to that service in Southwark Cathedral. In the latter part of this century the theological foundations of the western church have been severely undermined. This has happened in a cultural context in which homosexuality has become increasingly accepted as a legitimate lifestyle without any moral stigma. Is it all that surprising that such a service was held in a church building belonging to the principal denomination of England? Sadly not. Is it all that surprising that a self-confessed evangelical bishop could participate and preach in such a service? Sadly not. Those who want to remain true to Scripture and its moral standards will have to stand fast and to do so confident that they are standing where countless others have stood down the centuries.

## About the author

Ken Brownell is an American from New England. He graduated from Harvard University and completed a Ph.D in modern British history at St Andrews University in Scotland. Ken studied theology at the London Theological Seminary, lectures for the Prepared for Service training course and is at present pastor of East London Tabernacle Baptist Church. He is also the editor of the theological magazine, *Foundations*. He is married to Alison and they have two children.

### Chapter 2 notes

1   **D. Sherwin Bailey,** *Homosexuality and the Western Christian Tradition,* Longman, Green & Co. 1955.

2   See ref 1, pp 1-28.

3   **John Boswell,** *Christianity, Social Tolerance and Homosexuality—Gay People in Western Europe from the Beginning of the Christian era to the Fourteenth Century* University of Chicago Press 1989 (hereafter CSTH); and The Marriage of Likeness—Same Sex Unions in pre-Modern Europe, HarperCollins 1994 (hereafter ML).

4   **John Richard Neuhaus,** 'In the case of John Boswell', Evangelical Review of Theology, XIX, 19 (1995), p 65. This article was originally published in the American journal *First Things.*

5   **Michael Vasey,** *Strangers and Friends: a new exploration of homosexuality,* Hodder & Stoughton 1995.

6   **Eva Cantarella,** *Bisexuality in the Ancient World,* trans. Carmac O Cuilleanain, Yale University Press 1992, pp 160,162,173; see also **Peter Coleman,** *Christian Attitudes to Homosexuality,* SPCK 1980, p 162; **Aline Purelle,** 'Family under the Roman Empire', in A History of the Family, ed. Audie Burguire, Polity Press 1996, p 297; **Peter Brown,** *The Body and Society—Men, Women and Sexual Renunciation in Early Christianity,* Faber & Faber 1988, p 79.

7   See ref 6, Cantarella, pp 191,193.

8   The Didache, 2.2, in Ancient Christian Writers, VI, trans. James A Klest, SJ, Mercier Press, 1948, p16, page 34

9   Apostolical Constitutions, VII.3, in Ante-Nicene Christian Library [hereafter ANCL], XVII, T&T Clark n.d., pp179, 228.

10  **Justin Martyr,** First Apology, XXVII, in ANCL II, T&T Clark, 1879, p 30.

11  **Tertullian,** Against Marcion, quoted in Bailey, p 82.

12  **Lactantius,** *The Divine Institutes,* VI.23, in ANCL XXI, T&T Clark, 1871, p 411.

13  See ref 6, Cantarella, p 188.

14  See ref 6, Cantarella, p 14; ref 1, p 89; ref 3, CSTH, p 121; ref 6, Coleman, p 87.

15  **John Chrysostom** as quoted in ref 3, CSTH, p 121.

16  **John Chrysostom,** Homilies on Romans, IV (1.26-27) in Library of the Fathers of the Holy Catholic Church VII, John Henry Parker 1844, pp 44-52.

17  **Augustine,** *Confessions,* III.8.15, trans. John K. Ryan, Doubleday & Company 1960, p 87.

18  **Augustine,** *Concerning the City of God against the Pagans,* XVI.30, trans. Henry Bettenson, Penguin Books 1984, p 692.

19  See ref 1, pp 86, 91; ref 6, p 127.

20  See ref 3, CSTH, p159.

21. See ref 3, pp. 22,160.

22  See ref 3, ML, pp 10, 11, 190, 191, 199.

23  See ref 4, pp 66,67

24. **David F. Wright,** 'Homosexuality', in the Encyclopaedia of Early Christianity, Garland Publishing Company 1990, p 435.

25  **David F. Wright,** *Early Christian Attitudes to Homosexuality*, Studia Patristica, XVIII.2, Cistercian Publications 1989, pp 330, 333. Wright has also written, 'Homosexuals or page 35. Prostitutes: the meaning of arsenokoites in 1 Corithians 6:19; 1 Timothy 1:10', Viglae Christianae, 38, 1984, pp.125-153.

26  **J.R. Wright,** *Boswell on Homosexuality; A Case Undemonstrated,* Anglican Theological Review, LXVI.1, June 1984, pp 87f.

27  See ref 1, p 99.

28  **Reay Tannahill,** *Sex in History,* Hamish Hamilton 1980, p 156; also see ref 1, pp 92-97.

29  See ref 1 p 106.

30  See ref 3, CSTH, p 190.

31  See ref 3, p 218.

32  **Aelred of Rievaulx,** *On Spiritual Friendship,* trans. Mary Eugenia Laker SSND, Cistercian Publications 1977, p.131.

33  See ref 32, p.26; also ref 3, CSTH, p 222.

34  **Caroline Bingham,** *The Life and Times of Edward II,* Wiedenfeld & Nicolson 1973, p 54; see also Pierre Chaplais, Piers Galveston—Edward II's Adoptive Brother,

Clarendon Press 1994, pp 11,13.

**35 Christopher N.C. Brooke,** *The Medieval Idea of Marriage,* Cambridge Univesity Press 1989, pp.266-7.

**36** See ref 3, CSTH, pp 191, 238ff.

**37** See ref 6, Coleman, p 131.

**38** Boswell, CSTH, p.215

**39 Henri Bresc,** *Europe: Town and Country,* in Berguire, p 452. page 36

**40 John D'Amico,** *Renaissance Humanism in Papal Rome,* Johns Hopkins University Press 1983, pp 92, 93.

**41 David Greenberg,** *The Construction of Homosexuality,* University of Chicago Press 1988, pp 305, 307; see also ref 1, p 134.

**42** See ref 1, p 112.

**43 Arthur Holmes,** *Natural Law,* in the New Dictionary of Christian Ethics and Pastoral Theology, ed. David J.Atkinson and David H. Field, Inter-Varsity Press 1995, p 619.

**44 Thomas Aquinas,** *Summa Theologicae,* 20.25; 28:84; 43:47; 43:245, Blackfriars in association with Eyre & Spottiswoode 1964-1980; see also ref 1, p 117; Richard Lovelace, Homosexuality and the Church, Fleming H. Revell, 1978, p 19.

**45** See ref 1, p 119.

**46** See ref 3, CSTH, pp 303ff.

**47**. **Martin Luther,** *Lectures on Genesis,* in Luther's Works, III, ed. Jaroslav Pelikan, Concordia Press 1961, pp 239, 251-5.

**48 Martin Luther** as quoted in ref 44, Lovelace, p 19.

**49 Joel Harrington,** *Reordering Marriage and Society in Reformation Germany,* Cambridge University Press 1995, pp 37, 215.

**50 John Calvin,** *Commentary on Genesis,* Banner of Truth Trust 1975, p 496.

**51 John Calvin,** *Commentary upon Romans,* Calvin Translation Society 1849, p 33.

**52 John Calvin,** *Commentary upon 1st Corinthians,* Calvin Translation Society 1848, p 209.

**53 Heinrich Bullinger,** *The Decades, I,* Cambridge University Press 1849, p 418.

**54 Thomas Goodwin,** Works, X, Jas. Nichol 1865, p. 320.

**55 David Clarkson,** Works, III, Banner of Truth 1985, pp 231-2.

**56 Richard Baxter,** *Christian Directory in The Practical Works of Richard Baxter, I,* Soli Deo Gloria 1990, pp 437, 453.

57  **Matthew Henry,** *Expositions of the Old and New Testaments,*
    Henry G.Bohn 1846, Genesis 19:4.

58  See ref 57, Judges 19:22-30.

59  **Jeremy Taylor,** *Holy Living and Dying,* George Bell & Sons, 1898, p 447.

60  **Andrew Fuller,** Works, III, Sprinkle Publications 1988, pp 75,77.

61  See ref 41, pp 303-28; Lawrence Stone, The Family, Sex and Marriage,
    Wiedenfeld & Nicolson 1977, pp 492, 541.

62  **Simon Shama,** *The Embarrassment of Riches,* Fontana Press 1988. pp 601-6.

63  See ref 6, p 152.

64  **John Knox and Gerald Cragg,** *Romans* in The Interpreter's Bible, Abingdon Press, p 402.

65  **Karl Barth,** Church Dogmatics, III.4, T.&T. Clark 1961, p166.

66  See ref 44, Lovelace, pp. 23, 24.

67  **Helmut Thielicke,** *The Ethics of Sex,* Jas. Clarke & Co. 1964, pp 269ff;
    Lovelace, pp 24-27.

68  **Alan Shead,** Homosexuality and the church: historical survey, in *Theological
    and Pastoral Responses to Homosexuality,* Explorations 8, ed. B.G. Webb,
    Open Book 1994, pp 7, 8.

69  **Norman Pittenger,** *Time for Consent—A Christian's Approach to Homosexuality,*
    SCM 1976.page 38

70  **J.J. McNeill,** *The Church and the Homosexual,* Darton, Longman and Todd 1977.

71  **Letha Scanzoni and Virginia Mollenkott,** *Is the Homosexual My Neighbour?*
    Another Christian View, SCM 1978; **Virginia Ramey Mollenkott,** *Sensuous
    Spirituality,* Crossroad 1992.

72  **Pim Pronk,** *Against Nature—Types of Moral Argumentation Regarding Homosexuality,*
    Wm. B Eerdmans 1993, pp 322, 324.

73  See ref 68, pp 18ff.

# Just genetics?

What are the causes of homosexuality? Medical practitioner **Dr Peter Saunders** examines the changing medical perceptions and asks, "Is it nature or is it nurture?"

The term homosexuality was coined by Benkert in 1869. The prefix 'homo' comes from the Greek word meaning 'same', the opposite of 'hetero' or 'other'. The Oxford Dictionary defines homosexuality as 'being sexually attracted only by members of one's own sex' but there is no universally accepted definition among clinicians and behavioural scientists. There is even less agreement as to its cause.

Part of the problem is that not all people are exclusive in their sexual inclinations. There is a spectrum ranging from those who have never had a homosexual thought in their lives, to those who experience nothing else. In the 1940s Alfred Kinsey conducted a major study[1] into sexuality and classified subjects on a continuum from 0 (exclusively heterosexual) to 6 (exclusively homosexual) with grades of bisexuality (attraction to both sexes) in between.

Another difficulty with definitions is that sexual desire may or may not correlate with sexual behaviour. Some people with exclusively same-sex erotic fantasies may never proceed to homosexual activity, and in fact may live in long-term heterosexual relationships. Others with sexual desire only for the opposite sex may, under extreme circumstances (such as in prisons or during wartime), participate in homosexual acts. The term 'sexual orientation' is now commonly used to describe the predominant sexual preference.

### Changing perceptions

Medical perceptions of homosexuality have changed. In the 19th century it was attributed first to moral degeneracy and later to mental illness. In the early 20th century it was credited to hormonal imbalance, psychosocial influences and more recently biological factors. Many now see it simply as a natural variant like handedness or skin colour.

As recently as 1967 in the United Kingdom, homosexual behaviour between consenting adults in private was a criminal offence at any age. In 1974 the American Psychiatric Association voted to drop homosexuality from its official list of mental disorders (DSM II) and in 1994 the British Medical Association (BMA) Council joined in calls for the lowering of the age of homosexual consent.

This change in perception rests on the presupposition that homosexual orientation is biologically determined and unchangeable and much of the current literature focuses on the need to help homosexuals embrace their sexuality and cope with discrimination. Some within the American Psychiatric Association are now calling for an official ban on therapy to change the condition (reparative therapy).[2]

Now that homosexuality has attained 'nonpathological status' it is increasingly difficult to ask fundamental questions or to carry out research which challenges the prevailing view. As one commentator [3] has put it 'this is an area, *par excellence*, where scientific objectivity has little chance of survival.'

### Vested interests

It is difficult not to bring one's own preconceptions to scientific investigation. The temptation (consciously or unconsciously) is to view the facts selectively in order to prove the rightness of one's own prior convictions. Many researchers are quite open about having an agenda other than the mere pursuit of scientific truth. If sexual orientation is not fixed then, according to US law at least, homosexuals may not be protected from 'discrimination'.[4] Bailey and Pillard, two of the most prolific medical researchers in the field (and leading advocates for the view that homosexuality is inborn) have commented that 'a biological explanation (of homosexuality) is good news for homosexuals and their advocates'.[5] Another author has suggested that if homosexuality is a purely biological phenomenon, 'society would do well to re-examine its expectations of those who cannot conform.'[6]

Researchers who have the added motivation of changing public opinion will be guided along certain channels in their work and there are now powerful interests in the scientific community attempting to prove that homosexuality is uniform across time and culture and therefore 'natural', that sexual orientation is established early in life, that it cannot be changed even with 'treatment' and even that homosexuals are in some way genetically superior and therefore favoured in the evolutionary process.

### The influence of media and pressure groups

Journalists can also bring their private social agendas to bear by selective and sensational reporting of research findings. Tenuous conjecture is then interpreted to a gullible public as certain conclusion.

Gay rights activists have used sympathetic academics and a supportive press to seek minority status for homosexuals and the abolition of all forms of perceived discrimination. Practising homosexuals, they argue, should be given equality in the workforce, in social welfare and in being able to marry and raise (adopted or artificially conceived) children. The strategy, as outlined in books by gay authors, such as *The Homosexualisation of America* and *After the Ball* is as follows: divert attention from what homosexuals do, make homosexuality a topic of everyday conversation, portray homosexuals as 'normal and wholesome' in every other way, and portray those who disapprove of homosexual behaviour as motivated by fear, ignorance and hatred.

It is, of course, quite appropriate for the public to be responsibly informed about scientific discoveries, but twenty-second soundbites cannot do justice to complex controversies, especially when those holding a contrary view are not given the opportunity to respond. 'The first to present his case seems right, till another comes forward and questions him.' (Proverbs 18:17).

### Balancing word and world

Of course we have to be careful not to fall into the same trap ourselves, by selectively using scientific findings to bolster our own position. We need to cultivate an openmindedness which neither gullibly accepts nor quickly rejects new data, but which rather tests the claims of scientists rigorously. The biblical injunction to 'enquire, probe and investigate it thoroughly' (Deuteronomy 13:14) is surely relevant here.

We can expect that just as the Bible will lead us to question whether we have interpreted the scientific facts correctly, so scientific discoveries may lead us to question whether we have interpreted the Bible correctly. We need to balance revelation and science, the Word and the world, in a humble search for the truth knowing that science and Bible properly interpreted should not contradict each other.

### The limitations of Science

When it is next announced in the press (as it inevitably will be) that scientists have discovered a 'gay gene', or a difference in the brain structure of homosexuals for instance, we should evaluate the evidence for such a claim carefully before jumping to conclusions one way or the other.

First, we need to ask whether the research has been replicated elsewhere. Often other studies will have been published which come to opposite conclusions. If the issue has never been addressed before, we need to wait to see if independent investigators can repeat the study and come to the same conclusions. A classic example of this kind of error was the Kinsey Report.[7] For decades, researchers adopted Kinsey's figure of ten percent for the incidence of homosexuality in the general population, not realising that this estimate was based on a poorly designed study of a non-randomly selected sample population, 25% of whom were (or had been) prison inmates. The figure stood unchallenged largely by default until quashed by contemporary research. The finding in a recent British sex survey,[8] that only one in 90 people had had a homosexual partner in the previous year, is much more in keeping with the figure of 1-2% now generally quoted.

Secondly, we need to look at the response from the rest of the scientific community. Other researchers may examine the findings of the study in question and not agree that they warrant the claims made. When it was announced recently that homosexual orientation had been mapped to a small section of the X chromosome,[9] the media uncritically propagated the news as fact. However, an editorial reviewing the findings published shortly afterwards in the British Medical Journal[10] was far more cautious. Unsurprisingly this was not given the same high profile in the popular press.

Thirdly, we need to ask whether there are confounding variables in the study which could be distorting the results. If subjects for a study are not randomly selected from the general population or if like is not being compared with like, then the results can be skewed. For example subjects for a key study[11] claiming to prove that homosexuality has a genetic basis were actively recruited through homophile magazines, hardly an unbiased sampling process.

Fourthly, we need to ask whether an apparent link between, say, homosexual orientation and brain structure, is a direct effect or not. In other words does the brain difference cause the sexual orientation or vice versa? Or alternatively, is the observed difference a consequence of some third factor such as the disease process AIDS?

Fifthly, we must avoid simplistic solutions to complex problems. As science progresses it becomes clear that nature is far more complex than we first imagined. With homosexuality the lack of any real consensus regarding cause should make us suspect that we are not dealing with simple cause and effect.

### Nature or Nurture?

Having laid this framework we now proceed to examine the evidence put forward. What is it that makes one person experience homosexual thoughts and another not? Is homosexuality something genetic or is it a result of upbringing? Is it biological or psychosocial? Or, to use biblical terminology, are people 'born that way' or 'made that way by men'?(Matthew 19:12). Furthermore, if nature or nurture (or both) are involved, then what part does personal choice play in a person adopting a homosexual lifestyle?

Opinions on these questions differ widely among leading researchers. Some, like Boston psychiatrist Richard Pillard,[12] conclude that 'homosexual, bisexual and heterosexual orientations are an example of the biologic diversity of human beings, a diversity with a genetic basis'. Others, like Van Wyk and Geist,[13] contend that 'biologic factors exert at most a predisposing rather than a determining influence'. Still others hold the middle ground. Let us review the evidence.

## Nature arguments

Those who advocate a biological cause have argued that homosexuals possess different hormonal mechanisms, brain structure or genotype. Such biological explanations may not be unrelated; as genes lay the blueprint for hormones which in turn influence body structure. We will look at each in turn.

## 1. Hormonal mechanisms

Hormones are chemical substances produced in the body which have specific regulatory effects on particular body cells or organs. Male sex hormones or androgens are produced by the testis and are responsible for the development of secondary sex characteristics like chest and pubic hair and a deepened voice. Female sex hormones or oestrogens are produced by the ovary and bring about pubic hair growth and breast development. The release of these sex hormones, and indeed the development of the gonads (testis and ovary) themselves, are in turn regulated by other hormones called gonadotrophins (LH and FSH) produced in the pituitary gland at the base of the brain. These are in turn regulated by a third group of hormones (releasing factors) produced just above the pituitary in a part of the brain called the hypothalamus. A delicate balance is maintained.

At one stage it was thought that homosexuals were hormonally different (eg in their circulating levels of reproductive hormones), but this idea was abandoned when sensitive hormone assays became available and accurate measurements could be made.[14] However the possibility remains that hormones might play a part in the *prenatal development* of the brain, and hence in sexual orientation and behaviour.

Female rats exposed to androgens in early development exhibit 'mounting', a typically male sexual response.[15] By contrast, neonatally castrated male rats exhibit 'lordosis', a sexually receptive back-slouching position characteristic of females.[16] Is the rat brain being hormonally programmed in some way during foetal development? Could the same sort of thing be occurring in humans who later show homosexual tendencies?

There are limits in extrapolating these rodent studies to man. First, sexual behaviours in rats are under rigid endocrine (hormonal) control. By contrast in humans sex is not a reflex but a complex and conscious behaviour. There is no human equivalent for stereotyped 'lordosis' or 'mounting'. Second, human homosexuals engage in both receptive and penetrative intercourse; whereas in this model 'mounting' and 'lordosis' were gender-specific. Third, the prenatal hormone theory fails to explain the complexity and variability of the human sexual response with changes of erotic fantasies, modes of sexual expression and indeed even sexual orientation over time.

If the prenatal hormone hypothesis is correct we would expect to find a higher incidence of abnormal gonadal structure or function in homo-sexuals. We do not. We would also expect to find a higher proportion of homosexuals among patients with disorders involving androgen excess or deficiency. Again, extensive reviews of the literature suggest that this is not the case.[17,18] For example there is also no evidence that children resulting from hormonally treated pregnancies develop homosexual tendencies.[19]

Some very rare medical conditions, in which the affected person's sexual status is ambiguous, have however been put forward as providing evidence for a hormonal cause of homosexual orientation. One example is testicular feminisation. Affected individuals are genet-ically male (ie: have XY chromosomes) and have testes which are normal but remain in the abdomen. They also have normal appearing female external genitalia. Often these individuals do not come to medical attention until after puberty, when they present with amen-orrhea (a failure to menstruate) and infertility. On psychosexual testing they are indistinguishable from heterosexual genetic females in terms of sexual arousal and erotic imagery.[20] However because they are raised as females (because they look like females), this does not prove that sexual preference is hormonally programmed, rather than environmentally conditioned.

Congenital adrenal hyperplasia is a condition in which genetic females are exposed to excessive levels of androgens produced by the adrenal gland, resulting in masculinised (part-male, part-female) genitalia. The vast majority of women with congenital adrenal hyperplasia develop heterosexual interests and there is no consistent evidence for an increased incidence of lesbianism in this condition. Even if this were shown to be the case, it would be almost impossible to show that this was due to a hormonal effect on the brain rather than the psychological effect of having masculinised genitalia.

Of course, it needs to be stressed that the vast majority (99%) of homosexual people have no measurable hormonal abnormality. The case for a hormonal cause of homosexuality remains as yet unproven.

## 2. Brain structure

Could homosexuality be the result of differences in the structure of the brain? Again studies in rodents have aroused suspicions.

The hypothalamus, situated at the base of the brain, is an important hormone control centre. Within its substance lie 'nuclei', tiny bundles of nerve cells each no bigger than the head of a pin. Because of their minute size they can only be properly examined at autopsy. In rats one of these nuclei (SDN-POA) is sexually dimorphic, that is, it is a different size in males and females. This has fuelled speculation that similar differences may exist in humans, not only between sexes but also between homosexual and heterosexual people. Much current research involves examining microscopic portions of post-mortem brain tissue, in an attempt to prove that these variations exist.

In 1984, two scientists named Swaab and Fliers claimed to have found a hypothalamic nucleus which was larger in men than in women.[21] Later, however, they were unable to establish a link between its size and sexual orientation.[22]

In 1991 LeVay, a neurobiologist, dissected the brains of 35 males and reported that the size of another hypothalamic nucleus (INAH3) in homosexual men was smaller than its counterpart in heterosexual men and the same size as that of the women.[23] The study was highly publicised, but again there were reasons to be cautious. Firstly the numbers involved were small. Secondly most of the homosexual men with abnormal hypothalamuses had died of AIDS. Thirdly, it was not apparent how the anatomical area involved could have had a bearing on sexual behaviour. Fourthly, even if it could have, it would remain to be proven that the structural change was the cause rather than the result of the altered sexual orientation. Finally, other researchers have pointed to technical flaws[24] and the findings of the study have not yet been confirmed by other researchers. A number of other hypothalamic structures have been shown to be sexually dimorphic, but without any yet being clearly implicated in regulating sexual response.

In addition to the hypothalamus, the commissures (bundles of nerve fibres joining the two sides of the human brain) have been extensively examined. Allen and Gorski, again in a well-publicised study, reported in 1992 that the anterior commissure was smaller in heterosexual men than in homosexual men and heterosexual women.[25] However there was considerable overlap between the three groups and again the majority of homosexual subjects had AIDS.

There have also been claims that the corpus callosum (a much larger commissure) may be female-typical in homosexual men, but the 23 studies reported thus far have yielded conflicting results.[26]

In summary we have currently uncorroborated reports that three different brain structures may possibly show structural variation with sexual orientation. However in each study the sample size was small, the possible relation between the structure and sexual preference has not been established and the confounding effect of AIDS has not been adequately addressed.

### 3. Genetic studies

In the human body there are 100 trillion cells, each possessing a nucleus containing more information than an average laptop computer. This information is written on 46 chromosomes, arranged in 23 pairs, each pair consisting of one chromosome from each parent. The chromosomes are constructed from coils of a ladder-shaped molecule called DNA which makes up our genes. The genetic language has an alphabet of four letters (bases) and if we were to take the entire amount of information in any one cell nucleus and print it out 1,000 letters to a page it would fill 3,000 books of 1,000 pages each. The letters are grouped together into three letter words (codons) strung together into sentences (genes). Each of the 100,000 genes in the body carries the instructions for the production of a specific protein. Proteins perform a vast variety of actions from determining the detailed structure of our organs, to transporting chemical substances from one part of the body to another, to controlling the thousands of chemical reactions that are occurring in our different cells. In so doing they govern everything from handedness to eye-colour, from appearance to temperament.

There are about 6,000 known genetic diseases (disorders resulting from spelling mistakes in the genetic language which can be passed on from parents to children), and 21,000 children in the UK are born with one each year. However these conditions vary widely in their severity, frequency, mode of inheritance and expression. Some are lethal (such as those causing many miscarriages), while others may produce no discernible difference at all. Some (like Down's syndrome) are common while others are extremely rare. Some (like Huntington's disease) if passed from a parent will be expressed in the next generation, while others (like cystic fibrosis) may skip generations completely or simply create a predisposition for the disorder rather than guaranteeing its occurrence.

Could homosexual orientation have a genetic component? Could it even be entirely genetically programmed?

The possibility of a genetic basis for homosexuality has been recognised ever since Kallman evaluated the twin siblings of homosexuals and found that 100% of identical twins but only 12% of nonidentical (fraternal) twins were also gay.[27] While he used a biased sample (most were mentally ill and institutionalised men), and his results have never been reproduced, there have been further studies attempting to show that homosexuality runs in families. The most famous of these are two studies by Bailey. The first showed that 52% of the identical twins of gay men were also gay, while only 22% of non-identical twins were.[28] The second study gave corresponding figures of 48% and 16% for the twin sisters of gay women.[29]

There are reasons to be cautious in assuming that these observed effects were due to genes rather than upbringing. First, identical twins are more likely to be treated similarly by parents and others, especially if they have similar temperaments. Even in the same family children are raised in quite different ways. The fact that non-twin brothers are less likely to share a homosexual orientation than non-identical twin brothers suggests that environment plays a large part. This is because non-identical twins and non-twin siblings share the same proportion of genetic material. Second, neither study drew subjects randomly but recruited them through homosexual-oriented periodicals. This must at very least introduce the possibility that twins wanting to establish that homosexual orientation is genetic may have been more ready to apply. Was the sampling really unbiased? Third, there has so far been only one small and inconclusive study[30] comparing the sexual orientation of twins who have been reared apart since birth; when in fact this is the best way of ensuring that environmental factors do not confuse the picture. Fourth, even if homosexual orientation is influenced by genetic factors, the presence of a 'gay gene' is not necessarily proven. We may simply be talking about a character trait which makes a child more likely to be treated in a way which might lead to a development of a homosexual orientation. Fifth, the authors' interpretation of their data has been cast into serious doubt by statistical reanalysis which found no difference between the groups.[31] Finally, even if we accept Bailey's results, we still have a large proportion of identical twins (-50%) who develop different sexual orientations despite allegedly sharing the same prenatal and family environment.

With the rapid advances in our ability to unravel the genetic code, researchers are now trying to discover where on the 46 chromosomes each of the 100,000 known human genes is located. This international collaborative effort, known as the human genome project, is now well under way, and understandably there are attempts to locate a gene for homosexual orientation.

In 1993 Hamer, a geneticist working in the field, claimed to have done just that in a paper published in the journal *Science*. He reported that 33 of 40 homosexual non-twin brothers had homosexual relatives on their mothers' sides with similar DNA markers in a region of the female X chromosome known as Xq28.[32] There was considerable media interest in what came to be known as the 'gay gene' but also, as mentioned, less enthusiasm in the medical press.[33] An article in *Nature* commented, 'Were virtually any other trait involved, the paper would have received little public notice until the results had been independently confirmed'.[34] The study sample was small, the results have not yet been confirmed by other researchers, and there is not as yet any indication of how frequent the Xq28 sequence is in the general population. One researcher who reanalysed Hamer's data stated, 'Using the more appropriate (statistical) test I compared several pairs of relatives... there is no evidence for a maternal effect... Until these results are replicated... they should be viewed with extreme scepticism'.[35]

In fact no 'gay gene' as such has so far been located, let alone had its component DNA sequenced. Even if a gene is discovered, this may simply carry the instructions for a character trait rather than homosexual orientation as such. Furthermore even if a genetic link is established for a small proportion of individuals in one section of the gay community, it does not follow that it underlies or explains all homosexuality in all individuals. We know, for example, that a small proportion of breast cancer, but by no means all, is linked to one particular predisposing gene.

As outlined above, interest has focused on finding a 'gay gene' in other species. Biologists Ward Odenwald and Shang-Ding Zhang at the National Institutes of Health in Bethesda, Maryland, created a storm of media publicity with their claim to have transplanted a gene into fruit flies which produced homosexual behaviour.[36] As it transpired these flies were bisexual rather than homosexual and no lesbian flies were produced. The complexity of the human sexual response, in comparison with the far simpler reflexes in invertebrates, should lead us to beware of hasty conclusions.

Overall there is some evidence in small studies that genes may have some bearing on the later emergence of a homosexual orientation. However many questions remain. If homosexual preference (as opposed to homosexual behaviour) were truly genetic, why is it not observed in species other than man? Why do a large proportion of identical twins vary in their sexual orientation? Why does sexual preference change over time, or with therapy? (Masters and Johnson, in a five year follow-up of sixty-seven exclusively homosexual men and women, reported that 65% achieved successful changes in their sexual orientation after behaviour therapy.[37]) Clearly we are not dealing with a simple causal link.

Genetic factors may play a part in the development of homosexual orientation, but they are not the full story. Terry McGuire, Associate Professor of Biological Sciences at Rutgers University, New Jersey, urges us to be circumspect about alleged research findings:

'Any genetic study must use (1) valid and precise measures of individual differences, (2) appropriate methods to ascertain biological relationships, (3) research subjects who have been randomly recruited, (4) appropriate sample sizes and (5) appropriate genetic models to interpret the data.... To date, all studies of the genetic basis of sexual orientation of men and women have failed to meet one or more of the above criteria.'[38]

While we may not ever find a 'gay gene', there is however increasing evidence to suggest that personality variants (in particular novelty seeking, harm avoidance and reward dependence) may well be inherited.[39] These could theoretically predispose to the development of a homosexual orientation given the right (or wrong) environment.

This leads us to evaluate the role of nurture.

### Nurture arguments

The pure biological view is that homosexual orientation is programmed in the genes, fashioned by hormones, and displayed in brain structure. The pure psychosocial view is that the environment writes upon the developing child, in the same way that someone might draw lines on a blank sheet of paper. Both embrace a type of determinism; in the first the individual is the product of the interactions of chemical reactions, in the second he (or she) is programmed by social forces.

As with the biological arguments, I will consider nurture arguments under several headings, although it should be obvious that they interrelate. Let us consider then the cultural environment, the family environment, the peer-group environment and the moral environment.

## 1. The cultural environment

The cultural view is that sexual conduct is determined by the society in which one grows up. In other words, we learn sexuality in much the same way that we learn cultural customs. Whereas biological sex is set at birth, gender-specific behaviour develops in a cultural context. The interplay of tradition, religious belief and political factors lays a framework for acceptable behaviour which become increasingly ingrained until they eventually feel natural.

The evidence for this is the diversity of sexual behaviour across cultures and across history. There are cultures where homosexual behaviour is so uncommon that there is no word for it in the language.[40] Similarly, homosexuality as we know it today (long-term relationships between consenting adults), did not exist in Western culture before the nineteenth century.

## 2. The Family environment

Most nurture theories focus on the pattern of the parent-child relationship. Male homosexuals are more likely to emerge from families where the father is disinterested, remote, weak or overly hostile and the mother is the dominant disciplinarian and warmest supporter.[41] In the same way lesbians may result from families where there is a breakdown of the mother-daughter relationship.

This view has been popularised by Elisabeth Moberly, who has come to the conclusion that homosexual orientation is the result of unmet same sex love needs in childhood.[42] Martin Hallett, Director and Counsellor at True Freedom Trust, a Christian ministry to Christians struggling with homosexuality, has found that the majority of male homosexuals counselled identify very much with this lack of intimate bonding with the father or any other male role model.[43] As a result, the heterosexual identity is not established, and the unaffirmed child later as an adult suffers from a lack of confidence and fear of failure in heterosexual contacts. He tries to meet those unmet same-sex needs through sexual relationships. When these fail to satisfy the result may be an even more compulsive and promiscuous lifestyle.

Sara Lawton,[44] a Christian counsellor specialising in lesbianism and sex-abuse, similarly sees the root of female homosexuality as an unmet need for mother love which becomes sexualised in the adult. This can be compounded by repressed trauma (eg the mother tried to abort her), adoption, prolonged separation through illness or sexual abuse.

The parent-child relationship can also be disturbed through death or divorce. Saghir and Robins found that 18% of homosexual men and 35% of lesbians had lost their father by death or divorce by the age of ten. The figures for heterosexuals were 9% and 4% respectively.[45] The vast majority (up to 70%) of homosexual adults describe themselves as having been 'sissies' or 'tomboys' as children.[46] This is despite the fact that most adult homosexuals fit neither the effeminate male nor masculine female stereotype. While a higher percentage of homosexuals than heterosexuals exhibit some degree of gender nonconformity, we cannot generalise to all cases. Heterosexuals can come from situations of poor same sex bonding, whereas homosexuals can come from families where the parent-child relationships were good.[47]

However, amidst the enthusiasm to find a biological cause, the extensive experience of counsellors and the memories of homosexuals themselves need to be taken into account. Thomas Schmidt, in an excellent, wide-ranging review of the literature has commented: '...since developmental theory is now out of fashion, homosexuals are either not asked about or no longer 'remember' childhood problems. It is certainly suspicious that, to my knowledge, not a single study of early childhood among homosexuals has been conducted since the early 1980s.'[48]

### 3. The peer group environment

The forming of a homosexual identity takes time. Before adolescence most people consider themselves heterosexual and for the majority these thoughts are reinforced by the peer-group. However, for the child who doesn't 'fit in', the masculine female or the nonmasculine male, identification with the opposite sex peer group may prove easier, especially if there is experience of rejection by same sex peers. The male child in this situation may be socialised as a girl and vice versa. This can lead to gender confusion at adolesence and later identification with others of the same sex who are suffering from the same feelings of isolation. In this context the acceptance of the homosexual label can bring security, self understanding and acceptance; at a level which has never been experienced by that individual before.

Identification with the gay culture, or 'coming out', has many rewards in terms of escaping from conflict, reducing the pain of rejection and providing human contact. In other words, just as peer pressure enhances a sense of sexual identity in those who eventually become heterosexual, so peer pressure can similarly reinforce homosexual feelings and behaviour. A network of supportive friends and perhaps a long-term homosexual relationship can be powerful forces driving people into and keeping them within the gay community.

Whether heterosexuals can be recruited into homosexuality is a complex issue, but a disproportionate number of male homosexuals were sexually molested as children. Education promoting the idea that homosexuality is just a genetically programmed normal variant will certainly lessen any stigma and make it easier for those with confused gender identity to enter the gay community.

## 4. The moral environment

In all societies children grow up with a set of instilled values giving them a sense of right and wrong. To a large extent the conscience will be shaped by the parental environment. Children who are seldom punished will quickly cease to feel guilt when they cross boundaries. On the other hand if standards are arbitrarily or unfairly imposed, or if the parents are not themselves good role models, children may rebel against their consciences.

Personal conscience can thus be underdeveloped through liberal upbringing, or blunted through disuse. This tendency will be intensified if the public conscience itself is changing, as it certainly is with regard to homosexuality. When homosexuality was regarded as degeneracy there were powerful social pressures preventing its expression. Now that one can incur the wrath of the politically correct for suggesting that homosexuality is anything other than a natural variant, the tables have turned.

The present author's opinion concurs with that of Bancroft: 'It remains difficult, on scientific grounds, to avoid the conclusion that the uniquely human phenomenon of sexual orientation is a consequence of a multifactorial developmental process in which biological factors play a part, but in which psychosocial factors remain crucially important'.[49]

## The role of personal choice

Some react against advocates of a strong nature or nurture model, by arguing that sexual orientation is a myth, and that homosexuality is a matter of simple choice. This is understandable. All of us have a sense, that at least in some small way we are the masters of our own destiny. We are not solely genetic machines any more than we are blank slates on which experience writes. While most authors recognise the possible importance of both nature and nurture, often too little attention has been given to the ways in which these factors interact, or to the role of personal choice.

At some point every practising homosexual makes a choice to indulge in homosexual fantasy, to identify with the gay community or to have homosexual sex. And regardless of the strength and power of the temptations encouraging that choice, regardless of the biological and psychosocial forces operating in any individual, that choice is always wrong. However we must not make the mistake of ignoring the role of nature and nurture in making those of homosexual orientation what they are.

## An interactive model

While there will always be those who support one model of causation, be it nature, nurture or choice above all others, the majority of scholars concede that many factors are involved. Heredity and environment are both important and personal choice is clearly involved too. How these elements interact in any one individual may differ and this explains why one or more of the biological or psychosocial ingredients may be lacking in any one case.

For example, a boy with a biological predisposition to 'girlish' behaviour is born into a dysfunctional family where the father is remote and the mother smothering. He grows up with little moral training into a society where homosexuality is viewed as a normal variant. He experiments with homosexual behaviour in adolescence and finds companionship and identity through a longterm homosexual relationship at university, before entering the gay subculture in a large city.[50]

At any point the process may be interrupted or diverted; if the biological disposition is not there, if the family dynamics or society's attitudes are different, or if a conscious choice is made not to proceed. But the process is complex and multifactorial, different for each individual.

This should leave us with a humble and open attitude, willing to learn more from scientific research, and the testimony of skilled counsellors and gay people—so that we can come to understand and respond to the factors involved in any individual case.

### What is natural?

Explaining **how** a homosexual orientation may develop, and understanding **why** some individuals are more susceptible than others does not start to answer the question of how people **should** behave.

There is often an unstated assumption that strong feelings should determine behaviour, whereas in fact this is not accepted in almost any other area of life. We do not believe for example that a strong desire to smoke or to drink should be rewarded with the provision of cigarettes or alcohol. Nor do we accept that lust legitimises adultery or that envy sanctions stealing or greed.

Many of the desires we have, if acted upon, lead to damaging not only other human beings but ourselves as well. As the Bible succinctly puts it: 'There is a way that seems right to a man, but in the end it leads to death' (Proverbs 14:12), or 'the heart is deceitful above all things and beyond cure' (Jeremiah 17:9). God calls us to resist evil desires, not to act on them, but rather to obey him with the strength his Spirit gives.

The Gay Rights Lobby presupposes that what comes naturally is good. By contrast the biblical world view is that the whole world and human beings themselves are polluted by sin which has affected our bodies (and this must surely include our genes), our minds, our wills and our feelings. Consequently our biology, our thoughts, our choices and our desires are not what they were intended to be. In the biblical scheme 'natural' (as in Romans 1:27) means not 'what comes naturally' but rather 'what God intended (and intends) us to be'.

## Summary
While Christians will see both homosexual orientation and behaviour as evidence that we live in a fallen world, we must not retreat into a simplistic analysis that sees homosexual behaviour simply as arbitrary personal choice. The exact means by which sin exerts its effects on societies and individuals is only in part discernible to us as sinful human beings. It should come as no surprise to discover that even our genetic code, hormonal functions and body structures are affected by it. The ageing process itself, for example, is a consequence of sin and yet mediated by these same factors. Why not then a predisposition to homosexual orientation? In the same way we should not be surprised that our upbringing may have profound effects on our temperaments and personalities.

This is not to deny that all of us, homosexual or heterosexual, are sinners by choice. But we are also sinners by nature both by virtue of living in a fallen world, and by being sinned against by others.

Regardless of what may come to be known in the future about the relative contribution of nature, nurture and personal choice to the development of homosexuality, its complete healing will only be found through repentance, faith, forgiveness, regeneration and ultimately resurrection of the body in a new heaven and a new earth.

## About the author
Born in New Zealand, **Peter Saunders** qualified MBChB in 1982, later completing specialist training in General Surgery (FRACS). He worked in New Zealand and Kenya (with AIM) before doing a two year

diploma in theology at All Nations Christian College, Hertfordshire. Since 1992 he has been in full-time Christian ministry as Student Secretary for the Christian Medical Fellowship. He speaks and writes regularly on issues at the interface of Christianity and medicine and is a member of the Independent Chapel, Spicer Street, St Albans. Peter is married to Kirsty (also medically qualified) and they have three sons. In his chapter Dr Saunders investigates the causes of homosexuality.

### Chapter 3 notes

1   **A Kinsey et al,** *Sexual Behaviour in the Human Male*, WB Saunders, 1948
2   **C. Socarides and B. Kauffman,** *Reparative Therapy* (letter), American Journal of Psychiatry, 1994, 151:157-59
3   **J Bancroft,** *Homosexual Orientation: The search for a biological basis*, British Journal of Psychiatry, 1994, 164:437-440
4   **R. Green,** *The immutability of (homo) sexual orientation: behavioural science implications for a constitutional (legal) analysis.* Journal of Psychiatry and Law, Winter 1988, pp 537-575.
5   **M Bailey and R Pillard,** in *Opinions and Editorials*, New York Times, 17 December 1991, p19
6   **A Bell et al,** *Sexual Preference: Its development in Men and Women,* Bloomington, Ind: Indiana University Press, 1981, p219.
7   See ref 1 above
8   **A Johnson et al,** *Sexual attitudes and Lifestyles,* Blackwell Scientific, 1994, cited by A. Tonks, "British sex survey shows popularity of monogamy", *British Medical Journal,* 1994, 308:289.
9   **D Hamer et al,** *A linkage between DNA markers on the X chromosome and male sexual orientation,* Science, 1993, 261:321-327
10  **M. Baron,** *Genetic linkage and male homosexual orientation,* Archives of General Psychiatry, 1993, 48:1089-1096
11  **J Bailey and R Pillard,** *A genetic study of male sexual orientation,* Archives of General Psychiatry, 1991, 48:1089-1096
12  **R. Pillard and M. Bailet,** A Biologic perspective of heterosexual, bisexual and homosexual behaviour, Archives of Sexual Behaviour, 1984, 13:505-544.

13   P Van Wyk and C Geist, *Psychosocial development of heterosexual, bisexual and homosexual behaviour*, Archives of Sexual Behaviour, 1984, 13:505-544

14   H. Meyer-Bahlburg, *Psychoendocrine research on sexual orientation: current status and future options,* Progress in Brain Research, 1984, 61:375-398.

15   R Goy and B McEwen, *Sexual Differentiation of the Brain*, Cambridge Mass: MIT Press; 1980

16   H Meyer-Bahlburg, *Sex hormones and male homosexuality in comparative perspective, Archives of Sexual Behaviour, 1977, 6:297-325.*

17   H Meyer-Bahlburg, *Sex hormones and female sexuality: a critical examination*, Archives of Sexual Behaviour, 1979, 8:101-119
     See also reference 12 above

18   W. Byne and B. Parsons, *Human Sexual orientation: The Biologic Theories Reappraised,* Archives of General Psychiatry, 1993, 50:228-239

19   See reference 18 above.

20   J. Money et al, *Adult heterosexual status and fetal hormonal masculinisation,* Psychoneuroendocrinology, 1984, 9:405-414.

21   D Swaab and E Fliers, *A sexually dimorphic nucleus in the human brain*, Science, 1985, 228:1112-1114

22   D. Swaab and M. Hoffman, *Sexual differtiation of the human hypothalmus: ontogeny of the sexually dimorphic nucleus of the preoptic area*, Dev Brain Research, 1988, 44: 314-318.

23   S LeVay, *A difference in hypothalamic structure between heterosexual and homosexual men*, Science, 1991, 253:1034-1037

24   See reference 19 above.

25   L Allen and R Gorski, *Sexual orientation and the size of the anterior commissure in the human brain*, Proceedings of the Naional Academy of Sciences, USA, 1992, 891:7199-7202

26   See ref 18 above, p 235.

27   F Kallman, *Comparative twin study of the genetic aspects of homosexuality*, Journal of Nervous and Mental Disease, 1952, 115:288-298

28   J. Bailey and R. Pillard, *A genetic study of male sexual orientation,* Archives of General Psychiatry, 1993, 50:217-223

29   J Bailey et al, *Heritable factors influence sexual orientation in women,* Archives of General Psychiatry, 1993, 50:217-223

**30** **E. Eckert et al,** *Homosexuality in monozygotic twins reared apart* British Journal of Psychiatry, 1986, 148: 421-425

**31** **T. McGuire** *Is Homosexuality Genetic?* A critical review and some suggestions, Journal of Homosexuality, 1995, 28 (1-2) 115-145

**32** See ref 9 above.

**33** See ref 10 above.

**34** **M. King,** "Sexual orientation and the X" *Nature,* 1993, 364: 288-289.

**35** See ref 31 above.

**36** **L. Thompson,** "Search for a Gay Gene", TIME magazine, 12 June 1995, pp 52-53.

**37** **W Masters and V Johnson,** *Homosexuality in Perspective*, Little, Brown and Co, 1979

**38** See ref 31 above.

**39** **C. Cloninger,** *A systematic method for clinical description and classification of personality variants*, Archives of General Psychiatry, 1987, 44:573-588

**40** See ref 3 above.

**41** **A Bell et al,** *Sexual Preference: Its Development in Men and Women*, Bloomington:Indiana University Press, 1981, pp41-62, 117-134

**42** **E. Moberley,** *Homosexuality: structure and evaluation,* Theology, 1980, p.83.

**43** **M Hallett,** *Homosexuality*, Nucleus, January 1994, pp14-19

**44** **S. Lawton,** *Key Issues in Counselling Lesbians,* Lecture 8 in Signposts to Wholeness, True Freedom Trust, 1994.

**45** **M Saghir and E Robins,** *Male and Female Homosexuality: A Comprehensive Investigation*, Baltimore:Williams Wilkins, 1973

**46** See ref 39, pp 17-31, 191-203.

**47** **R Friedman,** *Male Homosexuality:A Contemporary Psychoanalytical Perspective.* New Haven, Conn:Yale University Press, 1988, pp33-48

**48** **T. Schmidt,** *Straight and Narrow? Compassion and Clarity in the Homosexuality debate,* IVP, 1995, p 215..

**49** See ref 3 above, p439

**50** Adapted from **T. Schmidt,** ref 48, p 151

# The Bible and sexuality

**Paul Brown** summarises the teaching of the Bible on the whole subject of sex and marriage

People today seem to want two things that are complete contradictions. On the one hand, they want an ordered society and stable marriages with love and security where children can be brought up with the affectionate care of two parents who are both committed to each other and to their children. On the other, they also want to be free to express their sexual desires without any limits imposed on them from outside, to enter into sexual relationships without the commitment of marriage, and to change their partners if they feel this will be best for them. It has, however, never been possible to have one's cake and eat it, and a society that tries to do both is heading for trouble.

A great deal of the present problem arises because people tend to think that morals, or at least sexual morals, are the concern of the individual, and not of society as a whole. What right has anyone else, so the argument goes, to tell me how to live my life? What right has society to impose upon me standards of sexual behaviour that I either feel I cannot live up to, or that I simply don't want to live up to? So a sort of *laissez faire* situation has arisen: some believe in marriage as a lifelong commitment, and that is fine and good for them; others adopt alternative lifestyles and that is good for them—but no-one has the right to query or criticise at all. It is into this picture that homosexual relationships fit.

No-one can pretend that the present situation in society is one with which anyone can be happy. The breakdown of marriage; the large numbers of one-parent families; children insecure and unloved, perhaps not knowing who their fathers are; sexually-transmitted diseases; the sexual abuse of children and paedophilia; all these things and many others make for unhappiness and misery and a tragically disordered society. Christians wish to speak out, with compassion and deep concern, and say that these things ought not to be and do not need to be. God has given us his pattern for our lives in the Bible, and it is the neglect, perhaps more accurately in many cases, the rejection, of what he has said which has led to things being as they are.

## The creation pattern

The accounts of creation in Genesis 1 and 2 give us the pattern of marriage that God presented in the beginning. Speaking particularly of Genesis 2:21-25 Gordon Wenham says, 'The story therefore needs to be closely read, for in its often poetic phraseology are expressed some of the Old Testament's fundamental convictions about the nature and purpose of marriage.'[1] But more important than this, in turning to these chapters we are taking our cue from Jesus Christ. When asked a question about divorce he replied, 'Haven't you read... that at the beginning the Creator "made them male and female", and said, "For this reason a man will leave his father and mother and be united to his wife, and the two will become one flesh"? So they are no longer two, but one. Therefore what God has joined together, let not man separate.' (Matthew 19:4-6).

Genesis 1:27,28 reads, 'So God created man in his own image, in the image of God he created him; male and female he created them. God blessed them and said to them, "Be fruitful and increase in number; fill the earth and subdue it. Rule over the fish of the sea and the birds of the air and over every living creature that moves on the ground." '

This indicates clearly two features of human beings as created. First, they were made in the image of God, a point which is repeated for emphasis. Secondly, God made them male and female. After the image of God, the most significant feature is gender differentiation. They were created as sexual beings; physiologically distinct, with the natural desires and emotions, and psychological differences,[2] that belong to male and female. There was not, of course, the slightest tension between being in the image of God and being sexual beings.

As male and female God blessed them. Their sexuality, including its expression in all the mutuality of love culminating in sexual inter-course, had his approval and distinct blessing. The first obligation that God laid on human beings at the very beginning was, 'Be fruitful and increase in number; fill the earth...' Nothing could underline the naturalness, goodness and centrality of human sexuality more emphatically than the fact that the first obligation God placed upon the people he had made required the expression of their sexuality in intercourse. When God saw everything that he had made, he saw that it was very good (v31), and that included the fact and expression of sexuality.

Genesis 2 fills out the picture considerably. Here the creation of the first man and of the first woman is spelled out in detail, complementing the general, overall picture of chapter 1. The first point for comment is the fact that the man was lonely and incomplete by himself (v19). It is God who acknowledges this, and he who supplies the remedy. God did not make another man to meet Adam's need, he made the first woman. Adam's incompleteness had a sexual dimension and required someone human but also different from him. Wenham comments on the phrase 'a helper suitable for him', 'The compound prepositional phrase "matching him," ... literally, "like opposite him" is found only here. It seems to express the notion of complementarity rather than identity. As Delitzsch (1:140) observes, if identity were meant the more natural phrase would be "like him".'[3] So Eve was made for Adam, and Adam finds that Eve supplies the companionship that he lacked. Eve was made from Adam's side to indicate that her purpose was to be his companion, and also to show that the man and the woman belong together. They complement each other, find fulfilment in each other and reach their true potential in partnership together.

Secondly, it was God himself who not only formed Eve from Adam's rib but also 'brought her to the man' (v22). God her Creator 'gave her away'. The joining of Adam to Eve, and their uniting as one flesh was not simply permitted by God, or even mandated by God. He actively brought it about.

Thirdly, it is clear that the example of Adam and Eve is intended to set a pattern for marriage. This was why Jesus Christ referred to this chapter, quoting verse 24. The relationship established in marriage is one which is to take precedence over the parent/child relationship. It is one which is close and exclusive, 'a man will...be united to his wife'. So close is this unity that the verse continues, '...and they will become one flesh.' This undoubtedly includes a reference to sexual union (as Paul insists, 1 Corinthians 6:16); but it almost certainly goes beyond it. The physical union is an expression and symbol of the joining of two persons; in the words of Jesus, 'So they are no longer two but one' (Matthew 19:5). The word translated 'wife' is actually 'woman', it is the 'his' that makes it appropriate to translate 'wife' here and in the next verse. In Hebrew (and in Greek) there is a greater emphasis on gender; 'a man will be united to his woman.'

Fourthly, when God brought the woman to the man Adam broke out in an exclamation of wonder and joy in a couplet which could be called the first love poem.4 Once again it is the fact that the man and the woman belong together that is stressed. The woman was taken out of man, she is bone of his bone and flesh of his flesh, and now they are joined together again and become one flesh.

Finally, the goodness and innocence of the relationship between the first man and woman is brought out by verse 25, 'The man and his wife were both naked, and they felt no shame.' There was nothing about their union which was inconsistent with true righteousness nor with the closest fellowship with their Creator. Their mutual nakedness was open and pure.

From this brief survey of Genesis 1 and 2 it is possible to consider some of the practical emphases that emerge.

### Sexuality

Any Christian view necessarily involves the idea that God as Creator made humans men and women, but the Genesis account stresses this in a way which might not have been anticipated. Involved in sexuality are strong emotions and desires. The yearning for companionship, the desire for sexual fulfilment, the desire for children and for family life are deeply embedded in the human psyche and are all inter-related so that the satisfaction of only one of these components is inadequate. All the desires that arise from our creation as sexual beings are God-given. They are not to be under-rated or marginalised. We all have to recognise our sexuality and come to terms with it in the context of the life to which we are called to live by God.

## Marriage

Old Testament Hebrew does not have words which are the real equivalent of our 'marry', 'marriage'. The most usual term for marry is, literally, 'to take a woman', and this is what is found in Genesis (e.g. 4:19; 6:2; 11:29). We would, perhaps, have been glad if God had spelled out precisely what marriage is, what constitutes a marriage, and the roles, responsibilities and relationships between husbands and wives in a short section of the Bible. However, this is not what God has chosen to do. Genesis 2 presents us with a pattern from which we have to draw out implications in the light of the rest of Scripture that apply to life and circumstances today. This passage certainly indicates the central importance of marriage for human beings. The male/female differentiation finds its primary fulfilment in marriage; marriage is the basic, fundamental relationship for human beings made in the image of God. The picture which emerges here is developed in the rest of the Old Testament and is confirmed in the New Testament. 'The ethical ideal is that sexual activity is to be confined within faithful, heterosexual marriage, normally lifelong, and Jesus is recorded as upholding this in his own teaching (Mark 10:1-12; Matt. 5:31-32; 19:3-9; cf. Luke 16:18; 1 Cor. 10-11).'[5] The joy and fulfilment of marriage is celebrated in a number of passages such as Proverbs 5:15-19; 31:10-31; The Song of Songs; and Ephesians 5:25-33.

## The Family

The command of God 'be fruitful and increase in number' implies the family. Once children began to be born the first family came into existence. It is clear that from the very beginning it was the intention of God that children should be brought up by a man and his wife. The fact that children are conceived by an act of love between parents, together with the fact that God began the human race with a single couple—he could have started with a community if he had wished to—indicate that this is so. It is sometimes stressed today that the Bible speaks much more of the extended family than is customary among Western countries today. This is so and we should learn from it, but it should not be used to undermine the importance of the nuclear family. The human race began with a nuclear family; the commandment, 'Honour your father and your mother' (Exodus 20:12) shows its central importance, an importance which comes to a climax in Ephesians 5:22 to 6:4. Children are to be brought up within the context of a stable, loving relationship between husband and wife. Nearly everyone recognises the importance of this, though not everyone is prepared to follow out in practice what it demands. It is also within the family that children learn to relate to other people, to recognise authority, and to consider the needs of others and the good of the whole family unit. This has profound implications for society; and as children grow older they interact more and more with the wider family and other families in society.

## Divine Institution

It needs to be stressed that marriage was instituted by God. The whole emphasis in Genesis 1 and 2 is on what God has done. Marriage is a gift of God; it is an expression and evidence of his goodness. But though it is a good gift, it is not a gift to be tampered with or altered according to the desires of human beings. The divine authority of the Creator lies behind the whole arrangement revealed in Genesis 2:18-25. Marriage is between one man and one woman; it constitutes a unity which takes precedence over every other relationship, a unity which is ordained by God so that Jesus can comment, in the light of this passage, 'Therefore what God has joined together, let not man separate.' (Matthew 19:6) It is the divine authority that lies behind the marriage pattern of Genesis 2 which our Lord is highlighting. In days when people believe that sexual ethics are simply the concern of the individual it has to be stressed that it is God who sets the standards for sexual behaviour, indeed for all human behaviour both individual and social. God's pattern, and God's law, are authoritative and human beings are accountable to him for their response to the standards he has set. It is not surprising that unbelievers reject what God has laid down; those who take seriously their commitment to Scripture are both committed to personal obedience and to bear their witness to what God has said to people today.

## Singleness

In the light of what has been said so far it is essential to make some reference to singleness. There is no doubt that Genesis presents marriage as the norm for human beings as they were created, and the Old Testament takes this for granted. So much is this the case that there is no word for 'bachelor' in the Old Testament. Are we to assume that singleness is part of the derangement which has come about as a result of the Fall? This question is not answered in Scripture. It is nowhere even hinted that singleness came about in this way and idle speculation leads nowhere. What we do know is that in the New Testament the single condition is shown to be the will of God for some people (1 Corinthians 7:7), and it is clear that for Christians there can be real spiritual advantages resulting from singleness (1 Corinthians 7:25ff.). Vera Sinton says, 'So the Christian perspective on the biblical material is that, while the first created human beings, Adam and Eve, were a married couple, in the new creation the second Adam, Jesus Christ, was a single man. Singleness and marriage are parallel routes for loving and serving in the world and preparing us for life in the resurrection community.'[6]

Singleness is at least part of life for everyone and may be the will of God for an individual for the whole of life. Many of those who marry will spend a significant number of their years as single. In the light of Genesis 2 we can deduce that singleness means that sexuality cannot be expressed in intercourse, as that lies at the heart of the marriage unity, 'one flesh'. While the Bible does not say that intercourse constitutes, or institutes, marriage, consummation is an essential element because marriage is, by definition, a union between two people of different sex. It is worth pointing out that refraining from sexual intercourse is obligated on all who are not married. Those who desire relationships with those of the same sex are not being discriminated against in this matter; the same prohibition, difficult though some may find it to bear, lies upon all who are unmarried.

## Justification for this approach

This way of approaching the subject through Genesis 1 and 2 has been criticised by Michael Vasey in his book, 'Strangers and Friends'. One of his main criticisms is that the 'standard argument' 'does not reflect on the cultural diversity found in human relationships. It imposes on scripture the domestic ideals of the nuclear family—a husband and wife with their children enjoying domestic bliss in protected isolation from wider society.'[7]

This can be answered in various ways. First of all, those advancing the argument never intended 'to reflect on the cultural diversity found in human relationships'. Their concern was to discover what the Bible said about marriage and sexual behaviour. Secondly, there is no reason to suppose that those who use this argument necessarily have an ideal of the nuclear family 'in protected isolation from wider society'. Thirdly, he actually answers this point himself when he writes, 'These great chapters are intended to provide the backcloth to the whole complex story of the ordering of human society. When the text says, "Therefore a man leaves his father and mother and cleaves to his wife, and they become one flesh" (Genesis 2:24), it is implying not the isolation of a married couple from the wider society but the creation of a new unit within society, as noted in the earlier discussion on polygamy, "one flesh" refers to the creation of a new kinship group (cf. Genesis 29:14).'[8] Quite so. It is a society based on a network of relationships broadening out from the first marriage and linked again and again by new marriages. As Calvin says, 'God could himself indeed have covered the earth with a multitude of men; but it was his will that we should proceed from one fountain, in order that our desire of mutual concord might be the greater, and that each might the more freely embrace the other as his own flesh.'[9]

In Old Testament terms 'the cultural diversity of human relationships' was not to include homosexual relationships. Vasey writes of 'The modern 'intuitive' sense that same sex love is somehow contradicted by Genesis 2:18-25..'[10] Does he think that anyone in Old Testament days would have supposed that Genesis 2:18-25 included same sex love, or could have included it? And would Jesus Christ have supposed so? The bishops write, 'But from the fact that [Jesus] supports with his own authority the statement in Genesis that in the beginning God created humankind male and female, and uses that as a basis for ethical guidance (Matt. 19.3-9; Mark 10.1-12), it is not unreasonable to infer that he regarded heterosexual love as the God-given pattern.'[11] Many people would put the argument in somewhat stronger terms than that.

## The fall and its effects

The creation pattern of Genesis 1 and 2 is followed by the account of the fall of Adam and Eve into temptation and direct disobedience to God's command. The rest of the Bible shows how far-reaching the effects of that disobedience were (see, for example, Rom.5:12-21). Genesis does not explain its significance theologically, but the beauty of the first two chapters gives way to a very different atmosphere in the latter part of chapter 3, in chapter 4 and then on throughout the book, and the whole Bible. There is no suggestion that the first sin was sexual in any way, but it is clear that the results of the fall have affected every area of life including the sexual.

The first effect on Adam and Eve was that they felt ashamed of their nakedness. Their sexual difference became a source of embarrassment to them. The relationship between Adam and Eve was also obviously deeply affected. Adam blamed his wife for what had happened and the ominous words of verse 16 announced a tension between the sexes that is only too apparent today, 'your desire will be for your husband, and he will rule over you.'[12] As Genesis unfolds chapter 4 introduces us to bigamy; chapter 6 to lust; chapter 9 to indecent exposure; chapter 19 to intended homosexual rape and incest. The fall, and sin as a principle of evil within human beings, is seen to have profound effects upon sexuality and marriage. The first act of disobedience leads to disobedience to the creation pattern for marriage.

The Bible makes it clear that sin affects every part of human nature and every area of human experience. The effects of sin are physical, psychological and emotional as well as moral and spiritual. Just as the natural creation has been spoilt by the fall and the curse (Genesis 3:17-19), so also people's bodies have been affected. Genetic disorders, physical disability and hereditary disease all have to be traced back to the disorder in the created realm which was introduced as a result of the original human disobedience. People's minds and emotions are also affected; some suffer from learning disabilities, others from inherited tendencies to depression or other psychological disorders. The original goodness of the creation has been lost and there are many tragic situations.

There are also effects in the sexual realm. There can be deformities affecting the sexual organs. Some people can never have children of their own. We live in a world of much pain and suffering where we need to love and help each other. What we must not do is to think that by disregarding God's word we can somehow alleviate the pain and improve the situation. In the long term it will be found that deviations from God's way are always detrimental. There may be several reasons why some people are sexually attracted to those of the same sex, or perhaps to those of both sexes. Some physically belong to one sex yet emotionally feel they belong to the other and sometimes go to the extent of changing their sex by operation. It is neither possible nor necessary to consider all the variety of conditions possible, for we live in a greatly disordered world.[13]

Homosexuality in terms of orientation, desire and temptation has to be looked at as one of the effects of the fall. This is not to single out homosexuals in any particular way. All human beings are deeply affected by the fall; and sin has corrupted the hearts and desires of us all, 'There is none righteous, not even one' (Romans 3:10). Romans chapter 1 which speaks of 'shameful lusts'[14] and 'unnatural relations' (v.26), goes on to speak of people becoming 'filled with every kind of wickedness' (v.29) and specifies all sorts of other evils which are, sadly, the common heritage of people as they now are.

## Two implications

Because humanity is fallen it is not right for people simply to say, 'God made me as I am.' No-one suffering any disability or conscious of a bias to a particular sin or sins can simply accept their condition as one intended and made by God. This is a difficult and sensitive point. What we are as individuals undoubtedly comes about in the over-ruling providence of God, yet we cannot put down the fallenness of our humanity or our inner tendencies to sin simply to creation by God.

God has made us as we are and put us into our own circumstances not just for us to accept either as good in themselves, but often also as challenges to faith, obedience, and to prove his grace and power. One person suffers from debilitating migraines; another from bouts of depression which may include temptations to self-pity, perhaps suicide, and may involve evil obsessive thoughts; another simply has a violent temper. None of these conditions is good; all involve temptations to be resisted, inner battles to fight, things about ourselves which cause us shame and perhaps near despair, but there is grace in Christ and the power of the Holy Spirit available to those who repent and seek that grace and power believingly.

It is also quite wrong for us to affirm, or thank God for, or celebrate a state of affairs brought about by the fall. It is not a good thing for a person to be born with cystic fibrosis; nor is it a good thing for a person to have a homosexual orientation. To celebrate or rejoice in something which deviates from God's will can never be right, and it is tragic when professed Christians believe that God tolerates departures from his pattern.

It is quite clear that in the Old Testament God tolerated, though he did not approve of, people departing from the creation pattern for marriage. This is so in two respects. First, God tolerated polygamy. Even within the line of the covenant people—even among some of the most godly men of faith—polygamy is found. It is not explicitly condemned, though its disastrous results are quite clearly exhibited, especially, for example, in the stories of Jacob and David. Secondly, God also tolerated divorce. This was permitted and regulated under the Mosaic legislation, even though it clearly contradicts God's original intention. As Jesus forcefully put it, 'Therefore what God has joined together, let man not separate.' (Matthew 19:6). In view of this toleration of polygamy and divorce it is striking that there is no such toleration of homosexual relationships. Rather, homosexual acts are strongly condemned in the Mosaic law, and there are no examples of homosexual relationships among godly people in the Bible. Those who wish to see a sexual or erotic element in the relationship between David and Jonathan are introducing something which is not there in the text. The idea that because it was a particularly close and deep friendship, described as 'love…more wonderful than that of women', it must therefore have been sexual begs the question. Such words could just as easily mean that it was of a completely different nature from that of a sexual relationship.

Perhaps the example of David and Jonathan ought to be considered a little further because it is really the only place in the Bible where it is even possible to see a homosexual relationship. Both David and Jonathan were married and had children, and David, the one who speaks so movingly of the depth of their love and friendship, clearly had strong heterosexual desires. Vasey accepts that ' There is no suggestion here of a genital relationship between the two men.'[15] If there had been this would, of course, have been an extra-marital homosexual relationship. A further point can be added. The writer of 2 Samuel exposes quite clearly David's adultery with Bathsheba, and God's discipline both in the death of the child and the longer term consequences in his family (2 Samuel 11 and 12; note 12:10-14). In the light of this, is it likely that a writer from the Israelite prophetic tradition, with a background formed from passages like Leviticus 18:22; 20:13, would simply pass over a sexual relationship between David and Jonathan if he knew that is what it was? But if *he* didn't know that it was, how can anyone now decide that it was, when we only have his account to refer to? The close same sex friendship revealed in this story certainly points to the value of such friendships. However, the atmosphere of sexual innuendo in which we now live increasingly means that there is a fear of such friendships and contributes both to the loneliness of singles and to the withdrawal of married couples into each other and the family.

It is worth diverging a little more from the main theme to notice the strong emphasis on friendship that there is in Scripture. Think not only of verses like Proverbs 17:17, 18:24, 27:6,9,10, but of examples like Ruth and Naomi (Ruth 1:16-18; 2;11,12; 4:15) and Jesus and John (John 13:23). David seems to have made close friends easily, with Hiram (1 Kings 5:1), Ahithophel (2 Samuel 15:31; Psalm 41:9; 55:20,21), Hushai (2 Samuel 15:37; 16:16), and Barzillai (2 Samuel 17:27-29; 19:31-39). There must surely have developed deep bonds of friendship between Moses and Joshua, Elijah and Elisha, and between

Paul and several of his colleagues, Barnabas, Silas and Timothy. It is striking that Abraham is picked out as the 'friend of God', and that Jesus emphasises the closeness of his relationship with his disciples by calling them 'friends' (John 15:13-15). True friendship is a Christian virtue and especially necessary for those who are single (see 2 Timothy 1:16-18). The relationship between David and Jonathan is to be seen in the light of this perspective on friendship, not through the eyes of those whose sexual inclination makes them read into it what is not there.

## Forgiveness and restoration

Against the background of the fall and consequent human sin comes the incarnation of the Son of God and his saving life and death. He has come 'to save his people from their sins.' He forgives all sins, the only exclusion is the blasphemy against the Holy Spirit, which is certainly not identified with any sexual sin. Rather it is to be understood in terms of the hostility exemplified by many of the scribes and Pharisees to the truth spoken by Jesus Christ and attested with miracles (Matthew 12:31,32; cf. vv.22-24). All sexual sins and deviations from God's pattern for sexuality can be forgiven through the sacrificial death of Christ, and are forgiven when repentance and faith in Jesus take place. John 8 records Jesus' attitude towards a woman caught in the very act of adultery. His words are striking, 'Then neither do I condemn you…Go now and leave your life of sin.' (John 8:11) We cannot assume that at this point the woman had repented, this is what Jesus is urging her to do. There is tender compassion on the part of Christ, but also a clear instruction that the woman must turn from her sin. He still has such an attitude of combined compassion and faithfulness to those who fall into all kinds of sins. It is this attitude which his followers must also exemplify.

## The power of the Holy Spirit

The gospel does not simply offer forgiveness; there is also the promised gift of the Holy Spirit (Acts 2:38). In 1 Corinthians 6:9-11 Paul says, 'Do you not know that the wicked will not inherit the kingdom of God? Do not be deceived: Neither the sexually immoral nor idolaters nor adulterers nor male prostitutes nor homosexual offenders nor thieves nor the greedy nor drunkards nor slanderers nor swindlers will inherit the kingdom of God. And that is what some of you were. But you were washed, you were sanctified, you were justified in the name of the Lord Jesus Christ and by the Spirit of our God.' It is the last words which are important for our purpose here. Over against what the New Testament calls unclean, or evil spirits, and also the lusts and passions of our fallen nature (see, for example, Ephesians 2:3) there is the Holy Spirit. Not only is he the agent of the new birth in the experience of conversion (John 3:1-8), but as a person he takes up residence in and control of every Christian. He is a power for holiness, goodness, and right living according to the will of God. Unfortunately his power and inward working are too often overlooked or undervalued in these days. For the New Testament, a Christian life is a life lived by the new power of the Spirit. This does not mean that all evil desires are simply eradicated from our hearts, nor that temptations are not sometimes very powerful; it is not a guarantee of an easy or painless life. It does ensure grace and strength to resist temptation, and enables progressive growth in likeness to Jesus himself. Single people, those who have been widowed or divorced, those who are attracted to someone who is married, or being married are attracted to another person, or who are attracted to someone of the same sex, may have fierce battles with desire and temptation, but the Holy Spirit is more powerful and there is both the hope of victory and also forgiveness and restoration for those who fall.

### Final observations

In conclusion there are several observations which should be made.

### Disordered sexuality

It has been apparent throughout the discussion that there is no case for isolating homosexual relationships and treating them separately or differently from heterosexual relationships. The Bible picture is quite clear. Sexual intercourse belongs to marriage, and marriage is between a man and a woman. Whatever the origin of homosexual orientation, there is no case for allowing homosexual people any other standard than for heterosexual people. Homosexuality is but one part of a spectrum of disordered sexuality. Homosexuals ask for Christians to treat them as a special case and to apply to them standards that do not apply to all people created by God. This is something that cannot be done.

There seems to be a fundamental ambiguity running through Vasey's book. On the one hand he speaks as if gays (the word he prefers) constitute a definite group with clear characteristics—sensitivity, artistic ability—who are especially open to aspects of truth and God, 'What is it about their (the churches') understanding of Jesus Christ that leads them to a poorer grasp of some fundamental Christian insights than the gay movement?'[16] But on the other hand he constantly stresses that homosexuality has to be understood against the various cultural backgrounds in which it occurs. When he considers possible causes for homosexuality he says, 'The complexity of the pattern should be sufficient to warn against over-simple identification of 'causes'. It should be clear that the homosexuality of individuals needs to be seen as one element within a wider complex social discourse. There is no possibility that its 'cause' can be limited to certain elements of genetic make-up or personal biography.'[17]

Might it not be better then, in these circumstances, to concentrate upon the fact that homosexuals are primarily people. Anne Atkins writes, 'A Christian I know, whose sexual feelings are entirely directed towards men (and who lives a life of chastity), tells only close friends about his homosexual orientation. "I'm more than just one aspect of myself," he says.'[18] All people struggle with desires that could get out of hand, and with temptation. Homosexuals who want to express themselves in genital sex will inevitably set themselves apart from the larger part of society at that point. But those who accept biblical standards will not set themselves apart. They will be free to relate widely with persons of both sexes, to make close friendships and to be involved in church and society. It will be said that this will be very difficult for them. So it may. But life is difficult for very many people. God's standards are high. Many struggle with their sexuality and sexual temptation. All of us need compassion, understanding and care; all at times need rebuke and warning; all of us are tempted to justify and legitimise what we want to do, and to make ourselves special cases to whom the normal rules do not apply.

## Marriage again

Marriage prior to the fall would have been joyful, harmonious and fulfilling. Perhaps Milton, who so beautifully pictures the mutual joy of Adam and Eve, is not far wrong when he imagines Satan's envy and hatred as evoked by their nuptial bliss:

'Live while ye may,
Yet happy pair; enjoy, till I return,
Short pleasures; for long woes are to succeed!'[19]

Long woes!—is the picture in Genesis now just an unattainable ideal? Do we have to make the best of the situation accepting that fornication, adultery and homosexual relationships are here to stay? From one point of view we do, for these things will certainly continue until the time of Christ's return. However, not only does God's common grace mean that there are many lasting, happy marriages and people living fulfilled single lives, God's saving grace gives forgiveness and enables a new start to be made. The new birth and a relationship with Jesus Christ affects and changes every area of life. On the other hand immoral acts and an immoral lifestyle, though forgiveable, bring the judgement of God upon people. This is what gives an urgency to Paul's words in 1 Corinthians 6, 'Do you not know that the wicked will not inherit the kingdom of God? Do not be deceived: Neither the sexually immoral nor idolaters nor adulterers nor male prostitutes nor homosexual offenders nor thieves nor the greedy nor drunkards nor slanderers nor swindlers will inherit the kingdom of God.'

Those who plead for a type of homosexual 'marriage' underestimate what the Bible teaches about marriage. Of course there can, and should be, close friendships between people of the same sex (along with cross-sexual friendships also). It is also true that many marriages in the present day are unsatisfactory and many break down. But for true bonding and the intimate companionship and unity which is at the heart of marriage God made a man and a woman and brought them together. Though the emotional and psychological differences between men and women are not absolute, the differences are real, just as are the physical differences. The unity of marriage is only possible between those for whom God designed it. The evidence suggests the reality of this. As the Report of the Free Church of Scotland for 1996 says, 'The high incidence of promiscuity among homosexuals, many times higher than among heterosexuals, surely indicates the extreme difficulty, the impossibility almost, of establishing a faithful, stable homosexual relationship, which indicates in turn that homosexuals do not "fit together" emotionally, or domestically.'[20] Moreover homosexual 'marriages' are of necessity barren. They are relationships which in themselves cannot issue in children and family life. The fulfilment open to most heterosexual couples is closed to homosexuals in the very nature of the case. Christians cannot but be distressed at seeing people taking a route which can never result in the natural outcome of sexual relations, and which is likely to be inherently unstable and unfulfilling.

### Growing as a sexual being

Christians have not always been very good at understanding or coping with sexuality. Even in New Testament times trends both to sexual denial (1 Corinthians 7:1-9) and to sexual licence (Revelation 2:14,15; 20-23; 2 Peter 2:13,14) are seen. It never has been easy to live in a world where God's standards are known in the conscience (Romans 2:14,15) but where sin warps and drives the natural appetites (cf. Ephesians 4:17-19). Even more so is it difficult today when the media has such a powerful influence throughout society. Young people are particularly exposed, both to the media and to peer pressure.

It is important for churches to give clear and practical teaching, and especially for their members to model biblical attitudes to sexuality. This is necessary for the guidance of young people, for the churches to act as salt and light in the world, and for the glory of God. This is not just a vocation for married couples with young children, but for single people, for older couples and those who are widowed. We have to learn to accept our gender, to recognise the power, importance and essential goodness of sexuality, to submit to the divine institution of marriage as the place for sexual union, and to resist pressure from within and without to compromise God's standards. While doing this we are to develop a whole range of friendships and relationships with people of both sexes, for mutual enrichment and Christian testimony in a world of people, who though fallen, are yet made by God and retain aspects and vestiges of his image.

This will not be easy. It requires grace from God, and is likely to include falls, sins and the need for forgiveness and restoration on the way. Yet it is God's way and it is good. The goal is not happy marriages. The goal is the glory of God as married and single prove and demonstrate that the will of God is good, acceptable and perfect; that a lifestyle governed by his will in Scripture is beautiful and productive of good for all who are touched by it. That it is also deeply joyful and fulfilling is a bonus.

### About the author

Born to missionary parents, **Paul Brown** spent 8 years at boarding school, including 5 years at the co-educational Oldfeld House, part of Swanage Grammar School. He trained for the ministry at London Bible College and has a BD from London University and M Phil from the University of Glamorgan. He is the pastor of Dunstable Baptist Church and serves on the Theological Committee of FIEC. He is married to Mary; they have three children and five grandchildren.

## Chapter 4 notes

**1**   **Gordon J. Wenham,** Genesis 1-15, Word Biblical Commentary, Word Inc., UK edition, 1991; p.69.

**2**   See, for example, chapters 10 and 11 'You're a man, aren't you?' and 'Women are different!' in Men, Women and Authority, **ed. Brian Edwards,** Day One, 1996.

**3**   See ref 1, p.68.

**4**   In ecstasy man bursts into poetry on meeting his perfect helpmeet.' Wenham; ref 1, p.70. See also his discussion. **Milton** in Paradise Lost has Adam saying, on seeing Eve:
On she came,
Led by her Heavenly Maker, though unseen,
And guided by his voice, nor uninformed
Of nuptial sanctity and marriage rites.
Grace was in all her steps, Heaven in her eye,
In every gesture dignity and love.
I, overjoyed, could not forebear aloud:-
**John Milton,** Paradise Lost, Book VIII, lines 484-490.

**5**   Issues in Human Sexuality, A Statement by the House of Bishops of the General Synod of the Church of England, December 1991, Church House Publishing, 2nd impression 1993; 2.13; p.10.

**6**   V.M. Sinton, Singleness in New Dictionary of Christian Ethics and Pastoral Theology, **eds. David J. Atkinson and David H. Field,** IVP, 1995; p.791.

**7**   **Michael Vasey,** Strangers and Friends, a new exploration of homosexuality and the Bible, Hodder and Stoughton, 1995; p.115.

**8**   See ref 7, p.115,116. On 'one flesh' see also Wenham, see ref 1, p.71. Although I believe 'one flesh' refers in the first place to physical intercourse because of Paul's use of the phrase in 1 Corinthians 6:16, I accept the implication of a new kinship group—the family—which this brings about.

**9**   **John Calvin,** Genesis, Banner of Truth Trust, 1965 (reprint); p.97.

**10**  See ref 7, p.117.

**11**  Issues in Human Sexuality; 2.17, p.12,13.

**12**  See Wenham, ref 1 p.81,82; particularly his comments on Susan Foh's interpretation of 'desire'; 'a desire to dominate her husband.'

**13**  See, for example, the article on Transsexualism by E.R. Moberly in New Dictionary of Christian Ethics and Pastoral Theology, p.863,864.

**14** By ending a sentence here and beginning the next sentence with 'Even…' NIV loses the connection indicated by the Greek word gar 'for'. As **Leon Morris** comments, '[Paul] goes on to particularize with his reference to women exchanging natural relations for unnatural ones…' **Leon Morris,** The Epistle to the Romans, IVP/Eerdmans, 1988; p.92. 'Shameful lusts' therefore refers to homosexual desires, though 'sexual impurity for the degrading of their bodies' in v.24 is not limited in the same way and doubtless includes all types of illicit sexual behaviour.

**15** See ref 7, p.121.

**16** See ref 7, p.237.

**17** See ref 7, p.149.

**18** **Anne Atkins,** 'Sodom and Gomorrah and Southwark', *Daily Telegraph,* November 15, 1996.

**19** **John Milton,** Paradise Lost, Book IV, lines 533-535.

**20** Reports to the General assembly of the Free Church of Scotland, 1996, (E) Homosexuality; p.53.

# The Bible and Homosexual Practice

**Alex Macdonald** examines the specific teaching of the Bible concerning homosexual practice

What does the Bible have to say? That is the most crucial question on this or any subject for the Christian. Christians recognise the Bible as the source book and ultimate authority for Christian faith and life. It is God's Word. But today great doubt exists in the minds of many about the relevance and applicability of the Bible's teaching to the life we live in the post-modern world. Various scholars give the impression that the Bible has to be corrected for its cultural conditioning before it can be of any use to us as a guide book. At any particular point it may be clear what the Bible says, but the question is, what does it mean? This approach is employed with specific reference to what the Bible has to say about sexual matters in general and homosexuality in particular. It is argued that what the Bible has to say about homosexuality is culturally conditioned by the prevailing attitudes of the time and therefore not to be taken at face value as the authoritative Word of God. In this connection two points need to be made at the outset.

First, of course it is true that the Bible was given originally in several cultures, all different from our own. But does that invalidate the principle of its abiding authority? For instance, cultures share moral principles: a lie is a lie in any culture. Furthermore, why should God not make particular aspects of these cultures the expression of his will for all cultures? As a matter of fact the Bible is actually most often in criticism of the contemporary culture. The Lord Jesus and the apostle Paul are sometimes diametrically opposed to their cultures on moral as well as on spiritual matters. But the fact that they may at other points be in agreement with their cultures, does not invalidate their positions at these points. To think otherwise is to deny God's common grace. To believe in the Fall and original sin does not mean that fallen human beings get it wrong all the time and that the non-Christian world is as bad as it is possible to be, otherwise we would now be living in hell. Instead, even non-Christians have God's law written on their hearts (Romans 2:14,15). The morality of every culture is an approximation to the law of God. What C. S. Lewis called the *Tao or standard of right conduct is recognised by all cultures.*[1] At any particular point a human society may fall short of that standard and at that point the prophet or the apostle may contradict their culture, but the fact that at other points the prophet or apostle may agree with their cultures does not invalidate their claimed stance as speaking the Word of God.

Second, if any part of the Bible is culturally conditioned in the sense that it cannot be taken as authoritative, why not the whole Bible? By what criteria can we pick and choose? How can we say that the Bible's condemnation of oppression is not culturally conditioned, but its condemnation of homosexual practice is? Personal preferences? Contemporary consensus? If we go down that road, we lose all objective authority in the Bible as our guide book. In what meaningful sense can it then be said to be the Word of God at all? To give up parts of the Bible as being non-authoritative because culturally conditioned is to give up the whole Bible, and to give up the whole Bible is to give up Christianity. Nevertheless, it is often argued that we already adopt this approach to much of the Bible especially the Old Testament. For instance, we do not practice the ceremonial and civil law of the Old Testament. However, it is one thing to accept the teaching of the New Testament that these are fulfilled and abolished in Christ; it is quite another to say that the teaching of Jesus and Paul on sexual matters is culturally limited, when there is no indication in the New Testament itself that this is so. We have no right to indulge in our own interpretations which have no grounds in Scripture itself.

It is also argued that the Church in the past has rightly ignored the teaching of the New Testament in a specific area when it was seen as limited to a particular political culture. This is said of Paul's attitude to slavery, for example. However, this is to misunderstand the Apostle's position. If he did not believe slavery to be contrary to God's will, why did he counsel slaves to obtain their freedom if possible (1 Corinthians 7:21) and why did he counsel all Christians not to become slaves (1 Corinthians 7:23)? The fact that Paul accepted that slavery was legal in the Roman Empire did not mean that he accepted that it was right, any more than a person's accepting that homosexual practice between consenting adults in private is decriminalised in this country means that he believes homosexual practice is morally right.

In this area it is not the Bible that is culturally conditioned, but it is the views of those who wish to reinterpret the Bible that are culturally conditioned—conditioned by the culture of late twentieth century Western society, including its sexual culture and sub-cultures. If these views were critical of the pervading culture (as Jesus and the biblical writers so often were) they would command more respect.

## Love

When we turn to the Bible for guidance on sexual matters we are confronted with the fundamental reality of love. The concept of love in the Bible is far more extensive than sexual love, but it includes reference to sexual love. Love, God's love, defines our sexuality and not the other way around. God is love. In himself he is a mysterious community of persons, Father, Son and Spirit, each loving the others and being loved by the others. This is the fundamental Christian truth and of great relevance to every aspect of our lives, but in this context it is of particular relevance as the pattern for our love, including sexual love. God is not a single person in love with himself. Nor is he a trinity of identical and indistinguishable persons. Each of the persons is equally divine, but they have their own personal properties too—the Father begets, the Son is begotten and the Spirit proceeds from the Father and the Son. So, although they are the same in nature, they are not the same in personal properties. Each person loves the others who are the same but different, complementary but not identical. In this sense (and not in any sexual sense) God's love is *hetero and not homo—for the other, not for the same.*

God's creation of the human race reflects this same reality. He creates human beings in his own image. Too often this is thought of as only relevant to the individual—the individual's personhood and worth. But the original context clearly shows that God's image is expressed in a community of persons. He created them male and female. He created a human pair who were equally human (in that sense the same in nature), but different and complementary. This is God's pattern for human sexual love—'For this reason a man will leave his father and mother and be united to his wife, and they will become one flesh.' (Genesis 2:24) This is stated not only in Genesis, it is repeated by Jesus and by Paul. Nothing is clearer in the Bible's teaching on sexual love than this stress that it is God's will that human sexuality should be expressed only in the one-man-one-woman lifelong relationship of marriage. This is to be the reflection of God in the world, it is God's will for our benefit and he warns that tragic consequences flow from disregard for it. All this is set forth in the act of creation itself. God did not create several Eves for Adam, or several Adams for Eve. Nor did he create another Adam for Adam, or another Eve for Eve.

This is further emphasised when the marriage relationship of man and woman is used as an analogy of the redemptive relationship of Christ and his church. The classic passage is Ephesians 5:21-33, although it is a theme that runs throughout the Bible, Old Testament and New. The love of Christ for the church is not the love of the same, but the love of the other. The relationship (and even the love) is complimentary and asymmetrical. This is also true of marriage.

God has created human beings with sexual natures and it is his will that those sexual natures should find expression in the love of a man and a woman in marriage. It is a total misunderstanding of the Bible to think that the original sin was sex. It was not. It was the eating of a particular food that God had forbidden. If anything, the original sin was in the area of ecology, not sexuality! The true antidote to the present confusion in the area of sexuality is for the churches to emphasise the great positive gift of sexuality that God has given us and to seek to encourage all agencies, from the government down, to support and not undermine marriage.

## Friendship and homosexuality

However, having said all that, we must not forget that love is much wider than sexual love. In God's plan for human community, there is also non-sexual love—sisterly love and brotherly love *(philadelphia)* and the love of friendship *(philia)*. The great example in the Bible is the friendship between David and Jonathan. But even more significant is the fact that Jesus chose close friends—Peter, James and John, especially John. Such is the confusion of thought in our day that some infer that these friendships must have had homosexual dimensions. It seems that people are incapable of conceiving of love without a sexual element. Of course, Jesus also had friendships with women—Martha, Mary and Mary Magdalene—and these too were non-sexual. Such was the obsessive hatred of Jesus by some that if there was any slur they could have made on his relationship with women (or men), they would have done so. The fact is that there is not the slightest hint that these friendships had any sexual or erotic dimension. This stresses the desirability of strong, non-sexual friendships.

Just because there is an obsession with sex in general and with homosexuality in particular at the present time, does not mean that we should be steamrollered into a fearful shunning of same-sex friendships. Christians should stand against the insinuations often made regarding them and not indulge in such insinuations themselves. The Bible is not homophobic in the sense of encouraging fear of those of the same sex. Instead, it encourages strong, deep and loyal friendships without any sexual dimension.

## Homosexual orientation

Many see nothing wrong with homosexuality. They argue that the true homosexual is only acting in accordance with his or her nature. They are just born that way. Or it's just the way they were brought up. To put it in more technical language, they are homosexual not by virtue of a perverted choice, but as a result of genetic or environmental factors.

There are, no doubt, various causes of a homosexual orientation, and not all of them are the homosexual's individual responsibility. To apply Jesus' words about eunuchs (Matthew 19:12), some are born homosexuals, some are made homosexuals by men and some make themselves homosexuals. We must understand and accept that there may be those with genetic or hormonal variations which have predisposed them to homosexuality. While the jury may still be out on the existence of a 'homosexual gene', the possibility should not cause us an insurmountable problem, as we shall see. Furthermore, we must accept that there are those who, in childhood or adolescence, were terrified or disgusted by aggressive and over-dominating members of the opposite sex, or were deliberately abused and perverted by older people (often slightly older young people). To be fair in our application of Jesus' words, we must also recognise that there are those who have made themselves homosexual by deliberately seeking out homosexual activity for sexual pleasure.

However, does this mean that apart from the (relatively small) number of true perverts, there is nothing wrong with homosexuality? If that was the way they were created, should we not just accept that this is God's will for them? This might very well be the case if we had to deal only with creation, but we have to reckon with the Fall as well. The world is not now as it originally came from the good hands of God. The human race has rebelled and fallen into a state of sin and misery. We are born into an already fallen imperfect world and we bring an already corrupted human nature with us. Our personalities are complexes of all kinds of sinful desires. No aspect of our humanity escapes unscathed. Our sexuality is not immune. We may inherit various tendencies to rebel against God's order of things and we may respond in a sinful way to various evil influences we experience.

Does this mean that we are absolved of all personal responsibility for any deviation in our sexuality from the pattern laid down by God? No, no more than it does in the area of any of the other commandments of God—respect for life, property and our neighbour's reputation. When we have said all that can be said by way of understanding the causes of homosexuality, we have only explained some of the reasons for homosexual temptation, or orientation. We have done no more than what we could do in the case of a liar, an adulterer, an embezzler, a drunkard or a murderer. We have not proved that homosexual acts ought to be excluded from the biblical category of sin. However, it is important that the distinction be made between homosexual orientation and homosexual activity. We cannot blame a person for being tempted in a particular direction, otherwise we could blame Jesus, because he was tempted in all points as we are. Yet it is made clear that he was without sin. Normally, the individual is not responsible for his temptation. But he is responsible for his response to it. In practical terms, we are not entitled to judge that a woman is a lesbian just because she appears 'butch', or a that a man is a homosexual because he appears effeminate. They may both be struggling against a deep-seated orientation.

## Homosexual activity

What has the Bible to say specifically about homosexuality? As we have already seen, God's creation of the original human couple teaches that, whereas heterosexuality is good, homosexuality is not. When God saw that it was not good for the man to be alone, it was a woman he created for him, not another man. By this act God declared his will for human sexuality. This does not just mean that heterosexuality is the ideal and homosexuality is a kind of second best. In both Old Testament and New Testament homosexual acts are described as sins. Michael Vasey, in his book *Strangers and Friends* looks at various biblical texts in his attempt to show that the Bible does not condemn homosexual activity as such. We will now look at the five main texts.

## Genesis 18:16-19:29

In this passage we are told of the sin of the cities of Sodom and Gomorrah and God's judgement of them. Vasey attempts to prove that there is no implied condemnation of homosexuality in this passage at all.[2] He does this by referring to Ezekiel 16:49-50 where the sins of Sodom are described in terms of pride, greed and lack of love. However he ignores the fact that Ezekiel also describes their conduct as "detestable"—the same word that is used of homosexual sin in Leviticus 18:22. In addition, there can be little doubt that among their sins was the intention of homosexual rape. The angels who came to visit Lot in Sodom appeared as men, and it was they whom the men of

Sodom intended to rape. Furthermore, this visitation by the angels was clearly God's investigation of the outcry against the grievous sins of Sodom and Gomorrah (Genesis 18:20). It was the intended homosexual rape that sealed their doom. It was evidence of their total corruption. However, this passage taken by itself does not prove that every kind of homosexual sexual activity is wrong. It clearly shows that homosexual rape, like all forms of sexual violence of the weak by the strong, is wrong.

## Leviticus 18:22, 20:13

'Do not lie with a man as one lies with a woman; that is detestable.' (Leviticus 18:22) 'If a man lies with a man as one lies with a woman, both of them have done what is detestable. They must be put to death; their blood will be on their own heads.' (Leviticus 20:13) There is little dispute as to what these laws mean. Vasey agrees that 'these verses prohibit sexual intercourse between men.'[3] However, there is no indication in the text that this is limited to anal intercourse, as Vasey suggests. It is simply homosexual sexual activity as such that is indicated—one man acting erotically with another. Where there is more serious divergence of views, however, is concerning the question of whether this prohibition still applies. Vasey argues: 'Firstly, it can be seen simply as part of an arbitrary purity code abrogated with the coming of Christ . . . Secondly, it can be viewed as a witness to an unchanging creation pattern for human genital acts. Thirdly, it can be regarded as some sort of combination of the two.'[4] Vasey opts for the third, but does not make clear how the two can be reconciled. What is clear is that some aspects of the law are abrogated by Christ. Jesus abrogates the death penalty for sexual sin (not only in John 8:11, but also in his replacement of the death penalty for adultery with divorce, Matthew 19:9). In addition, he shows that the regulations concerning a woman's 'uncleanness' (Leviticus 18:19) are no longer valid, as he does not regard himself as contaminated by the touch of the woman with the issue of blood (Mark 5:25-34). But neither the Lord nor his apostles indicate that homosexual acts are to be excluded from the category of sinful behaviour (any more than child-sacrifice and bestiality, Leviticus

18:21,23, are to be excluded.) Instead, there are clear statements in the New Testament to the contrary—homosexual sex is still regarded as sinful. Any approach which appeals to the New Testament's abrogation of any Old Testament command must be on the sure ground of being able to show that the command is specifically abrogated or fulfilled, or belongs to a class of commands (such as ceremonial or judicial) which is generally abrogated or fulfilled. This cannot be shown in the instance of the commands against homosexual sin.

## Deuteronomy 23:17,18

These verses are not of great significance to our subject. They prohibit temple prostitution (both male and female) and the use of the earnings of ordinary male and female prostitutes in the worship of God. They clearly prohibit all kinds of prostitution, including homosexual prostitution.

## Romans 1.25-27

'Because of this God gave them over to shameful lusts. Even their women exchanged natural relations for unnatural ones. In the same way the men also abandoned natural relations with woman and were inflamed with lust for one another. Men committed indecent acts with other men, and received in themselves the due penalty of their perversion.' Vasey attempts to lessen the impact of these verses by arguing that they are the culturally conditioned views of the Roman world by a Jew and that they are not referring to loving homosexual relationships.[5] This comes across as very special pleading. Romans 1-3 is a whole. Here Paul is showing that 'all have sinned and fall short of the glory of God' (3:23)—Jew as well as Gentile, but whereas the law could not put us right with God, Jesus Christ does. Paul shows the development of sin from the Fall and included in this development is homosexual behaviour. Discussion of Paul's use of the word 'natural' is not particularly significant. What is clear is that Paul is categorically describing as sinful the abandoning by men of sexual intercourse with women in favour of sexual intercourse with other men. It is this, together with his use of the expressions 'inflamed with lust' and 'committed indecent acts', that demonstrate that the Apostle's view is that homosexual sexual activity is sinful. This ought not to be considered a culturally conditioned view any more than his view of greed, envy, murder, strife, deceit, malice and gossip (v.29). He is simply confirming God's moral law.

### 1 Corinthians 6:9,10

'Neither the sexually immoral nor idolaters nor adulterers nor male prostitutes nor homosexual offenders nor thieves nor the greedy nor drunkards nor slanderers nor swindlers will inherit the kingdom of God.' This passage particularly shows that God declares homosexual acts to be sinful. They are contrary to God's will and, along with all other sins, merit his judgement and exclude the unrepentant sinner from the kingdom of God. It is argued by Vasey and others, however, that this along with other passages in the Bible that appear to be talking about homosexuality are in fact not talking about stable, loving homosexual relationships, but about homosexual rape, religious male prostitution and pederasty.[6] However, the key passages quoted above are quite clear. They use very plain language. They talk about lying with a man as one lies with a woman. In fact it appears that in 1 Corinthians 6:9 Paul possibly invented a compound Greek word for homosexual (*arsenokoites*), meaning precisely one who lies sexually with a man or one who beds a man when there were various other Greek words he could have used if he wanted to refer to homosexual rape, male prostitution or pederasty. Paul, or someone else before him, probably derived the term arsenokoites from the Greek Septuagint version of Leviticus 18:22 and 20:13 where the terms *arsen* (male) and *koite* (bed) are used.[7] Paul's use of this word, linked with the clear command in Leviticus, makes it abundantly plain that it is all homoerotic behaviour that is prohibited. It is not just homosexual rape, male prostitution or pederasty that is wrong. It is homosexual sexual activity as such that is wrong. All attempts to avoid the plain meaning of the words appear as very weak special pleading.

So, on the basis of Scripture the Christian cannot accept that homosexuality is natural in the sense of being in line with God's will for us.

The Bible teaches that a man and a woman are designed for each other sexually—they, and they alone, become one flesh. By contrast, both Old Testament and New confirm that homosexual sexual activity is included in the category of sin. Vasey seems constantly to miss the point. He seems to think that the Bible, for cultural reasons, condemns certain sexual practices, such as anal intercourse, irrespective of the sex of those involved.[8] What the Bible makes clear is that homosexual sex of any kind is included in the category of sin, along with the heterosexual sins of adultery and fornication. The Bible recognises only one sexual relationship which has God's approval—that is marriage.

### One sin among many

However, it must always be remembered that homosexual activity is only one sin among many. Yes, it is given as evidence of the judgement of God on a society, but so too are gossip, greed and rejection of parental authority (Romans 1:29-32). And yes, homosexual acts are among the sins that, if persisted in, exclude from the kingdom of God, but equally so do promiscuous heterosexual acts, theft, drunkenness and slander (1 Corinthians 6:9,10). There is nothing in the Bible that would single out homosexuals as worse sinners than any other sinners. Even if we accept that homosexual sex was one of the sins of Sodom we must remember what Jesus said to the city of Capernaum that refused to repent—'it will be more bearable for Sodom on the day of judgement than for you' (Matthew 11:24). This is not to dilute the significance of the fact that homosexual acts are sinful. To think so betrays a trivial view of sin. All sin is a horrendous affront to the goodness and purity of God and merits the judgement of God.

Nevertheless, homosexual sex is sin, and as sin it brings its own judgement, even in this life. 'Men committed indecent acts with other men, and received in themselves the due penalty for their perversion.' (Romans 1:27). Sin brings misery. Whatever a man sows that he shall also reap. AIDS is only the latest and most horrific result of uninhibited homosexual behaviour. Homosexual activity is not the only route by which AIDS is spread, but it is a fact that in America and Europe promiscuous homosexual activity was a major factor in the initial spread of the disease. However, some talk as if AIDS puts homosexual people beyond the pale altogether. We must resist such sub-Christian attitudes. The Lord Jesus helped people with all kinds of diseases and troubles without respect to how these may have been caused, and he resisted the judgemental attitude so prevalent in the society of his time (Luke 13:1-5, John 9:1-3).

## Homosexuality and judgement

Although it is clear that homosexual behaviour is sinful and therefore comes under the same condemnation as all sin, the apostle Paul says something rather different and equally important in Romans 1. There he is not teaching that one day God will punish the Roman world for its homosexuality. Homosexuality is itself part of the punishment. 'Therefore, God gave them over . . .' (v.24) 'Because of this, God gave them over . . .' (v.26) What is the sin for which homosexuality is the punishment? It is the sin of idolatry, of materialism, of worshipping the created thing instead of the Creator.

It is important to take account of the context. Paul is showing mankind's desperate need for the gospel: it is not just that man is miserable but that he is under the wrath of God because he has rejected the revelation of God and foolishly turned to idolatry. And this wrath is not only a future thing: it is being revealed now (v.18). But is wrath Christian? There are those who think that it is dishonouring to God to say that he is angry, as if he were subject to fits of rage like a human being. But that is to misunderstand the Bible. God's anger is not capricious, arbitrary and unpredictable like the anger of the gods of Canaan or of Rome. Nor does he lash out in rage; he is slow to anger. Nor has he given no warning. His will is revealed not only in the Scriptures, but also in the consciences of men (Romans 1:19; 2:15). But saying all that does not remove the concept of wrath from the Bible. It is there in Old Testament and New; in the teaching of Jesus and his apostles. To remove it is to de-christianise Christianity and to ask for a chaotic, unjust and meaningless universe where the righteous will always suffer and the evil will go scot-free.

How is God's wrath being revealed now? It is being revealed in his giving over of nations to immorality. The immorality will be punished, but the immorality itself is also a punishment. A nation where immorality, including homosexuality, is rife, is already under the judgement of God. Take our own nation. For over a century now the Bible has been attacked, undermined and rejected. People have turned from the only living and true God to gods of their own imagination and to material things. Therefore, ultimately, after due opportunity for repentance, God has punished spiritual adultery with physical adultery and all its dire consequences for society. He has punished the unnaturalness of idolatry with the unnaturalness of homosexuality. He has allowed the natural consequences to follow.

It must be emphasised that God's temporal judgements do not necessarily fall on individuals, but on groups and nations. Man is a communal creature and the actions of the individual affect the group and vice versa. This means that the homosexual tendency of an individual is not necessarily a sign that that person is under God's judgement. He may be a Christian struggling against temptation. But the very existence of his tendency is an indication that his group, his nation, his people are under the judgement of God. Conversely, this truth also applies to those of us who are not guilty of this particular sin. 'No man is an island . . . Never send for whom the bell tolls. It tolls for thee' (John Donne). That homosexuality is prevalent in our society is a sign that we are all under the judgement of God and are in desperate need of the good news of Jesus.

### Good news for homosexuals

Homosexual activity is sinful. There can be no doubt that this is the teaching of God's Word. But from the way many people talk, you would think that was all Christianity has to say to the homosexual. That is only the beginning, an important beginning, but only a beginning nonetheless. Because homosexual activity is a sin, homosexuals are candidates for salvation. That is what Paul's whole presentation in Romans 1—3 is all about. He is not writing about sin and judgement as if this was the complete Christian message. It is only preparatory for the revelation of God's love in the gospel. 'But now a righteousness from God, apart from law, has been made known, to which the Law and the Prophets testify. This righteousness from God comes through faith in Jesus Christ to all who believe. There is no difference, for all have sinned and fall short of the glory of God, and are justified freely by his grace through the redemption that came by Jesus Christ.' (Romans 3:21-24)

The Bible's emphasis on sin is not meant to drive us away from God to destruction and despair, but to show us our desperate need of the redemption accomplished by Christ and to call us to faith in him. After all the Christian message is one of forgiveness and only a person who has done wrong can be forgiven. We find the same emphasis in 1 Corinthians 6:9-11. After listing the lifestyles, including homosexual ones, which exclude one from the kingdom of God, Paul says to the Corinthian Christians, 'And that is what some of you were. But you were washed, you were sanctified, you were justified in the name of the Lord Jesus Christ and by the Spirit of our God.'

Corinth was a notorious centre of all kinds of vice in the ancient world and some of the Christians had been converted out of such a vicious background. There were Christians who had been male prostitutes and homosexual offenders, but they had been transformed by the grace of God. They were freed from the vices that had once enslaved them. We are not told if they were all able to establish normal heterosexual relationships. No doubt some of them were. But possibly others were called to a celibate life, which Paul mentions in the next chapter of 1 Corinthians as a specific option for some Christians. At any rate, they were all given the grace and strength to live a new lifestyle. The gospel is a message of hope and the church is a community of hope. The church of Jesus Christ is made up one hundred per cent of moral failures. But they are moral failures who have been given a new life and a new lifestyle.

### Practising homosexual a Christian?

'Glad to be gay.' Is that a Christian attitude? The Christian who has a homosexual orientation (or temptation) for whatever reason, cannot possibly be glad, because the existence of even homosexual orientation is evidence of the judgement of God against one's society. It is evidence of the outworking of the curse of the Fall. Homosexual practice is sinful: the Christian who is tempted by that sin cannot be glad. It should grieve him. It should make him long for that ultimate liberation from the curse of sin in the new creation (Revelation 22:3).

Can a Christian be a practising homosexual? If we mean by that 'Should a Christian be a practising homosexual?', the answer is a resounding 'No'. The Christian is committed to fight temptation and sin (Romans 6). But if we mean, 'Is it possible for a Christian to be a practising homosexual?', we must answer carefully. If the question is 'Is it possible for a person who has a settled practice of homosexual sin to be a Christian?', the answer, based on 1 Cor. 6:11, must again be 'No'. The person with a homosexual orientation who becomes a Christian turns from his sinful lifestyle to Christ who gives him a new nature and a new lifestyle.

This does not mean that the homosexual tendency necessarily dies there and then. In Romans 7, Paul speaks of the Christian's struggle with sin, and he admits that we may often lose that struggle. But the great question is, are we struggling? After every fall do we come broken to God in repentance and pick ourselves up to fight again and again, until the Lord will make us perfect in glory? There is all the difference in the world between that attitude and the attitude that says 'I'm glad to be gay!' The latter speaks out of all the arrogance of the unregenerate heart, the former out of the sadness and shame of the believer having fallen into sin.

### Civil rights and the homosexual

A relatively recent view known as Theonomy teaches that the church has been mistaken in its attitude to Old Testament civil law: the punishments in the Mosaic law, such as the death penalty for homosexuality should still apply.[9] But this is not only to ignore the specific example of Jesus in refusing to condemn the adulterous woman to death by stoning (John 8:3-11), and his specific teaching that the remedy for adultery is now divorce not death (Matthew 19:9), it is clearly contradictory to the whole tenor of his life. He was constantly in the company of people who, under Mosaic law, ought to have been condemned to death, but there is not the slightest hint that he thought they should be reported to the authorities. Rather the reverse—he showed them love and forgiveness. It is obvious that Jesus authoritatively ended such punishments which had served their purpose as part of the age of law. Jesus said to the adulterous woman, 'Neither do I condemn you. Go now and leave your life of sin.'

However, it is also clear that both Jesus and his apostle Paul believed in submission to the ruler. Jesus said, 'Give to Caesar what is Caesar's and to God what is God's.' Of the ruler Paul said, 'He is God's servant to do you good. But if you do wrong, be afraid, for he does not bear the sword for nothing. He is God's servant, an agent of wrath to bring punishment on the wrongdoer.' (Romans 13:4) It is clear therefore that the Christian is to submit to the authorities. The only exception is when the authority forbids you to do what God commands or the authority commands you to do what God forbids (Acts 5:29). What is not so clear is what happens when Christians come to have influence in society or even come to be rulers. In modern democracies rulers rule by consent, so politics is the art of the possible. But even if it were possible to legislate totally against homosexual activity again, would that be desirable? Christians may disagree about this, but it seems perfectly legitimate to follow the example of our Lord in not recommending civil penalties for sexual sin, while at the same time refusing to condone the moral sin. Furthermore, it is perfectly consistent with this view for the ruler to place restrictions on the advocating or advertising of what is regarded as immoral although not criminal. Equally, it is also consistent with this view that the age of consent for homosexual activity should be higher than that for heterosexuals, as it is a recognised fact that teenagers may very well experience a time of uncertainty about their sexual identity and it would be wrong to tolerate exposure to homosexual pressure at that stage.

In the final analysis, however, the Christian believes it is not the law that will change the homosexual, but grace. The law kills, but the Spirit gives life. Christians and Christian churches must be sympathetically aware of those with homosexual tendencies and must seek to show them the kindness and counsel that Jesus showed to the sexually immoral with whom he came in contact. We must always have the words of the Apostle ringing in our ears—"that is what some of you were" (1 Corinthians 6:11).

## About the author

Alex J MacDonald is a minister of the Free Church of Scotland. He took an M.A. degree at the University of Edinburgh and did his theological training at the Free Church College, Edinburgh. He has 24 years experience in the pastoral ministry and now ministers in a thriving church in the centre of Edinburgh. He is married with four children. Alex is a member of the City of Edinburgh Education Committee.

### Chapter 5 notes

1   **C. S. Lewis,** *The Abolition of Man,* Fount, 1978, p.15ff
2   **Michael Vasey,** *Strangers and Friends,* Hodder and Stoughton, 1995, p.125f
3   See ref 2, p.126ff
4   See ref 2, p.127
5   See ref 2, p.129ff
6   See ref 2, p.134ff
7   **David Wright,** *Homosexuals or Prostitutes?,* Vigiliae Christianae, 38 (1984), pp.123-53
8   See ref 2, p. 139
9   For a detailed critique of Theonomy, see relevant section of the Public Questions, Religion and Morals Committee Report in The Acts of the General Assembly of the Free Church of Scotland, Free Church of Scotland, 1997.

# Abusing the Bible!

**Brian Edwards** examines the way that supporters of homosexual practice use the Bible, with particular reference to the writing of Michael Vasey

Students are often warned that if they arrive at an interpretation of Scripture that appears rarely to have been considered in two thousand years of Christian history then there is a high chance that they are wrong. The logic of that advice is that the more times they are out of line with accepted interpretation then the higher the chance that they are consistently wrong!

In his book *Strangers and Friends - a new exploration of homosexuality and the Bible* (Hodder and Stoughton 1995), Michael Vasey appears either not to have heard that counsel or to be completely indifferent to it. On virtually every passage of Scripture that directly or indirectly touches on the issue of practising homosexuality he takes a view that is either novel or that violates accepted standards of biblical interpretation (hermeneutics). The more novel the interpretation of Scripture, the more likely it is being used to defend a very weak argument.

Michael Vasey, tutor of liturgy at the University of Durham, sets out to present a biblical case to defend his main thesis that the traditional evangelical opposition to homosexual practice is based upon a cultural position arising from misunderstood Bible texts, and that homosexual relationships are good in the sight of God provided they are loving, caring and committed. We must at least credit him with courage in attempting such a defence, and his pastoral concern is unquestioned.

When some evangelicals argued for bringing women into spiritual leadership in the church, it became clear that by the hermeneutic they were using they were unintentionally destroying the biblical foundation for the traditional Christian teaching on homosexual practice. And so it happened. For the first time in two thousand years some of those who profess to be loyal to the Bible are concluding that, after all, the Bible is on their side in defending caring homosexual practice; we are now to believe that what the Bible condemns is only erotic homosexual behaviour. Since Vasey has trawled through the Bible for every conceivable argument, it is hard to imagine anyone improving on his position. I want to examine his handling of the biblical text; but before I do so, I would like to assess his hermeneutic in another area that provides us with an example of his mind-set.

### Ailred and Christian Friendship

Michael Vasey uses as a model the life and writings of St. Ailred, a twelfth century Cistercian monk who read all he could on the subject of Christian friendship and finally decided 'to write my own book on spiritual friendship, and to draw up some rules for chaste and holy love'. Vasey's conclusion is that 'His own writing and the biography of his disciple, Walter Daniel, provide ample evidence that erotic attraction to men was a dominant force in his life, that the sexual activity that preceded his call to the monastic life was with male friends at the court of King David I of Scotland, and that profound emotional friendships with men continued to be an integral part of his life... Not only does Aelred (Vasey consistently spells the name this way) treat gay love in adolescence and in adult life without embarrassment, it is clear that he lived in a time when this caused no comment or difficulty.' (*Strangers and Friends* p 83-84).

I refer to Vasey's handling of St. Ailred, not because it matters too much what the Abbot of Rievaulx in the Middle Ages thought about homosexual relationships, but because in expounding Ailred's view Vasey reveals his own faulty hermeneutic. He presumably relies on the fact that few, if any, of his readers will have even heard of, let alone read, *Christian Friendship*. Reading it, and my translation is by Hugh Talbot and published by The Catholic Book Club in 1942, a very different picture emerges. The whole treatise was intended to keep friendships pure and spiritual, and Ailred's models were David and Jonathan, Philip and Nathaniel, John and Andrew, and Christ himself 'as the most tender of all friends'. The translator comments that Ailred saw all friendships as regulated by the Christian law and that 'intimacies which pretend to meet this need by pandering to the lower passions, must not be entertained. They are not true friendships at all. They will not satisfy man's nature, but rather, leave it empty and discontented.' He refers to an Anglo-Saxon hermit, Richard Rolle, who warned that the company of women with men is 'wont to happen to the destruction of virtue'. Rolle could hardly be concerned for that if he accepted sexual contact between men.

But to return to St. Ailred. His purpose is to show what spiritual friendship is, and how it can be kept 'in harmony with the pursuit of holiness' (p.35) and he refers to Acts 4:32 as an example of true friendship. Would Michael Vasey have us believe that in the phrase 'All the believers were one in heart and mind' there is a hidden reference to homosexual sex? Ailred describes homosexual relationships plainly: 'Men who are attracted to one another by passion have no right to be called friends... They are deluded by a mistaken likeness of their union to real friendship... Yet they experience a certain amount of pleasure in spite of the fact that it is defiled by lust and avarice and licentiousness. Imagine then what real delight may be expected from real friendship... the more chaste it is, the more pleasure it gives' (p41).

The abbot then distinguishes between three kinds of friendship - sensual, worldly and spiritual - and describes them in this way: 'Sensual is based on the gratification of the lower instincts. Worldly friendship is stimulated by the expectation of gain. Spiritual friendship is sought by good men with a similarity of outlook and community of ideals' (p.42). Ailred elaborates on the sensual friendship by a clear description of homosexual actions which 'by gestures, glances, words, little services, one heart captivates another: one heart sets aflame another and an intimacy is begun. And once the wretched pact is made, they commit and allow to be committed for each other's sake, all kinds of shameful and sacrilegious deeds' (p.42). We may ask what this refers to if not homosexual sex?

Further, Ailred distinguished between the 'kiss of the body' and 'the kiss of the spirit'. He offers a few examples for the first: a sign of reconciliation, a sign of peace, a sign of Catholic unity, and a sign of love - in which, significantly, the bride and groom is his only example. He concedes that there are other forms, but these are 'detestable and abominable'. Again, if this is not a reference to homosexual acts, then what is it? The 'kiss of the spirit' is 'not by the touching of the mouth but by the union of hearts' (p.58). Ailred adds that 'There is another type of friendship based on the mutual gratification of evil passions. But I decline to speak of it. Friendship is far too good a name for it' (p.67). To the unbiased interpreter of history all this is perfectly clear.

Ailred, who for twenty years ruled over some three hundred monks, describes his own intimate friendships and there is never even a suggestion of sexual gratification. More significant is the fact that Ailred had a number of friends at the same time and never once in all the debates did he propose that a monk should have only one friend, and that for life; on the contrary he actually argues for the possibility of multiple friendships. If Vasey assumes these friendships were sexual is he suggesting promiscuous homosexual relationships? Of course not, but the facts and the logic have destroyed his whole case. The fact is that Ailred nowhere even hints that his definition of friendship includes homosexual sex - everything is plainly to the contrary.

Let St. Ailred make his own position clear: 'The primary obligation that binds any man is to keep himself chaste, to deny himself the indulgence of his passions, and to procure for himself every spiritual advantage. When he has made this the rule of self-love, let him follow the same rule in love of his neighbour' (p 116). During the last ten years of his life Ailred was painfully crippled with arthritis; monks would frequently come to him wondering if they could enjoy friendships without harm to their spirit, and Ailred would counsel them positively; but he recognised that even holy friendships could arouse unholy passions. His wise counsel warned: 'A true friend must not expect to gain anything from friendship beyond God, and the natural good of friendship itself' (p.88).

Vasey frequently refers to Anthony Thiselton's emphasis on taking into account the writer's 'horizon' as a principle of hermeneutics. In other words, we need to discover the assumptions and cultural expectations of the writer in order to interpret his writing. To do this with

Ailred must surely involve a recognition that the Abbot and his monks had taken the vow of sexual chastity and that his understanding of friendship must be seen in the context of pure, spiritual relationships. All that we have seen in the above summary confirms this. And in Ailred's *Christian Friendship* there is no evidence to the contrary.

Vasey's way of handling of *Christian Friendship* is precisely the same as the way he handles the Bible: he consistently reads into the text rather than out of it, selects only what he thinks points to his conclusions, and ignores all else. In addition he makes massive assumptions. Ailred's relationship with Henry, the son of David, King of Scotland, could hardly have been anything other than platonic since he himself describes Henry as 'a lovely, quiet, shy boy, with a natural majesty; he was chaste in body, grave in countenance, honourable in life: so often in church, so still at prayer, so generous to the poor, so reverent to age'. It was a life-long friendship. Ailred describes his love to Henry's father 'whom I loved beyond all mortal men'.

If all this is love expressed in sexual fulfilment, then Vasey has chosen a remarkably promiscuous example as his model! Vasey assumes that same-sex love may include a physical sexual involvement. That is the whole point of his book. No one denies deep and committed same-sex friendships, it is the sexual contact side that is under investigation. Vasey appears incapable of understanding a same-sex friendship and love that is pure and spiritual yet does not indulge the passions - but this is precisely Ailred's definition. If Vasey thinks that Ailred is typical of an age in which homosexual sex 'caused no comment or difficulty' then he has certainly chosen a strange example. No fair reading of *Christian Friendship* could come to that conclusion.

This excursion into Michael Vasey's treatment of the writing of St. Ailred of Rievaulx perfectly illustrates his handling of Scripture. I want to examine his hermeneutic under three headings: **selection, rejection and assumption.** By selection I refer to those arguments where he has chosen to take an interpretation of a passage or the meaning of a word that, whilst perhaps possible, is decidedly a unique or minority view. By rejection I mean those areas where Vasey chooses to ignore the unanimous agreement of commentators and the plain meaning of the passage in its immediate context. By assumption I am thinking of those narratives where he draws massive conclusions from minimum evidence. In every case Vasey is violating clearly accepted principles of interpreting any piece of literature, let alone the Bible.

### First, selection

When faced with possible alternative translations of a word it is always a temptation to choose the one that fits best with the conclusion we wish to come to. That is natural, and providing our conclusion is a sound one, then it may be a legitimate hermeneutical approach. However, when we select a minority rendering, or one that is so obscure that few if any seem to have considered it possible, then at least we need a friend to point out that we have fallen into temptation.

According to Vasey, the story of the centurion who appealed to our Lord to heal his 'servant' hides a significant concession on the part of Christ. The word translated 'servant' (Matthew 8:6) is in fact the Greek *pais*, which is a common word for 'boy'. Vasey concludes: 'It is a standard form for a servant, but also an affectionate diminutive often used in homo-sexual relationships' (p.120). Unfortunately Vasey offers us no evidence for this 'often' use of the word, so we have to do our own work to discover how common it is or whether it is used in this way at all. Certainly the standard Greek lexicons offer no such reference and neither is the word used in this way anywhere else in the New Testament; in fact the same word is used to refer to Christ himself (Luke 2:42). Since *pais* frequently refers to a 'son' it would be more plausible to suggest that it was the centurion's own son that is in focus here. Even if the word *pais* does have this homosexual connotation it would be a very minor use, and the total absence of this use elsewhere in the New Testament demands strong evidence before such an interpretation is adopted.

Alarmingly, if we do adopt Vasey's unlikely view of this passage, i.e. that the centurion used this 'boy' (*pais*) as his homosexual plaything, we have an example of Christ condoning 'pederasty' (anal intercourse between a man and a boy) since that word is composed of the words *pais* and *erastes* (lover). Is Michael Vasey really supportive of pederasty? And does he really believe that Christ was? On reflection

Vasey might consider that he had proved a little too much from his unusual interpretation of a straightforward passage of Scripture!

However, Vasey is eager to grasp the possibility that Jesus healed a known 'boy' - a homosexual servant used by the centurion - since this would speak volumes for Christ's response to gay relationships. Hermeneutical honesty forces Vasey at this point to concede with the amusing understatement: 'There is an element of speculation in this interpretation'! In reality it is total speculation based upon the unwarranted selection of an uncommon use of a word which is never used in this way elsewhere in the New Testament. We can only hope that students at Durham do not follow the same hermeneutical approach as their tutor!

Even more devastating to his cause is the fact that Vasey's interpretation of Romans 1:27, 1 Corinthians 6:9, and 1 Timothy 1:10, which we will come to shortly, depends upon the cultural 'horizon' of Paul condemning homosexual relationships only in the context of 'slavery, idolatry and social dominance' (p.136); allowing his argument that the centurion's 'boy' was his homosexual servant, we apparently have the spectacle of Christ endorsing the very thing that Paul condemned!

Another example of Vasey's selection is found in his treatment of 1 Corinthians 6:9 and 1 Timothy 1:10. In both passages the apostle Paul uses the word *arsenokoitai*, and Vasey rightly identifies these as two of the seven texts commonly used against practising homosexuality. The word is composed of two Greek words one of which means 'male' and the other 'bed'; it is not difficult to recognise the general meaning of the word. However, Michael Vasey believes that the New Testament references condemn only the erotic sexual behaviour of the cult male prostitutes of the first century and that we must therefore translate *arsenokoitai* by the phrase 'male cult prostitutes' rather than simply 'homosexual behaviour'. But neither the Greek lexicon of Grimm/Thayer, nor that of Bauer, even mention temple prostitutes in connection with this word, and the Greek translation of the Old Testament (the Septuagint) uses *arsenokoitai* to translate Leviticus 18:22 and 20:13 - which we will come to shortly.

As if to escape from this highly speculative selection of translation Vasey concludes: 'The problem remains that any translation is somewhat subjective' (p.135). That is just not true. It is only subjective when we dismiss the accepted meaning. However, even if we assume that it is correct to translate *arsenokoitai* by the phrase 'male cult prostitute', the question remains: what does the other word mean that Paul uses in 1 Corinthians 6:9? The New International Version translates this verse in part: 'Neither the sexually immoral, nor idolaters nor male prostitutes nor homosexual offenders'. Here the N.I.V. has chosen to translate *arsenokoitai* by 'homosexual offenders', and the following word by 'male prostitutes'. This word is *malakos*, which means 'soft, effeminate' and refers often to men and boys who allow themselves to be abused homosexually. Here then are two words, and if one refers to the temple prostitutes, what does the other refer to?

It is not good enough to suggest, as Vasey does, that both words are merely 'general terms' that have hidden within them 'both the horizon and the organizing categories of those who use (them)' (p.136). Paul wrote to be understood, and the Christian church has never had difficulty in understanding his 'horizon' or his 'organizing categories'. To the average interpreter of the Bible, given only the knowledge of the components of the two words, it is not difficult to realize that Paul could hardly be more explicit. If the Apostle had only a limited activity in mind he certainly did not make himself clear.

Wherever does the New Testament (or the Bible for that matter) affirm the purity of same-sex genital contact even in a loving, caring relationship? Selecting unusual responses to clear texts in order to reject accepted instruction on this subject, Vasey is still left with the total silence of Scripture on the positive side of the debate.

### Secondly, rejection

However we understand the early chapters of Genesis, most Bible commentators have agreed that if the first two chapters teach us anything at all, the divine plan for the husband and wife relationship is included—especially in the light of our Lord's endorsement recorded in Matthew 19:4-6. Apparently that is no longer the case. Vasey insists that Genesis 2:18-25 is not a mandate for the nuclear family but simply for the ordering of relationships in society; it is about the 'social nature of humanity and the mysterious duality of gender' (p.117). It is not clear what Vasey means by that, but I cannot believe that we needed Genesis to tell us that society is made up from two sexes and that they must get along together! For almost all commentators, Genesis 1-3 provides valuable information concerning the Creator's specific plan for the ordering of a fallen society. And the pattern is Adam and Eve, one man and one woman.

However, according to Vasey, the view of Genesis 2:24 as a mandate for life-long monogamy is 'not confirmed by the rest of Scripture' (p.116). Both this and the subsequent teaching of Jesus has as its primary thrust 'the creation of an affectionate community within which marriage is almost an irrelevance' (p.117).

This staggeringly naive statement is supported by references to the calling of the disciples, the women who served Christ, Peter's mother-in-law, Paul's renunciation of his right to take a wife with him on his travels, the greetings to Christians in Romans 16, and the apostle's instructions to Timothy concerning relationships in the church. It is as if the constant biblical refrain of domestic happiness between a husband and wife, and the explicit instructions concerning relationships between the two, just do not exist! The fact that all biblical society is ordered on the basis of the husband and wife unit, that the Song of Songs and Proverbs major on this very relationship, and that both Christ and Paul spoke at length on the subject (Matthew 19 and Ephesians 5 for example), is all totally ignored by Vasey. It is true that the New Testament does not suggest that the only possible relationship in society is the married one, but whereas it commends the celibate life, and affirms the heterosexual family unit, it nowhere orders the homosexual partnership. On the contrary, the only references to *that* relationship are decidedly negative. To reject the plain pattern of Genesis 2 by referring to the Old Testament polygamous marriages and the non-marriage of Jesus and Paul is hardly an argument against the pattern of the primary unit, let alone an argument in favour of same-sex genital relationships. What is significant is that the Bible is wholly silent on same-sex unions - except to condemn them.

Leviticus 18:22 and 20:13 provide what have been seen traditionally as two of the clearest condemnations of homosexual behaviour in the Bible. All that must change, according to Vasey's interpretation of these verses. He suggests that they can be understood in one of three ways. **First,** they can be seen simply as 'part of an arbitrary purity code abrogated with the coming of Christ'; **secondly,** they can be viewed as 'a witness to the unchanging creation pattern for human genital acts'; and **thirdly,** they may be regarded as some sort of combination of the two. Vasey inevitably opts for the third position: 'The prohibition of anal intercourse between men in Leviticus is part of a symbolic system which creates a cultural resonance that is hostile to gay people' (p.128). There is not a line of evidence to support such a position. Vasey admits that such passages have contributed to the Jewish view of homosexuality as the 'characteristic vice of the Gentiles' (p.128), but concludes that this is no more relevant to our contemporary culture than the fact that both Jesus and Paul spoke negatively of dogs and that there are no positive references to these poor animals in Scripture. Does he really believe dogs and human relationships are to be compared?

Vasey is rarely weaker than when dealing with these texts in Leviticus. Their meaning has always been plain to the Jewish and Christian expositor. The statement 'Do not lie with a man as one lies with a woman' is unambiguous and unqualified. However, they are now to be regarded as culturally limited and their prohibition has been cancelled by the coming of Christ.

Our response must be to draw attention to the context of Leviticus 18:22. It occurs in a list of sexual prohibitions which is largely adopted by civilized societies even today. Verses 20 and 21 refer to adultery and burning children in the fires of Molech, and verse 23 denounces bestiality. On what grounds, we may ask Michael Vasey, can he be sure that future cultural changes will not legitimize adultery and sexual acts with animals - not to mention Molech or incest? It is the Lord God who placed homosexual practice in the same context as bestiality, and then declared: 'This is how the pagan nations behaved and that is why I will destroy them' (v.24).

Vasey is rightly motivated by a compassion for people, but if we want to know how the compassionate Christ deals with practising homosexuals we have the clear pattern in his treatment of the woman taken in adultery recorded in John 8:11. He forgives her sin and urges her: 'Go now and leave your life of sin.' That has to be our model since nowhere is it recorded that Christ dealt with homosexuals and therefore it is our nearest comparison.

Perhaps the most dangerous part of Vasey's hermeneutic is found in his treatment of Romans 1:26-27: 'God gave them over to shameful lusts. Even their women exchanged natural relations for unnatural ones. In the same way the men also abandoned natural relations with women and were inflamed with lust for one another. Men committed indecent acts with other men, and received in themselves the due penalty for their perversion'. Vasey's response to this can be summarised as follows: **First,** Paul's argument is that all sexual desire, whether heterosexual or homosexual, has been corrupted by the Fall - and therefore his argument tells us nothing about the wrongness of homosexual sex but only the abuse of it. **Secondly,** Paul's use of the words 'natural' and 'unnatural' are reflective not so much of the order of creation but of what was considered natural and unnatural in his first century society. This is taken to be true also of the argument in 1 Corinthians 11:14. **Thirdly,** and aligned with the second, the passage throws light on the sort of homosexual behaviour that Paul had in mind; it was homosexual activity that arose directly from an idolatrous allegiance (vs.22-23), and in the first century was associated with slavery and exploitation. All this, according to Michael Vasey, was Paul's 'horizon' for this subject and it is far removed from the modern 'Gay Christian' agenda. He concludes that 'It is at least possible that Romans 1:26-27 should not have the sort of absolute force that it has to modern ears - ears that have often been tuned by an ignorance of gay experience, a cultural hostility to affectionate male friendship, and a mythological fear of the "sodomite"' (p.133-134).

Arguing in this way enables Vasey to conclude from Romans 1:18-32 that 'There is certainly an argument to be made that the man we know from his letters might be more at home today in gay rather than non-gay society. He shared Jesus' non-familial emphasis and lifestyle (1 Corinthians 7:25-35, 9). He treated no group or person as inherently unclean... He had strong non-sexual relations with women (Philippians 4:2; Romans 16). He had strongly emotional relationships with younger men (2 Timothy 1:1-8, 2 Corinthians 2:13). One might add that he experienced ostracism and desertion by the church (2 Timothy 1:15)' (p 133). Here is a mishmash of selective thoughts to which we must respond.

In the first place it is at the very least dubious to argue that Paul's reference to same-sex physical relationships in Romans 1 is merely limited by the 'horizon' of his day. The force of his words in vv.26-27 can never be limited in this way - unless we come to them with a committed agenda to defend homosexual practice. Are we soon going to defend prostitution by the same argument from v.26? And if the 'unnatural relationships' of women are neither lesbian nor promiscuous, what are they? And does not Paul, under the direction of the Holy Spirit, make himself abundantly clear by writing of men abandoning natural relations with women 'and were inflamed with lust for one another'? All reasonable hermeneutics demands that unless there is plain reason for taking it otherwise, the exchanging by men of natural relations with women for 'lust for one another' is a reference to homosexual sex - and nowhere does Paul qualify that. Vasey must understand that it is not necessarily 'cultural hostility' or 'mythological fear' that conditions the response of evangelical Christians to gay sex, but the plain teaching of God's Word.

To suggest that Paul treated no group of people as 'inherently unclean' is an incredible statement in the light of Galatians 5:19-21. Paul's phrase 'those who live like this' refers to people inherently unclean and sinful by the nature of their lifestyle; and of these he concludes: 'Those who live like this will not inherit the kingdom of God'. In 1 Corinthians 6:9-10, Paul similarly lists 'unclean' life-styles of those who, without a radical change, 'will not inherit the kingdom of God'. 1 Timothy 1:9-10 is yet another list of 'unclean' practices which includes slave-traders, murderers, liars, drunkards, idolaters, swindlers, the greedy, and practising homosexuals; these are life-styles that are plainly unclean - however they are to be understood.

Further, we may say that Vasey's conclusion that Paul would be more at home in gay rather than non-gay society is ridiculous - unless he uses the word 'gay' as a synonym for 'male'. But the word 'gay' in **our** 'horizon' does not refer to those who simply enjoy, or even prefer, same-sex company; it refers to a commitment to sexual relationships. To suggest Paul would enjoy such company, in the light of Romans 1:26-27 alone, demands a rejection of all that Paul and the New Testament has to say on the subject of sexuality. The fact that Paul may have been unmarried, had non-sexual friendships with women, strong emotional ties with young men (note the innuendo of Vasey in the word 'young'), and was abandoned by some of his friends when the pace of persecution got too hot, has nothing whatsoever to do with the issue of gay sexual relationships. It proves only that Paul was pretty much like the rest of us —straight and normal!

### Thirdly, assumption.

Under the title *Finding homosexuality in the Scriptures,* Vasey first draws our attention to 'a curious phrase' in 2 Samuel 3:29 where King David, in order to distance himself from the treacherous act of Joab in the killing of Abner prays that calamity will fall on the descendants of his Commander-in-Chief and that they will never be without 'anyone who has a running sore or leprosy or who *leans on a crutch* or who falls by the sword or who lacks food'. Although he does not discuss the meaning of the Hebrew word *pelech* Vasey is right to suggest that it may refer to the spindle rather than a stick or crutch; this is certainly the position taken by the Old Testament scholar S.R.Driver. However, it is Vasey's conclusion that is significant: 'It does point to the presence of a despised but tolerated group of men who could not conform to the sexually aggressive masculinity of the culture of the early monarchy' (p.119); then, whilst admitting that this does not 'absolutely prove that such contemptible men were involved in sexual activity in Israel' he concludes that, because it may do, it will support his position.

This is an incredible and self-defeating assumption. If we take the word as referring to the spindle and therefore agree with Driver that 'David's words are an imprecation that Joab may always count among his descendants - not brave warriors, but men fit only for the occupations of women' (*Notes on the Hebrew Text of the books of Samuel,*

Oxford, 1913 p.251), this does not even hint at homosexual activity; and if it did, it would tell us only of a practice despised in David's society –an argument against, rather than for, Vasey's position. We must expect a more plausible line of argument than this from a biblical scholar.

In the relationship between David and Jonathan, Vasey speaks of the 'homoerotic strand of this story' (see 1 Samuel 20:17 and 2 Samuel 1:26). But why the use of the word 'erotic', when he admits that there 'is no suggestion of a genital relationship between the two men' (p.121)? Vasey assumes that the very relationship of love between them was, in the eyes of Saul, a cultural disgrace since it 'ignores the heart of the sexual ethic of his culture'. This is based upon Saul's outburst in 1 Samuel 20:30: 'You have sided with the son of Jesse to your own shame and to the shame of the mother who bore you'. But it is a totally unwarranted conclusion to assume that Saul saw the friendship as effeminate. Saul's anger, as the following verse makes clear, stemmed from the fact that Jonathan's friendship with David threatened the political stability of the crown.

Because of his band of twelve disciples, Vasey argues that the friendships of Jesus 'resonate for gay people' (p.124). Vasey does not suggest that Jesus was gay but that he did have strong loyalty and friendship ties with men; he is at pains to show the close bond of love that Christ had with his male disciples. But all this is beside the point. No one doubts that Christ loved his disciples and enjoyed three years of close companionship with them. Most ministers of the gospel work closely with a group of male church leaders - so what does that prove? No one questions that men or women can enjoy deep same-sex friendships or that 'straight people are quick to see in the love and intimacy they experience a pale reflection of divine love' (p 124). The issue is whether these should ever involve genital relationships. That is what is meant in the whole homosexual debate. Vasey must not be allowed to assume that the proper same-sex friendships found in Scripture are a justification for the demands of the gay community. To conclude, as he does, that 'It is difficult to see why gay people should not be allowed the same freedom' (p 124) is a wholly unjustified quantum leap from the biblical and Christian ethic.

## Conclusion

A school board in New Hampshire, USA, has instituted a policy that prevents teachers from presenting homosexuality as an acceptable lifestyle. In response some parents and teachers claim that this would limit the way they teach, for example, Moby Dick! What in fact the rule prevents is the *misuse* of such stories as Moby Dick. It may be true that there were only men on board the *Pequod* and that Ishmael shared a bunk with another man, but the story has nothing to do with homosexuality. In a similar way Michael Vasey has trawled the Scriptures to net same-sex friendships and then to use them as God's imprimatur on caring gay and lesbian relationships. That is just dishonest hermeneutics.

The 'Queer Theory', as it is known in some quarters, reads all literature with a homosexual agenda; but it is neither accurate nor honest as Ken Brownell has shown in chapter two of this book. It is more than disappointing to find a professing 'evangelical' supporting such a distorted view of literature, especially when he turns the same approach to the Bible. By selecting only the emphasis he wishes to make, by rejecting the best authorities and greatest scholarship, and by drawing massively unwarranted assumptions from the silence of the text, Michael Vasey cannot escape the plain and cumulative evidence of Scripture that whilst same-sex friendships are good, homosexual genital sex is sin.

What is undoubtedly the saddest part of Vasey's hermeneutic from a pastoral point of view is that in failing to distinguish between same-sex friendships - which are healthy and right - and homosexual sex - which is unhealthy and wrong - he has implied that all men or women who form deep relationships within their own sex, or find great comfort and security in single-sex company, must be equated with the gay community. That is pastorally cruel, spiritually disastrous and biblically indefensible. If Michael Vasey had used his hermeneutic to show that such friendships were pure and to be encouraged, but that same-sex genital contact was to be condemned, he would have done a great service to the church in general and the gay community in particular. At the same time he would have been a workman 'who does not need to be ashamed and who correctly handles the Word of truth' (2 Timothy 2:15).

## About the author

**Brian Edwards** gained a Bachelor of Divinity degree from London University in 1963 and after a short period of teaching accepted a call to the pastorate of Hook Evangelical Church, Surrey where he remained for almost thirty years before taking up the three-year Presidency of the Fellowship of Independent Evangelical Churches. From 1998 Brian is engaged in an itinerant preaching ministry and continues with his writing. He has written a number of historical and theological books including *Nothing But The Truth* and *Revival - a people saturated with God*. Brian is currently chairman of the FIEC Theological Committee, and lectures for the Prepared for Service and Genesis Project training programmes. He is married to Barbara and they have two sons.

# A matter of culture?

**John Hall** looks at the arguments currently being used to justify homosexual practice

Many people finding themselves experiencing homosexual feelings suffer considerable anxiety and confusion. For those brought up in a Christian tradition this can be compounded by feelings of guilt and isolation-and fear of rejection too, should they seek help and advice. For others, their homosexual preference has become something of a crusade, a mission to overturn centuries of accepted morality, to challenge society and its institutions (especially the church), and to see the demise of Christianity as we know it.

Those who experience confusion, anxiety and rejection in relation to their feelings may be tempted to embrace a 'new ethic' of sexual licence which will warrant such feelings. It is vital therefore for Christians to be able to justify their own position and to be able to challenge the arguments of others, if a Christian perspective on sexuality and sexual relationship is to hold credibility amongst those searching for guidance and help. This chapter attempts to examine the major arguments which have been put forward as reasons for homosexual behaviour, and to offer a Christian response.

### The traditional view challenged
It is only in the last thirty or so years that the traditional Christian view of human sexuality has been seriously challenged by a minority group from inside, as well as outside, the Christian church. Up until this point it was commonly agreed by most Christians that heterosexual marriage in a lifelong relationship was the biblical norm and that anything outside such a relationship should be regarded as both unlawful and undesirable. However, a remarkable change has come about. Today, we now face a grave moral challenge to the traditional biblical teaching regarding human sexuality to the extent that some, who would call

themselves Christians, are now openly advocating a third lifestyle, namely that of same-sex marriages. The orthodox understanding of biblical texts concerning the nature of homosexuality, especially in the Old Testament, has been challenged and supposedly reinterpreted by those who hold these new views.

In this country there is little doubt that one of the major agents for this change evolved from the Wolfenden Committee in 1957, and the passing of The Sexual Offences Act of 1967. As a result of that legislation homosexual acts between consenting male adults ceased, within certain safeguards, to be subject to legal penalties.

The main safeguards were that the Age of Consent was deemed to be 21, the age of majority at that time; that privacy was observed; that coercion or prostitution in any form was banned, and that homosexual acts by members of the Armed Forces and of the Merchant Navy remained illegal. The act did not apply in Scotland or Northern Ireland, where male homosexual acts in all circumstances remained illegal. By contrast, it should be noted that 'homosexual' acts between women were not subject to legal restriction. Since this time things have changed rapidly. It is now possible, for example, for homosexuality to be treated more openly in the media. Books, articles and discussions concerning the subject have been published in abundance and people are now talking freely about their own homosexual behaviour. Hitherto this was virtually a taboo subject. Over this period of time homosexuality has become more acceptable to public opinion as a valid way of expressing love. Condemnation of same sex relationships has decreased in political, clerical and media circles (although public opinion generally is harder to gauge, and many homosexuals continue to face discrimination, abuse and even violence in our society). There has been a considerable rise in the number and power of gay and lesbian groups, for instance, Outrage and Stonewall and The Campaign for Homosexual Equality, which is an organisation that offers support networks and campaigns for greater equality of rights for homosexual people. These changes in society have had their effect on the church where increasingly the 'traditional' theological position is being challenged. To what degree the average Christian in the pew is aware of this or affected by it is unclear. What is clear is that such changes in attitudes are going to affect us all, either in this generation or the next, and that it is vital that we are aware and informed if we are to be faithful to God and uphold the teaching of Scripture. So what are some of the reasons given to justify homosexual practice? Six of these are discussed below.

## 1. It is no more right or wrong than heterosexuality (just as it is not wrong to have red hair, or be left-handed).

The question of what is right or wrong is a central one: it raises the question: Who sets 'the ground rules'? For Christians the answer must surely be God. And how does God convey these rules to us? 'By the teaching of Scriptural principles' would be the answer of an evangelical Christian. We accept the nature of sexual relationships as explained in Genesis 1-3 which contain God's creational ordinances. These are confirmed by the Lord Jesus Christ in Mark 10:6-9, 'But at the beginning of creation God made "them male and female." For this reason a man will leave his father and mother and be united to his wife, and the two will become one flesh. So they are no longer two but one.' For those who are not Christians and may reject Christian morality, normality comes through inherited customs and practices or reason. Trying to come to basic principles is of course, a veritable minefield, for what is 'normal' to one may well be 'abnormal' to another. Normality for the Christian is determined by the Creator, and this in turn is borne out by the physical and biological characteristics of male and female, which are meant to complement each other and so fulfil the creative purposes of God. So Genesis 2:24 states 'they will become one flesh'. Nature teaches us that this cannot be achieved in a homosexual relationship be it either of male or female orientation. It is not possible for such a union to conceive other life nor to find fulfilment and satisfaction in the biblical sense of completion. Rather it is an abnormal way of behaviour and contrary to the Creator's intended function. In the long term it does not create the true union intended by God at man's creation. In God's eyes homosexuals have become sexually deviant and therefore their practice cannot be said to be normal. In Romans 1: 24-27 Paul says that homosexuals have exchanged their God-given role functions and have developed unnatural practices.

## 2. It is a condition that is not within the control of those who practise it.

Some justify homosexual behaviour by arguing that homosexual preference is not a choice but a fact of life given from birth; it is linked with our chromosomes and possibly a "gay gene". That raises the question, Is there such a thing as genetic determinism? Contrary to what people may think or say, no 'gay gene' has actually been discovered and it remains in the minds of people as a theory. Richard Dawkins, of Oxford, the author of the book *The Selfish Gene* states:

'The body of genetic determinism needs to be laid to rest'. His conclusion is clear. 'Whether you hate homosexuals or whether you love them, whether you want to lock them up or "to cure them," your reasons had better have nothing to do with genes. Rather admit to prejudiced emotion than especially drag genes in where they do not belong.' [1].

It has been said that until 1973 psychiatry was generally agreed in its opinion that homosexuality was the product of mental and emotional disorders, the reason being that people were 'made' homosexual in their orientation through their life-forming situation and circumstances. [2] Professor LaGard Smith, states: 'We simply can't know all the subtle factors that may influence one's sexual orientation. If relational problems carry the most weight, as they seem to do, even those are complicated beyond belief. [3] In *Straight and Narrow,* Thomas E. Schmidt lists several possible reasons: '*Biological Causation theories, Social Construction, Early Childhood Environment, Moral Environment, Behavioural Reinforcement, Recruitment, Individual Choice*' All may have some causal effect at various stages of a person's sexual development.

Whatever may cause sexual desire, it still remains under the control of a person's individual control. When it comes to our moral acts our desires do not over-ride our wills. Our conduct is under the control of our wills, and Christians know that their conduct should always be under the authority of God's Word. Love is expressed most clearly by fulfilling the Law (Romans 13:10).

Some homosexuals wish to remain celibate, and others want to change how they respond to their sexual preferences. Homosexuals do not need to pursue their preferences anymore than their heterosexual counterparts who, outside of marriage, must exercise a disciplined response to their own kind of preferences. T. E. Schmidt says, 'Against this pressure, many secular therapists persist in offering help to clients who wish to change. Leadership in this endeavour is supplied by the National Association for Research and Therapy of Homosexuality (NARTH)...Researchers who have conducted follow-up studies report success rates of 30-50 percent for long term significant change in behaviour or orientation.'[4] Schmidt goes on to say, 'homosexual activists want to convince not only the public but *themselves* that change never occurs, because *if I exist, each of them must be haunted by the possibility that they, too, might find the power to change.*' Paul reminds the Christians in Corinth of what they used to be like, and what a remarkable transformation has taken place as the result of the work of the Holy Spirit in their lives. He states:

' Do not be deceived: Neither the sexually immoral nor idolaters, nor adulterers nor male prostitutes nor homosexual offenders nor thieves nor the greedy nor drunkards nor slanderers nor swindlers will inherit the kingdom of God. And that is what some of you were. But you were washed, you were sanctified, you were justified in the name of the Lord Jesus Christ and by the Spirit of our God' (1 Corinthians 6:9-11).

There are Christians and Christian organisations, in this as well as in other countries, who are exercising a remarkable ministry among homosexuals. Such is the effect of their work that men and women are coming out of homosexuality and finding a new "life-style" in Christ. Amongst these is Leanne Payne, whose book *The Broken Image* [5] stresses the loving, prayerful ministry that is bringing forgiveness and relational healing to those seeking help . The power of the gospel is still effective in helping us all to find sexual fulfilment in our God-given roles.

### 3. It can be superior to other expressions of love.

Some people who practise homosexuality claim that as far as they are concerned it can be more beneficial and superior to expressions of heterosexual love. They maintain that a one-to-one relationship without any of the distractions of having children makes for something which is deeper and more permanent. Other commitments could weaken the relationship and so make it harder to survive the pressures of life and the hostility of society.

Michael Vasey makes this very point in his book, 'Strangers and Friends'. 'By contrast, many gay people and gay cultures play a very positive part in recovering and embracing gender and gender complementarity. One example is the sort of friendship that gay men often have with women. Another is the cultural exploration of gender identity in which gay and lesbian subcultures are involved and to which the whole of society is indebted. It is precisely non-participation in heterosexual marriage that makes this possible.'[6]

This argument, while containing elements of truth, is of course a fallacy: statistically speaking relationships between homosexuals are frequently very brief indeed. Schmidt, quoting Bell and Weinberg 1981, states, ' We can quantify the phenomenon of homosexual promiscuity, especially among males, more specifically. The numbers are astounding. Bell and Weinberg found that 74% of male homosexuals reported having more than one hundred partners during their lifetime, 41% more than five hundred partners, 28% more than one thousand partners. 75% reported that more than half their partners were strangers, and 65% reported that they had sex with more than half their partners only once.' He continues, 'And overall, only 8% of homosexual men and 7% of homosexual women ever had relationships that lasted more then three years.'[6] One major factor that emerges in homosexual orientation is that many find it difficult to establish any kind of stable relationship with people of either sex. It is as though there is a psychological orientation which prevents them from going too far into any commitment without reservations on a long term basis.

Another factor to be borne in mind is that, 'Over 90% of men and over 95% of women who had a partner of the same sex also had a partner of the opposite sex. Exclusively homosexual behaviour is rare!' (Christopher Townsend).[8]

## 4. It harms no one.

This line of argument is not sustainable when we consider the biological nature of the human body. A basic lesson in human anatomy will reveal the dangers involved in the misuse/abuse of the sexual organs. Medically there is a long list of possible infections that can be picked up in a variety of ways. Among them is, 'a common disease called amebiasis, which causes inflammation of the rectum and colon, resulting in severe diarrhoea and cramps. It is estimated that it effects some 25-40% of homosexual men.'[9] Amebiasis is said to be linked mainly to oral-anal contact, and may take place indirectly by transportation of the infection from the anus to finger and mouth during foreplay or when using saliva as a lubricant for anal intercourse. That is indeed a heavy price to pay for this form of love.

Add to this that Thomas E. Schmidt states, ' for instance in the year 1994 in the United States of America approximately 250,000, 70% of those who died, were men who had sex with men, and at least that many more homosexuals are currently HIV infected. The level of infection among homosexual men is approximately 30%, with estimates ranging from 20% in a Pittsburgh study to 50% in a San Francisco study.'[10]

Practically speaking these relationships do little or nothing for the development of the personality nor do they mature the human character. The reverse is so often true: many people are uncertain and frightened by the instability of the relationships that they fail to achieve. The realisation that no lasting commitment can be guaranteed does nothing to help a person's confidence or self esteem.

Mental breakdowns, feelings of guilt, rejection, fits of depression, loneliness, alcoholism, drug dependency and even thoughts of suicide are not uncommon in such relationships. Jack Burton, speaking on behalf of homosexuals, put it like this, 'Time and again I am driven to this conclusion: when it comes to basic issues like warm, friendly acceptance of people, the ability to love widely and to respond to friendliness without fear, the quality of tenderness and vulnerability in our relationships—gay and heterosexual stand together, sharing a common humanity, differently but equally bewildered, equally hesitant. equally conformist, equally lonely. God intended us to love. But dust we are and unto dust we shall return. The design of our Maker seems ambitious, and beyond our present capabilities. Our efforts to communicate, to relate, to love are clumsy—sometimes laughable, sometimes deeply moving in their ineffectiveness.' [11] There is both a wastefulness and sadness mixed in together in the statement of what might be possible—if only!

## 5. It is a human right.

One of the cardinal principles in this age of post-modernity is that each person should be allowed to decide what is right or wrong for him or her in their particular set of circumstances. This is a radical change in traditional patterns of thinking. Rights should certainly be used to promote freedom, equality and to combat prejudice on the grounds of race, colour, creed, gender or sexual orientation. In principle most of us would wholeheartedly support those aims. But have rights become too individualistic, and has community responsibility been set at a very low ebb? The plain fact of the matter is that you cannot have 'rights' for everyone without at the same time accepting responsibilities from everyone. Responsibilities must be to yourself and to others in your community.

Many attempts have been made to distinguish between acts done in private and acts done in public so that the one may be seen as right, while the other may well be regarded as wrong. In the radical cultural changes that are going on around us, the crucial issue is, whether we as a society will give legitimacy to moral relativism, or whether we will make a stand for moral absolutes. Homosexual behaviour and abortion happen to be at the forefront for many people who are facing this moral dilemma. But the basic question is, is it possible for our society to recognise and accept biblical morality as traditionally taught and understood?' Can we define it? And can we impose biblical standards and authority on people who may think differently?

It is against this background that a document was published in 1978 entitled, 'Towards a Charter of Homosexual Rights'. It was sponsored by 174 prominent citizens who came from many walks of life politically, academically and religiously—an impressive list. It was particularly strong in its condemnation of the Christian Church, and accused it of fear and ignorance. It laid claim for homosexuals to have full civil rights and liberties. It also encouraged homosexuals to disclose their sexual preferences. In the list of its beliefs is this statement:

'We believe that homosexuality is not a disease, or a disability, but a natural sexual orientation in a human minority, variously estimated between 4% and 10% of the human race. This estimate is increasingly supported by modern medical knowledge, and by ordinary human experience. Homosexuality in no way impairs normal physical, creative or spiritual development, and is consistent with the highest attainment in every human profession. Homosexuals are a cross-section of humanity, differing in no perceptible ways, other than in sexual orientation, from their fellows.'[12]

Although this document is supported by a substantial number of clergy there is not one single reference, either directly or indirectly, to the Bible or its teaching concerning human sexual relationships! Human rights are important for all of us, but for the Christian they cannot be based upon human reason. God's word alone is the basis for true human rights, and we must remember that at the last he is the Judge before whom we must all one day give an account.

## 6. It allows individuals and groups to fulfil themselves and establish a new identity.

Should homosexual practices be made publicly acceptable and should those who do them be encouraged to come out into the open and be accepted as 'the third sex'? This is what the Campaign for Reason had in mind when it produced its *Charter for Homosexual Rights* in 1978. Professor Oliver O'Donovan states: 'The new Gay/Lesbian consciousness presents itself as the bearer of a social agenda, the 'eroticisation of society', as it is often called, which implies the systematic criticism of the traditional heterosexual organisation of social relationships as a form of oppression.'[13] This is borne out by the Lesbian and Gay Christian Movement in its Statement of Conviction, which says, 'It is the conviction of the members of the Lesbian and Gay Christian Movement that human sexuality in all its richness is a gift of God gladly to be accepted, enjoyed and honoured as a way of both expressing and growing in love, in accordance with the life and teaching of Jesus Christ. Therefore, it is their conviction that it is entirely compatible with the Christian faith not only to love another person of the same sex but also to express that love fully in a personal sexual relationship.'[14] It is the last twelve words with which we would want strongly to disagree. As a result of this thinking among homosexuals there is a desire to have something like a marital status to give public acknowledgement and acceptance of this abnormal lifestyle. Deep down they do not want to be considered odd or out of step with anybody else. They believe that this is a practical way of dealing with any possible guilt feeling, and a chance to be acceptable amongst heterosexuals.

### The present dilemma

Concern with homosexual issues may be seen in the light of the various liberation movements that have been current since the Second World War. These have manifested themselves in various ways: the Civil Rights movement, the Feminist movement, and the sexual freedom movement. These in turn can possibly trace their roots back to the teachings of Karl Marx, Sigmund Freud and Friedrich Nietzsche. While Marx undermined the institutions of the family and marriage, Freud undermined the concept of human responsibility in areas of sexual morality, and Nietzsche turned away from the morality of Christian faith saying that truth is whatever enhances power. God is dead!

A combination of such thinking has turned many people away from the authority and teaching of the Bible and opened a door into an age of 'free thinking' This has affected society as a whole, and has also rubbed off on the Christian Church to such an extent that in most things it is the world that now sets the agenda for morality while the Christian Church falls into line with its thinking.

It is not surprising that sexual ethics, along with many other disciplines, have ended up in the melting pot of reinterpretation and pluralism, which in turn encourages individualism and opposition to the moral law. Objective truth and absolute standards for moral behaviour have become for many just the smile on the face of the Cheshire cat in the tree. 'Anything goes' expresses the profound selfishness that lies at the heart of all human sin. It is this tide of free-thinking that has encouraged the homosexual lobby to press forward with its demands for equality and acceptance, while so many others have looked on and remained silent.

The service to celebrate the 20th Anniversary of the Lesbian and Gay Christian Movement recently held in Southwark Cathedral, plus the exhibition and workshops in a nearby hall, reveal the determination of the Movement to press home its aims and objectives. Writing in New Directions, Reformer says, 'At the centre of the L.G.C.M.'s ethos is the notion of self-expression. However, I have been startled at the way that my right to express myself has been censored, and that, because the assumption is that theological conviction is merely a product of personal bias, it is not just my convictions that have been despised, but my personality. Liberalism is proving itself once more to be the enemy of tolerance. And that is why now is the time to draw lines.'[15]

Perhaps the most important change in thinking is the claim that the Bible does not speak out against homosexuality, or that it is ambivalent in what it teaches. Michael Vasey's book [6] 'Strangers and Friends' has in many ways crystallised such thinking. Chapter 8, entitled, 'What does the Bible say?' challenges the traditional understanding of Bible texts in such a way that leaves the door open for those who wish to embrace a liberal approach to sexuality. Vasey put a strong emphasis on the 'cultural environment' of the times in which the Bible was written. He equates the cause of the emancipation of slaves with the need for the acceptance of a homosexual lifestyle.[16] (This is the same hermeneutic which was used by some to justify the ordination of women in the Church of England.)

Vasey's book has undoubtedly brought the homosexual debate, along with other fundamental issues regarding Bible authority and interpretation, to the top of the conservative evangelical agenda across all denominations. To adopt his hermeneutical conclusions, and accept his particular approach to the various cultures in Scripture and what he describes as 'modern conceptual frameworks'[17] is for many to open the door to the comment, 'You can make the Bible say what you want it to say'. That flies in the face of traditional Biblical scholarship which commands both authority and respect.

Our theological beliefs concerning homosexuality must be clear and Biblical and they must be expressed with the utmost compassion and sensitivity possible to both heterosexual and homosexual.

This issue has life and death consequences for those concerned. The effects on the life-span which have been given are said to be considerable, 'The median age of death for homosexuals, however, was virtually the same nationwide and, overall, less than 2% survive to old age. If AIDS was the cause of death, the median age of death was 39. For the 829 gays who died of something other than AIDS, the median age of death was 42 and 9% died old.'[18]

In a recently published article on the issues concerning homosexuality David Field says, 'To explore the ways in which God's *agape* standard can be applied would need another chapter. Let me conclude this one by making just two suggestions:

The first is that Christians should be in the forefront of those who protest when homosexuals are treated unjustly. That is because love and injustice are incompatible. Whenever homosexual people are the object of snide humour on the television screen or harsh penalties in law-courts, genuinely loving Christian people ought to be the first to stand up in their support. Any minority group which suffers discrimination should have full Christian backing in the struggle for their legal and moral rights.

My second suggestion is also a requirement, if biblical standards are to be kept. Those who accept the Bible's veto on homosexual *behaviour* must go out of their way to express genuine love for homosexual *people.*'[19]

In the light of what has been said, we all need to exercise a Christian love and concern that will bring honour to the Lord Jesus, and which will influence for good those he came to save. Pastorally many fences may have to be repaired, and bridges rebuilt if we are to maintain a Biblical position and show compassion to those who need the love and forgiveness that Jesus Christ offers to *all* of us. Only then may the required help, healing and restoration be effected. We do need repeatedly to realise that none of us is without sin.

### Where does the Church of England stand?

Within the Church of England the recently published Report by the House of Bishops, *Issues in Human Sexuality* has highlighted the confused and ambivalent situation that sometimes exists. Like the curate's egg, the Bishop's Report is good parts. But in its desire to offend as few as possible, while upholding the principle that human sexuality should be heterosexual, it makes a distinction between what is permissible in terms of the sexual behaviour of the laity and the clergy.

Speaking of homosexuals in the life of the Church it states: 'This means that certain possibilities are not open to the clergy by comparison with the laity, something that in principle has always been accepted.' While the Report has not been approved by the General Synod of the Church of England, it has clearly moved away from the traditional teaching which the Church has held previously. General Synod in 1987 passed by 98% majority stating that, homosexual practice 'is to be met by a call to repentance'. No other statement on the issue has been debated, let alone approved by the General Synod since then.

### What is the current Evangelical position?

In 1995 The Church of England Evangelical Council, being aware of the confused situation that existed regarding the subject of human sexuality in the minds of many people issued 'The St. Andrew's Day Statement'. This was an examination of the theological principles affecting the current homosexuality debate.

In order to clarify their position they said there, along with many other things, 'In addressing those who understand themselves to be homosexual, the Church does not cease to speak as the bearer of this good news viz., ( Salvation through faith in Jesus Christ). It assists all its members to a life of faithful witness in chastity and holiness, recognising two forms or vocations in which life can be lived: marriage and singleness (Genesis 2:24; Matthew. 19:4-6; 1 Corinthians 7). There is no place for the Church to confer legitimacy upon alternatives to these.' This had the effect of clearing the air among Evangelical Christians. But there is still much work to be done theologically if evangelicals are to present a united front in the future.

## About the author

**John B. Hall** is the Rector of St. Nicholas Church in Tooting, South London. He serves in a multi-racial and multi-cultural parish where over 50 different languages are spoken. The Church is seeking to reach out to this community with the love of the Lord Jesus Christ, and to bring the Gospel of his saving grace to all who need to know its saving power.

Married with five children, John was a sailor in the Merchant Navy when he became a Christian, and felt God's call to the ministry.

### Chapter 7 notes

**1** *The Daily Telegraph,* July 17 1993, p.12

**2** **Marshall Kirk & Hunter Madsen,** *After the Ball* 1989 p.88

**3** **F. LaGard Smith,** *Sodom's Second Coming* 1993 p. 78 Harvest House

**4** **Thomas E. Schmidt,** *Straight and Narrow* I.V.P. 1995 Chapter 7 p.155

**5** **L. Payne,** *The Broken Image* Kingsway 1981

**6** **Michael Vasey,** *Strangers and Friends* Hodder and Stoughton p.58

**7** See ref 3, p.106

**8** **Christopher Townsend,** *Cambridge Papers* June 1994, Vol 3, No 4

**9** See ref 3, p.119

**10** See ref 3, p.122

**11** **Jack Burton,** *Our Common Humanity* p.11

**12** Campaign for Reason, *Towards a Charter of Homosexual Rights* p.5 1978

**13** **Oliver O'Donvon,** Latimer Comment *The Question of 'Gay' Carers* p.5 *no date*

**14** LGCM leaflet, *Aims and Objects*

**15** Reformer, *New Directions* December 1996 p.29

**16** See ref 6, p.140

**17** See ref 6, p.48

**18** **Cameron Playfair,** *The Longevity of the Homosexual before and after the AIDS epidemic* Omega 1994

**19** **Melvin Tinker,** *The Evangelical Crisis* Christian Focus 1995 p.184

# More equal than others?

Discrimination is a growing claim among homosexual activists. **Roger Hitchings** suggests a basis for responding to their claim for special treatment and sets out some of the implications that arise

Prejudice, ignorance, apathy and fear lead to discrimination. Discrimination denies our human dignity, our freedom to be ourselves, and our place in a free society. When even one person is deprived of these basic human rights, we are all diminished. [1]

Justice for the deprived, fair dealing for the disadvantaged and deliverance for the oppressed, all of these feature prominently in the teaching of the Bible.[2] They are hallmarks of a truly Christian approach to social justice. The history of the Christian church overflows with fine examples of men and women who have identified with those who were poor and disadvantaged. They have defended the cause, and fought to establish the rights, of those who have experienced injustice and cruelty, and they have even sought to change societies' values in regard to such groups. British history in particular provides extensive witness to this. Their view of justice and fair dealing was informed by a Bible-based understanding of truth and righteousness, and took full account of the fact that, with God, justice involves a rejection of sin and sinful behaviour.[3]

Evangelical Christians will therefore seek to be at the forefront of opposition to prejudice and discrimination which robs fellow human beings of their dignity and exposes them to oppression and devaluation. Yet it is just here that we find particular challenges being raised by the proponents of gay rights.

Many of those who pursue an active homosexual lifestyle, or at least support an individual's right to do so, argue that for generations there has been systematic oppression and injustice against them born out of prejudice and discrimination.

They would claim that they have been robbed of their essential human dignity, they have been denied the freedom to be themselves, and have been forced to be secretive and surreptitious in expressing their personal sexuality. Now the time for redress has arrived. They claim that their lifestyle is quite natural and their behaviour quite legitimate, and they should receive equal treatment with everyone else in society.

Some activists for practising homosexuals even demand to be given more favourable treatment than others across all aspects of life in order to make amends for the long history of mistreatment. Such positive discrimination, it is suggested, is their right because of the accumulated debt in western society; a debt created by the intolerance, cruelty and persecution they have endured. And where ingrained prejudice and discrimination continues to be held or pursued, it should be challenged and opposed by affirmative actions on behalf of gay people by those who exercise power. Others would simply assert that as human beings they have a right to choose their own lifestyle and that the prejudice against homosexuality can only be eliminated by some form of positive discrimination.

The objective is for a homosexual lifestyle to be given the same status as heterosexuality. To be heterosexual is of course to be attracted to a person of the opposite sex, but the term is also used to cover that set of values which asserts that the only legitimate sexuality is that between people of opposite sexes. The goal of 'gay rights' campaigners is that an active homosexual lifestyle should be affirmed as being totally legitimate —a valid choice in sexual practice. And in pursuit of this the radical wing, which is so prominent and vocal, wants special privileges that can only be at the expense of traditional Christian morals and values.

The concept of 'rights' is being subtly misused by homosexual activists. It is sometimes claimed that 'gay rights equals human rights'. The Christian Institute has pointed out that, 'sexual practice is a moral choice. It is not a religion. Nor is it a physical or generic characteristic. It is a choice.'[4] To establish this point they refer to studies which demonstrate that social factors, rather than genetics, lead to most homosexual practice. The claim that homosexuals are 'born that way' does not bear detailed scrutiny.

Alongside specifically homosexual men and lesbians who are demanding positive action to establish their rights, are people who view themselves as bisexual and pursue intimate relationships with people of both sexes. They see this as a legitimate choice, part of their inalienable rights of freedom. The promiscuity implicit in bisexual activity is clear. A straight person or a gay person can be faithful but a bisexual person can never be faithful. Bisexuals are generally powerful supporters of gay rights.

In this context it should be noted how much the campaign for the legitimisation of homosexuality also fits in with those trends in society which are generally leading to a decline in moral values.

It is in this climate that many Christians find themselves facing complex and difficult challenges. At base many of us wish to show love and compassion to gay and lesbian people, as we do to all. Following the example of our Lord in John 7:53 - 8:11, we would show love and understanding while upholding the high moral values of God's law, which for us is truth. But when we speak in this way we are cried down as intolerant and rejected as out-dated. How do we respond then to the demand that civil rights equal gay rights? How do we maintain our position and integrity in the face of the apparently hostile forces of equal opportunities, which can be a challenge to more traditional values? How do we cope with the siren cries for positive discrimination? To add to the potential confusion these demands sometimes come from those who claim a Christian worldview.

This chapter aims to clarify the situation at present, to suggest a basis for response to the claim for special treatment, and to set out some of the implications that arise.

### Equal opportunities policies

Many organisations seek to demonstrate their own tolerance and define how they deal with the complexities of a modern pluralistic society through formal policy statements. These will reject discrimination and promote equality of opportunity within the organisation's activities. Such equal opportunities policies are very wide ranging.

'It is the City Council's intention to operate fair systems where its citizens whether they are black, white, male, female, whether they have a disability and regardless of their age, sexual preference, race, nationality, religion, marital status, or culture, can be assured of being treated in an equitable manner.'

'The City Council will produce its own Equal Opportunities Policy which will cover all its activities. All members and employees will be required to act in tune with its principles and to deliver services accordingly.
'In pursuing this commitment to a policy of equality of opportunity and to maximise its effectiveness, the City Council attaches the highest importance to ensuring that suppliers, traders, contractors, recipients of grant-aid and other bodies pursue similar non-discriminatory policies and practices in all their activities.'

Statements of this kind which express and define a commitment to equal opportunities are produced by public bodies (such as the Local Authority, Police Service, Fire Service, Health Authority, Health Trusts etc.) and many other organisations across all sectors of the community. In general they should not necessarily be seen as threatening but rather as an attempt to set a moral direction to the dilemma of how to cope with such a diverse society. Sometimes 'non-discriminatory policies and practices' may be developed as what is often termed 'anti-discriminatory practice'.

In constructing such policies there are guidelines and recommended codes of practice which have been produced by the Equal Opportunities Commission, the Commission for Racial Equality, the Department of Employment and the National Council for Voluntary Organisations.[5] Professional bodies, such as the Law Society, and most national umbrella charities have also produced guidelines for their member organisations. On the issue of discrimination a distinction will usually be made between direct and indirect discrimination, and the range of categories covered may be extended to include carers or those with responsibility for dependents, trade union activities and political affiliation.

The legal framework within which such policies are currently formulated is defined by five Acts of Parliament. These are: Sex Discrimination Act 1975 (and its Amendments 1986); Equal Pay Act 1970 (and its Amendments 1983); Race Relations Act 1976; the Rehabilitation of Offenders Act 1974 and the Disability Discrimination Act 1995.[6] In general, we may say that it is unlawful to discriminate on racial grounds, sex or disability in providing access to services, facilities or goods, and in employment practices. There are, however, many situations where discrimination is not specifically unlawful, for example in relation to age, sexuality and in most cases religion.[7] Provisions included in the European Union's Amsterdam Treaty (Clause 6A) agreed in June 1997 may lead to changes in these areas in time, some of which could well have an adverse effect on Christian values.

But equal opportunity policies will usually go beyond the mere legal framework. Nevertheless, it is important to note that none of the Acts mentioned encourages positive action and indeed, they make most positive discrimination unlawful in the areas of employment and service provision. There is limited provision for some positive action (such as advertising particular posts for people with disabilities or from ethnic communities) but this is generally in terms of under-representation of specific groups and even here the scope is extremely restricted.

A further key piece of legislation which inhibits positive discrimination is section 28 of the Local Government Act (1988). Under this local authorities, and by extension organisations funded by them, cannot intentionally promote homosexuality. Furthermore they cannot publish materials with the intention of promoting homosexuality or encouraging teaching in any maintained school that homosexuality is acceptable as a family relationship.

There is of course great diversity across the United Kingdom as far as Equal Opportunities policies are concerned, and Christians in some parts of the country will undoubtedly face more challenging situations than in other areas. This diversity will be particularly found across employers and some (particularly multi-nationals) are now developing 'human resources policies' which are sympathetic to gay and lesbian workers. These policies will, for instance, encourage specific gay and lesbian groups and introduce same-sex domestic partner benefits.

## Equal Opportunities and Anti-Discriminatory Practice

Although the legal framework is quite restricted, and in some people's eyes restrictive, there is ample scope through more general equal opportunities policies and structures to develop a much wider response to and attack upon discrimination. It is now generally accepted that all forms of discrimination are unacceptable and should be eliminated. However, there is still a general failure to address the conflict that inevitably arises when what some people define as discrimination represents another person's deeply held views and established life principles. Too often the deciding factor as to what is to be accepted is popular opinion or whatever is 'politically correct'. In numerous situations Christians find themselves being wrong-footed by such attitudes on the issue of homosexuality.

Anti-discriminatory training provided for employees is a particular area that clearly highlights the dilemma. In order to implement an equal opportunities policy such training will be considered essential and increasingly the area of sexuality is being addressed.

Thus in one recent training course for probation officers there was a session on 'Tackling Homophobia'. I will quote from the training material to show how directly it challenges fundamental biblical values:

The term Homophobia was coined in the 70's by an American psychologist. Currently, the term is used to describe the fear of loving or being intimate/sexual with someone of the same sex and the hatred of those feelings in others. Homophobia derives from heterosexism which is the name of the oppression of lesbians, gay men and bisexual people and is based on a set of beliefs which assume that heterosexuality is the only natural, normal and acceptable sexuality.... A little later on we read: 'Western culture provides us with very clear messages about what expressions of sexuality are 'right' and 'wrong' ... The only sexual behaviour that is really okay has to take place in the context of heterosexual marriage and ultimately be about producing children (compare the way we deny the validity of same-sex sexuality with the way we deny the sexuality of people with disabilities and older people). Lesbian, gay and bisexual sexualities challenge and threaten the rules not only about acceptable sexual behaviour, but also traditional ideas of what it means to be female and male.'[8]

The document continues in this vein telling participants to begin '*by assuming you are homophobic*', and raising a whole range of very loaded questions. While complaining of ignorance, prejudice and stereotyping it exhibits all of these towards heterosexuals. By these definitions the Bible is heterosexist and therefore prejudiced and to be rejected.

Training materials, of course, are not statements of the policy of the organisation. However, such an emphasis is no longer the domain of extremists, it is increasingly an accepted approach. Within training and academic circles there are different emphases and perceptions. Trends in the humanities and social sciences may not be reflected in science and engineering. Similarly different establishments and courses will exhibit different priorities. Nonetheless, homosexual propaganda is generally accepted and promoted. Without being labelled as such it is positive discrimination on behalf of practising homosexuals. At the same time of course it is full-blown discrimination against Bible-believing Christians.

How then do Christians respond to this? In the first place we are against unreasonable or unmerited discrimination. In fact some of the more restrained equal opportunities policies will contain phrases such as 'less favourable treatment which cannot be justified' or 'treated less favourably...not on the merits of the case'. We abhor and resist racism and discrimination against people with disabilities. We hate the unjust oppression of deprived minorities and the blatant misuse of power to disadvantage the weak in society. Indeed, even in the case of practising homosexuals, it is the practices and claims to normality and legitimacy we oppose, not the individuals themselves. We seek to love lesbians and gay men, and we have no fear of befriending them but seek to do good to them. While this is our basic position, it must be reinforced by positive action on our part as we show love and concern. In this way we earn the right to challenge.

But secondly, we expose the false assumptions about, and misrepresentations of, our position. To do so we need to think through our position and marshal our arguments. It is important to be cogent. Nevertheless a protest on biblical grounds will often be immediately dismissed and laughed out of court. We may effectively demonstrate the internal inconsistencies and errors of fact in much of the presentations made, yet still there will be rejection. But since when was rejection a disincentive to a Christian witness? We may expect to be rejected but we can look to God to honour our testimony.

Thirdly, we do have rights. Where Christian principles are openly at stake we must speak up. The very policies that expose us to attack, or place us in moral dilemmas, give us the right to state our view and defend ourselves. In the areas of employment and service delivery we also have the legal safeguards already mentioned, to which as citizens we may appeal. This is of course a difficult area but one we should not shun.

### Equal Opportunities and Working with Diversity

British society is increasingly multi-racial and multi-cultural and contains within it a vast range of differing and divergent value systems. Responding to that diversity, and containing and resolving the inevitable conflicts, is seen as one of the great challenges that has to be faced. The concept known as 'Working with Diversity' has therefore been developed. At its simplest, this means that everyone should accept other people's views and values as being legitimate and should work alongside them without questioning. Policies and practices are developed in such a way that unnecessary challenges to individual positions are avoided, or at least these individual positions are tolerated and allowed. Clearly in such a framework ideas of absolute truth are dismissed.

Such relativism is in itself full of contradictions and impracticalities. The reader will be able to identify the weaknesses and there are a number of useful books available which explore the subject.[9] For

Christians this relativism poses one great problem - we have received absolute truth in the inspired Word, the Bible, and the revelation of Jesus Christ, who is himself the Truth. We can and must show respect to other religious and moral positions, but acceptance and approval are not alternatives available to us when it means an implicit or explicit denial of that truth. In situations that involve support of the practice of homosexuality and a gay lifestyle we cannot be relativistic. But even here the issues to be resolved are very often complex and deeply personal. Individual situations often require individual responses; we must always avoid over-simplification of the issues.

On the other hand we must be realistic and relate to the processes that are in place. We do not necessarily compromise our position if we invoke the principles of working with diversity in order to ensure we get a hearing. Our position may not be popular, or even to some people acceptable, but in the diversity that exists we have a legitimate viewpoint. It goes without saying that we should not raise concerns or objections when there is no principle at stake or expectation that we should in some way compromise our personal values.

Within the concepts of equal opportunities and working with diversity there is, at the very least, the right to withdraw and not to take part. However I am suggesting that in some situations we may wish or even need to go further and insist on being heard. These are always matters of personal judgment and it is not wise to lay down rigid formulae for how we might respond to the whole range of situations that can and do arise. But we should not feel totally without opportunity to present our case.

Of course in some employment situations (such as teaching, social welfare or probation work) the challenges may be very great. A refusal to follow a particular policy or undertake a specific piece of work may result in a disciplinary response. Using the concept of working with diversity will at least provide one ground of defence. While it has distinct limitations because it is so relativistic, it can be useful in some circumstances. It may not reduce the cost of standing up and being counted but it does allow a viewpoint to be aired, and bias against a Christian position to be exposed.

## The agenda for a positive change

The goal of full acceptance sought by gay activists is a vision that covers every aspect of life. It aims to achieve recognition for homosexuality as a normal and natural way of life. And to some degree, the campaign has already been successful with public opinion becoming increasingly sympathetic.

There is a significant level of support within the Houses of Parliament, with members of all parties in both Houses being prominent in their backing of the various campaigns. Nevertheless, there has also been a principled stand by a number of MPs and peers which to date has resisted attempts to change the law. It is important that Christians support these men and women as strong efforts are made to loosen the legal restraints and to establish the claim for normality by the gay lobby.

This support for equal status for homosexuality is also found in Europe. A new Article 6A included in the Amsterdam Treaty of the European Community states:

'Without prejudice to the other provisions of this Treaty and within the limits of the powers conferred upon it by the Community; the Council, acting unanimously on a proposal from the Commission and after consulting the European Parliament, may take appropriate action to combat discrimination based on sex, racial or ethnic origin, religious belief, age or sexual orientation.'

While this clause will undoubtedly be used in employment matters, it may also be used for a whole raft of other changes. The European Court of Justice could well be used to interpret this article to implement, for example, 'intra-community' rights so that provisions made in one state can be claimed in another. Thus a homosexual couple moving from one country to another could seek the same tax, benefits and property rights as a married couple in the country where they settle. It should be noted that strictly the European Court of Justice is an economic court.

Proposals are also being promoted for a future devolved Parliament in Scotland to guarantee 'equal rights' to gay men, lesbians and bisexuals, and to give some priority to this issue.[10]

The arguments and efforts for change by politicians are matched by the influence of many prominent people in the world of arts and entertainment who strongly promote positive attitudes towards homosexuality. Gay activists also have a massive presence on the Internet which they use most effectively to present their case. The generally permissive sexual values of our culture all create an atmosphere conducive to further changes. That there is a clear agenda for change there can be no doubt. We may identify six particular issues that form priorities for changes.

## Repeal of Section 28 of the Local Government Act (1988)

It has already been shown how this piece of legislation has exercised some restraint on the promotion of homosexuality as a legitimate lifestyle. Prior to 1988, there had been cases of teachers being put under extreme pressure to teach the normality of a homosexual way of life and in addition, literature was given to children that reinforced the same message. However, section 28 is now claimed to have severely repressed teachers and denied them the opportunity to present 'the whole picture on sexuality'.

In addition, gay campaigners blame section 28 for inhibiting the ability of public libraries to display appropriate information on homosexuality and of having a detrimental effect on the arts with over fifty plays failing to be produced.[11]

The validity of these claims is questionable and it may be observed that ingenious ways have been found to circumvent the provisions of section 28. Its full significance has not yet been tested in the courts and so claim and counter-claim may be made about its impact. Its main value surely lies in the fact that it represents a statement of public policy against the promotion of homosexuality as a lifestyle and as an acceptable family relationship. The abolition of section 28 would be a major achievement for the gay community.

It is sad that some leading politicians wish to remove section 28. It is equally sad that few Christians appreciate the importance of such an eventuality. There is a great need to be aware of the issues at stake and alert to the changes that may be mooted.

It is not alarmist to anticipate that if this change in the law were achieved, the pressures felt by some teachers in the mid-1980s and the literature aimed at children at that time would all resurface. If the explicit literature giving AIDS information is a yardstick we may well feel concern at what may be produced. There is a great need for vigilance if our young people are to be protected from polluting and degrading materials.

## Introduction of a Sexual Orientation Bill

Attempts have been made to introduce legislation concerning sexuality which would parallel the Sex Discrimination, Race Relations and the Disability Discrimination Acts, or at least to amend these Acts so as to cover sexuality. To be accorded equal status within a legislative framework with women, racial groups and people with disabilities would again be a major achievement for the gay community. However, such a bill could potentially inhibit and even imperil the expression of contrary views in some circumstances, including Christian views.

A European Parliament resolution in 1984 called for an end to workplace discrimination against lesbians and gay men but this has not been implemented. Whilst that proposal might well be acceptable, it would not be the end of changes that would be sought. Indeed, homosexual rights are now included in the European Union's own staff regulations, and further demands for change have been sanctioned by the Parliament.

The sympathetic attitude of the courts in recent years towards transsexuals has been seen by many within the gay community as a source of great encouragement. The emphasis on sexual orientation and on the emotional pressures felt by transsexuals is guaranteed to attract public sympathy. However, it is extremely important to distinguish between this particular issue and the way it is being used by those wishing to further legitimise homosexual practice.

## Lowering the Age of Consent

This issue continues to be a source of major concern to the gay lobby. The Sexual Offences Act (1956) prohibited homosexual practice *'whether in public or private'*. In the subsequent Sexual Offences Act

(1967), this prohibition was modified so that in limited circumstances these practices were permitted between males over twenty-one. In 1994 the age of consent was reduced to eighteen in an amendment to the Criminal Justice Bill.

'Stonewall', the homosexual lobby group, and the 'Tory Campaign for Homosexual Equality' (TORCHE) have stated they will continue to press for the age of consent to be lowered to sixteen.[12] However, it has to be noted that some Christian lobbyists argue that, though the age of consent is eighteen, in practice it is sixteen.[13] This is certainly confirmed by the Crown Prosecution Service's flexible prosecution policy in respect of male homosexual offences.[14] At the core of this policy is a consideration of what is termed 'in the public interest'. In essence, offences need to be either very serious or very public to attract any prosecution. Thus adolescents of sixeen or seventeen face increased danger. Amnesty International has announced that it will consider any gay man between sixteen and eighteen as a prisoner of conscience if he is charged under the amended legislation. They have condemned discriminatory ages of consent between heterosexual and homosexual activity as appearing specifically to criminalise homosexual conduct.[15]

This pressure is in spite of significant evidence of the dangers to adolescent males. A British Medical Association funded study demonstrated that gay men under twenty-one are at higher risk of HIV infection than those above twenty-one.[16] This same study also showed that a significant percentage of homosexual men wished they were not homosexual and would change if they could. Studies in San Francisco, which has the liberal legislation being sought in Britain, show high increases in a number of sexually transmitted diseases over the decade since the laws were relaxed.[17] And a study of gay telephone helplines[18] confirmed the evidence of the SIGMA study referred to above that many homosexuals actively recruit adolescents. It should be noted that many adolescents have had a homosexual liaison before they identify themselves as homosexuals - an issue raised in the SIGMA study relating to the process of maturing in adolescent males.

The pressure for change has been increased by appeals to the European Court of Human Rights in Strasbourg, which would appear to be favourable to the homosexual case. A further element in this however is the desire that any legislative change should address more than just the age of consent. Anya Palmer of Stonewall says:

..'it's better to have a Bill which deals with the whole package of criminalisation of gay male sex which was never fully decriminalised in 1967, not just dealing with 16.' [19]

The potentially horrifying effect of these moves has been demonstrated by prominent gay rights campaigners speaking in defence of sex with children.[20]

## Acceptance of 'Gay Marriage'

Same-sex 'marriage' is a further area where change is demanded. It twins with the efforts of lesbian couples to borrow sperm and seek DSS benefits to allow them to have babies, and the placing of foster children with gay or lesbian couples. This is a major effort to usurp marriage and the family. Marriage and the family may not hold the place of significance in ordinary people's value systems they once did, but they are still highly valued institutions. That is why public opinion polls have shown strong opposition to the adoption of children by lesbians and homosexual men.[21]

The Children's Act does give children certain rights of choice, and it is being claimed that they are increasingly choosing gay foster parents themselves and would welcome the opportunity of adoption.[22]

This campaign for 'gay marriage' and its consequences is gaining ground. There is a subtle euphemism used by some advocates in respect of 'gay marriage' - they talk of 'partnership rights'. In the end it is to claim equal status for a same-sex partner as for a husband or wife. Such an assertion is strengthened by those clergy who offer blessing ceremonies.

This is, of course, an international issue. In the summer of 1996 a United States federal 'Defence of Marriage Act' was passed which defined marriage as 'a legal union between one man and one woman'. However in Canada in late 1996, a judge ruled that in defining 'spouse' the words 'male and female' should be replaced by 'two persons' and a

Hawaii court has considered legalising 'gay marriages'. It is now proposed by leading British politicians that a partnership law should be introduced for gay couples committed to a stable relationship which would confer some legal rights on the partners.

Already Denmark, Iceland, Norway and Sweden offer legal recognition to gay partnerships. Holland will follow as from 1 January 1998, allowing homosexual couples every right of marriage except access to adoption. The Law Commission is now advocating that cohabiting homosexual partners should gain the same rights as spouses, and this has been reinforced by the Court of Appeal in regard to tenancy rights. The European Court of Justice is also likely to back claims for employers to give spouse's rights to gay partners.

Normal families have children and so lesbian and gay couples have increasingly turned to surrogacy to achieve this goal. In other cases a lesbian and gay man have pursued a sexual relationship, with the child born of that union living in either the lesbian or gay household. In this way natural desires to be parents are satisfied and, in some eyes, same-sex unions are validated as normal. Sometimes these households are termed 'alternative family units'.

One argument advanced for establishing 'gay marriages' and 'gay parenting' is that heterosexual relationships (i.e. normal marriages) are so unstable and unsatisfactory for vulnerable children. It is both a campaign for equality and an attack on the fundamental institutions of society. It is also an issue for serious reflection by Christians as far as both our views and our conduct of marriage is concerned.

### Status in the Armed Forces

The ban on homosexual personnel serving in the armed forces is a *cause célèbre* for homosexual activists. Military chiefs remain adamant that it is unsuitable for a practising homosexual to be a member of any branch of the services and that has generally been supported by government ministers. However, legal challenges are being made and the issue will be considered by the European Court of Justice. In addition, political support to modify the position is growing and changes will undoubtedly be made.

The armed forces constitute a major pillar of the establishment in British society and therefore a vital area for attack by gay activists. To win full rights and acceptance here would constitute a major triumph.

## AIDS Reality Campaign

The history of AIDS and the response to it in Britain contains a record of deception in respect of gay men that is quite shocking.[23] In order to obtain funding 'everyone is at risk' was the key message, even though statistically the overwhelming majority of sufferers were gay men.[24] HIV had to be an equal opportunity virus. So tragically, much of the resources targeted on AIDS information and treatment have bypassed the homosexual community to the chagrin of sufferers, activists and medical personnel.

A new emphasis has therefore arisen which has been termed the 're-gaying' of AIDS. Its intention is to redirect health education and treatment where it is really needed. Thus the Terence Higgins Trust, the most prominent AIDS charity, has launched a new reality campaign aimed directly at gay and bisexual men. While the 're-gaying' debate is controversial within the homosexual community, the campaign itself is about targeting resources on the highest risk groups and is to be welcomed as a new honesty. However, it will not face the reality of the dangers implicit in homosexual practice and the smokescreen of legitimacy will still exist.

## Support for Positive Action

All of the above six concerns were addressed by a Resolution passed in the European Parliament on 8 February 1994. This resolution was initiated by the International Gay and Lesbian Association. In summary, it called upon the European Member States (para 5:20) to:

(a) decriminalise sexual activities between persons of the same sex
(b) apply an equal age of consent
(c) end 'unequal treatment' (i.e. of homosexuals and lesbians) under 'legal and administrative provision'
(d) (UK only) to repeal its 'discriminatory provisions' of Section 28

(e) work with homosexual organisations to create a separate category of 'violent crime against homosexuals'

(f) combat all forms of discrimination against homosexuals

(g) allow homosexual 'social and cultural organisations' access to support from public funds (something, it could be argued, the lottery does)

The resolution also calls upon the European Commission to present to the Commissioners a draft recommendation to seek to end:

(a) 'different and discriminatory' ages of consent

(b) prosecution of homosexuality as being a public nuisance

(c) all forms of discrimination in law

(d) storage by the police of electronic data on paedophiles

(e) the barring of homosexuals from marriage or an equivalent legal framework (i.e. of relationships)

(f) any restriction on the rights of homosexuals to be parents or to adopt or foster children.[25]

These six areas focus attention on how the demand for positive action is directed to every part of life and challenges Christian values at vital points. The campaigning and publicity feed off permissive attitudes in society, lack of understanding of the real impact of the issues, and a diet of misinformation. It is surely clear that there can be no ambivalence about these things for Christian people. To accede to the agenda set by the gay activists would be to deny fundamental elements of Christian teaching, expose our children to unacceptable literature and pressures, and concur with a more rapid moral decline in the whole of society.

It should be noted that while the information in this section is correct at the time of writing, this is a fast moving scene where changes are taking place all the time.

### The direct impact on Christian activity

As citizens, Christians are affected by all these issues and we have rights and responsibilities. But there are some very direct ways in which the pressures of the homosexual campaign impinge on the life of the church and on Christian activity.

## Christian Societies

There are many charities and voluntary organisations in Britain which owe their origin to the social concern of evangelical Christians and still retain some association with Christian values. There will be increasing pressure on such organisations in the future on these issues. The major battlegrounds will be those identified earlier: employment, training, and service provision.

We may illustrate the nature of the conflicts by looking at societies working with children, although similar illustrations could be brought from other areas such as Housing Associations or care of elderly people. Barnado's is perhaps among the more politically correct of societies and is seen by gay activists to be at the forefront of change. Dee Fleming, Barnado's equal opportunities advisor is quoted as saying:

'For a long time a number of committed Christians felt that anything to do with lesbians and gay men was contrary to the aims of the organisation. And there was a lot of reservation and concern over child abuse, paedophilia and homosexuality..... homophobic discrimination meant that it was difficult to be cut through. There's a lot of dead wood in the organisation and lots of old-fashioned language. We are taking steps to change the language, including the use of the terms 'wife' and 'husband', so that lesbians and gay men get the same rights in compassionate leave and pension terms as everyone else. I believe the situation can only improve.' [26]

Other children's societies are still more reserved on these issues. NCH Action for Children (formerly National Children's Homes) has a very broad equal opportunities approach which includes rejecting discrimination on the grounds of sexual orientation. In this they follow the Methodist Church's approach to lay employment. Within the ranks of the staff in NCH Action for Children, there is considerable diversity of opinion. As far as involving lesbians or gay men in service provision, there is some ambivalence. Thus in placing children with gay couples, each case is 'treated on its merits'. There is clearly a strong management will to effect more progressive change but how far that has filtered down the organisation is unclear.

Gay rights issues have produced quite a deep split within the

Children's Society and the evangelical influence appears to be fairly strong. A more 'traditional' position on matters of service provision has certainly attracted considerable criticism. Committed Christians within the Children's Society are striving manfully to uphold their position.

But the battles are not just internal. Strong pressures are being exerted on such societies by campaigning groups and from a social work world that is sympathetic to gay rights. Understandably, the societies will not wish to discuss such matters but these pressures are very real.

Other issues will also arise. Funding is increasingly difficult for all voluntary organisations and Christian societies are, by and large, not exempt. If, as is sometimes suggested, funding is to be tied to equal opportunities then a squeeze is likely to be applied to those societies taking a scriptural position on gay rights. And if the society is looking for work to be referred to them by the local authority or other secular agencies, then the potential for pressure increases.

Whether such scenarios will develop is unclear but the arguments are being made and gay campaigners have identified potential areas for action. It is quite astounding therefore that many organisations, smaller or more local than those already referred to, have actually given little thought to the issue. Christians involved in such societies need to be well prepared and need the support of other believers, and that is especially so if the changes in legislation identified in the gay agenda begin to become realities.

## Local Churches Involved in Social Action

Many local congregations reach out to their community not only in evangelistic efforts but also in seeking by practical means to meet the social needs they encounter. This may include a day nursery, an elderly people's lunch club, a mother and toddlers' group or a Residential Home. At various levels there will be encounters with the Local Authority and the issues of equal opportunities, and therefore gay rights, could well arise. Services being provided by a local church may involve seeking funding from the local authority or another agency.

There is a positive element to this that must not be missed. Our position is a valid and consistent viewpoint that can be powerfully stated. In expressing our position, in respect of practising homosexuals, we may both resist the pressures to conform on the basis of our faith-perspective and also define why we stand where we do.

## Christians at Work

Should we regard sexuality and sexual choices as neutral? For an increasing number of Christians working in a wide range of settings this is more than an academic question. The Rutherford Institute[27] is an international legal and educational services organisation specialising in the defence of religious liberty, family and pro-life issues. They report several cases of Christian social workers experiencing discrimination that relates to their views on homosexuality. One case involved a worker being replaced in teaching and training activities; others have been in relation to aspects of child care. The Probation Service Christian Fellowship has experienced conflict with the National Association of Probation Officers over these issues, although negotiations have achieved some degree of improved relationships. Other professions are facing potential threats and increasing challenges. These pressures could well be increased as the implications of Clause 6A of the European Union's Amsterdam Treaty are realised.

The issue is not only about sexual choices and lifestyles, it is also about freedom of speech and religion. The demand by gay activists for special treatment for homosexuals and for the removal of limitations on their rights implies a direct attack on Christian moral values. For individuals in work situations this can be extremely stressful. Personal isolation and vulnerability can create pressures beyond what would normally be expected in a professional context.

This situation will often be exacerbated by the absence of support from colleagues who fail to understand the argument that is made from Scripture. Indeed, even fellow Christians with whom we work may well not hold to the same position and will undermine the stand being taken.

In such situations the support of the local church, fellow believers and organisations such as the Rutherford Institute becomes absolutely vital. Opportunity to express the full nature of the problem within a local church or a structured group situation, and to discuss the sense of pain and difficulty, is very important for individuals. Empowering fellow believers through sympathy, understanding and informed prayer is a crucial role for Christian people. Of course, the issue of homosexuality is not the only moral dilemma faced in the decaying culture in which we live. But this does not diminish its reality.

## Christians and Education

The activities of gay activists in the University scene, their dominant involvement in student politics and the widespread acceptance of sexual freedom present particular challenges to Christian young people and their parents. There has long been a strong emphasis within schools against prejudice on the grounds of sex, race, colour, culture, religion and disability. Children are rightly taught to value all people as human beings and discrimination is spoken against. However a new emphasis on equal opportunities is being introduced. Undoubtedly sexual orientation will be added to this emphasis.

Reference has already been made to the impact of the repeal of Section 28 of the Local Government Act (1988). Alongside the general acceptance of homosexuality this will introduce a new climate in educational establishments. It should be recognised from what has been said already that much of the approach to equal opportunities, and especially aspects of homosexuality, are supported by a relativism which undermines all concepts of absolute truth.

The challenge to Christian truth will come from both what may be produced for and required of educational establishments in regard to the presentation of homosexuality, and the underlying value systems that promote the particular approach to equality.

## Christian Thinking and Living

While the situations outlined above are among principal areas where the direct impact of homosexual propaganda and campaigning is being felt, we need to note briefly that we are all potentially influenced in the way we think and live. The overall sympathy within our culture towards homosexuality and the diverse presentation of gay issues in a favourable light by the arts and media can easily undermine our own convictions and diminish our determination to take a stand.

This undermining of convictions is reinforced by so called 'gay Christians' who so effectively present their case. The apparent self-confidence with which they argue what they believe may strongly affect our own strength of conviction. It needs to be remembered that part of the confidence building strategy that 'gay Christians' adopt is built on what is called attacking the stigma and attacking the stigmatizer, and it is to a large degree therefore an artificial construction.[28]

## Positive responses by the local church

We began this chapter with a number of questions about how we should respond to the demands for preferential treatment by gay activists. We have answered some of those questions as we have sought to map out the areas of conflict. Now we must sum-up by highlighting four further elements in our overall response.

## The Authority and Teaching of the Bible

The basis for our position is not the changing tide of public opinion or the projections of a vocal minority in society. We have the eternal Word of God that does not change. Whether a first-year university student is being challenged to examine his own sexuality or an elderly lady is being confronted about her supposed bigotry, we are subject to, and witness of, that unchanging truth. In working this out, there is a vital role for that mutual support and encouragement that is so central to church life.

## Understanding a Confused World

The levels of misinformation and biased propaganda on the subject of homosexuality are high and we cannot all be expert in every aspect of a complex subject. But believers have a duty to understand the world in which they live. That requires effort and some discernment but it is essential if we are to bear effective testimony on this issue, especially because it is a matter of defending and expounding righteousness in a corrupt and very confused world. Christian people need to be alert and ready to take wise action as developments take place in society.

## Compassion and Love in Everything

If there is one core error in homosexual propaganda, it is the teaching that personal identity and sexuality are inextricably linked. True identity is surely only found in our identity in Christ through the gospel. There is healing and renewal for every type of person through faith in Christ. Whatever situation we face, true compassion and a desire for people's best interests must be paramount. There should be a welcome and friendliness about our churches that helps overcome fears and prejudice. Winning arguments is ultimately not as important as winning people.

## Testifying by Holiness and Wholesomeness

We reject a homosexual lifestyle and we refute the claims to positive discrimination and action. But our response must be positive. That requires holy, attractive, Christlike lives and wholesome relationships and friendships that exhibit a joyful relationship with God. These ultimately are the great testimony. The witness of godly, happy homes is a positive statement that cannot easily be dismissed.

## About the author

Originally trained as a Company Secretary, **Roger Hitchings** has worked for over twenty-four years as a service manager in the voluntary sector. After eighteen years working with visually impaired people in Bristol, he moved to Birmingham to work with older people. He is a frequent lecturer on issues relating to ageing. He has played a prominent role in innovative developments in respect of care of visually impaired people and also older people, and is a regular conference speaker.

He has held office in local churches in both Bristol and the West Midlands, both as a youth leader and church officer. He is a member of the Board of Governors of the London Theological Seminary, and is also a member of the Citizenship Committee of the Fellowship of Independent Evangelical Churches. He has recently taken up the pastorate of East Leake Evangelical Church.

## Chapter 8 notes:

**1** Introduction to a model equal opportunities policy current within the Age
Concern movement (Feb. 1997)

**2** For instance Psalm 82:3-4; Galatians 2:10; James 1:27.

**3** In the interests of fairness it should be acknowledged that Christian history also
has glaring examples of unjustifiable intolerance and extraordinary cruelty. Such
excesses cannot be excused. They do not however reduce the reality of the argument
of this paragraph.

**4** The Christian Institute, News Update 1997 No 2 - quoting 'New NIX Study Indicates
Homosexuality is Learned' by **Robert H Knight,** Family Research  Council, and King &
MacDonald study 1992 referred to in *Homosexuality and the Politics of Truth,*
**Jeffrey Satinover,** Baker, 1995

**5** Equal Opportunities Commission, Overseas House, Quay Street, Manchester M3 3HN
(tel. 0161 833 9244) Commission for Racial Equality, Elliot House, 10-12 Allington
Street,  London SW1E 5EH (tel. 0171 828 7022) Department of Employment - contact
local office National Council for Voluntary Organisations, Regents Wharf, 8 All Saints
Street, London N1 9RL (tel. 0171 713 6161)

**6** For fuller details, see **Sandy Adriandeck** and **James Sinclair Taylor,** *Voluntary Sector
Legal Handbook,* published by the Directory of Social Change

**7** Discrimination on the grounds of race or sex may constitute indirect  discrimination
(e.g. if religion is linked to ethnic origin). Lesbians may be protected under the Sex
Discrimination Act if they can show that they have been treated differently from the
way a man would be in the same situation. Transsexuals have been found to be covered
under the Sex Discrimination Act.

**8** **Val Lunn,** *Tackling Homophobia,* Association of Community Workers (ACW),
March 1993, Talking Point No. 141

**9** e.g. **Carson, D. A.,** *The Gagging of God,* Apollos, 1996

**10** *BBC Women's Hour,* 20 June 1997

**11** BBC Radio 4 *Today Programme,* 21 February 1997

**12** *The Case for Change - Arguments for an Equal Age of Consent,* Stonewall
Lobby Ltd., September 1997, p.11

**13** Christian Voice, P.O. Box 526, Sutton, Surrey

**14** **Sir Derek Spencer M.P,** the Solicitor General, *Hansard* vol 721, 14 March 1994

**15** *The Pink Paper,* 4 March 1994

**16**  **Weatherburn P et al,** *The Sexual Lifestyles of Gay and Bisexual Men in England and Wales,* Project SIGMA, HMSO, 1992

**17**  **Magnusa Rege J**, *Are 'Gay Rights' Right ?* Straitgate Press, Minneapolis, 1985

**18**  **Malcolm Macrat,** *How Can We Help You?* NCVO Bedford Square Press, London, 1989

**19**  Out This Week News, 13 July 1997

**20**  **Peter Tatchell** in the Letters page, *The Guardian,* 26 June 1997

**21**  Harris, 'JN29216' for Stonewall, February 1992 produced by the Harris  Poll Co.

**22**  *BBC Radio 4, Agenda,* 27 September 1997

**23**  *Daily Telegraph,* 10 December 1996

**24**  'Public Health Laboratory Service statistics show that of 12,565 UK Aids  cases only 161 were the result of UK heterosexual transmission'— quoted  in 'Now it's the Real Thing', **Sinn Garfield,** The Guardian, July 18 1996

**25**  reported by *Christian Voice,* July 1994

**26**  'Child Minding', *Pink Paper,* 4 March 1994

**27**  The Rutherford Institute, Abbey House, 4 Abbey Orchard Street,  Westminster, London SW1P 2JJ

**28**  See *Attacking the attacker; gay Christians talk back* **Andrew Yip,** British Journal of Sociology, Vol 48, Issue 1, March 1997

# High wall, wide gate

How can we reach out to homosexuals when they assume that they will be condemned in our churches? **John Woods** urges a Biblical approach that is is tough yet tender

One morning the phone rang in my study; it was our local television station asking if I would like to appear on their mid-morning chat show as part of the invited audience. The show *The Time and the Place*, is a programme which tackles a variety of moral issues, and the subject on this occasion was gay marriages. I and a number of ministers were present as were representatives of the gay community. At the pre-programme coffee time I and a pastor friend were asked if we were a couple! I have to confess that my reaction was one of amused embarrassment which turned into the realization that gay men do not conform to any of my preconceived ideas! While some people might fit into the stereotypes of gay or straight we have in our minds, others are not so easily categorized. Gays are people and must be treated with the respect that should be extended to all human beings. As I was not called on to speak, I had an opportunity to reflect on the debate and was left with four impressions.

First, we live in a moral maze in which people are not equipped to tackle today's big ethical issues. Secondly, the moral climate in our nation is increasingly being shaped by a secular mindset: a mindset in which the highest virtue is tolerance, where there are no moral absolutes and no moral authority above human reason. Thirdly, surprise that the debate stayed so long on what the church and the Bible have to say on the subject. Especially among the representatives of the gay clergy there was a desire to gain God's rubber stamp on a new code of behaviour. Fourthly, there is lack of understanding between conservative evangelicals and the gay community. We did not appear to be speaking the same language; our understandings of reality were poles apart. Any attempt at persuasion was fruitless; without inner transformation there is no prospect of consensus.

The evangelical church does not have a good track record when it comes to dealing with this issue in an even-handed way. It has led to double lives and repression, inappropriate guilt and despair.

### 'Look in the mirror before looking out of the window.' [1]

Before we consider standards in the churches we must face up to these faults. The following words written by Rod Beadles after research into the lives of gay men and woman within the evangelical church are worth weighing, 'On the evidence of this small piece of research it seems to me that there are a number of areas where the thinking and belief of the church are wrong. For example, if the evangelical church believes that the issue of homosexuality is one that exists outside its walls it is wrong. If it believes that every homosexual person within its walls lives a celibate lifestyle it is wrong.'[2]

If Rod Beadles is correct, and I suspect that he is, then many evangelical churches have a woefully inadequate grasp of the extent, depth and strength of homosexuality within their own ranks. We must take this issue seriously, as Rod Beadles concludes 'It seems to me that the issue of homosexuality is one of the major items to be faced by the church in general and the evangelical church in particular. It raises some complex questions such as the interpretation of scripture, and challenges some orthodox views on marriage and traditional family life. ... If the church believes that the problem is going to go away it is wrong.'[3]

### Homosexuality is not the greatest or only sin.

In the lists of sins recorded in Corinthians, 5:9-11 and 6:9-11, Paul makes it plain that sexual sins are not to be placed at the top of a league table of sins. On the contrary they rub shoulders with those 'socially acceptable' sins such as greed and slander. The latter is a notable inclusion; with its root meaning of 'insult-hurler', it perfectly describes the behaviour of those afflicted with homophobia. Unfortunately we are all too ready to label the outsider and treat him/her like a social leper, as if the eleventh commandment were, "Thou shalt not be different". If we are to be taken seriously we must stamp on the tendency to demean or bash 'queers'. In the film 'Philadelphia', which was Hollywood's attempt to tackle gay and AIDS related issues, we have a classic example of this attitude. The main character, played by the ubiquitous Tom Hanks, is a lawyer who has been dismissed from his law firm for having AIDS, which has been contracted within a homosexual lifestyle. In one scene he is entering the court house when a mean looking fundamentalist blurts out the slogan 'It was Adam and Eve, not Adam and Steve'. I somehow doubt whether anyone has been converted or persuaded out of the gay lifestyle by the hurling of such slogans.

If we are to speak forthrightly on this subject, and we must, then we should do so with love and understanding, not with suspicion and blind prejudice.

Lance Pierson, an evangelical who has had a struggle with a homosexual orientation echoes this warning: 'Homophobia is far more widespread than homosexuality. It is not recognized as a pathological condition; so it is largely untreated and unconfessed. Yet those with gay feelings instantly detect it. It wounds them, hammering into them that they are unlovable, unforgivable, unwelcome. We drive them away from our churches, where they assume they will be condemned. We distort their view of God by implying that he shares our hate of gays. Our passing remarks and sweeping generalizations in favour of "a hard line against gays" force any silent sufferers into the misery of secret loneliness.'[4] Evangelical elder statesman John Stott writes, 'I rather think that the very existence of the Lesbian and Gay Christian Movement, not to mention the "Evangelical fellowship" within it, is a vote of censure on the church.'[5]

The evangelical church must face up to the problem of its perceived hostility to gay people, and repent of it, if it is to recover its integrity and restore its ability to be an instrument that promotes significant change. For most heterosexuals there is a feeling of revulsion concerning the homosexual, and at times this may have more than a tinge of self-righteousness about it. While the adage 'love the sinner hate the sin' is a half truth which has been over-worked, as sinful human beings we would do well to direct our hostility toward actions not persons. People are more likely to change in a climate of loving acceptance than in one that has the flavour of suspicion.

How can we talk tough on this issue while remaining tender toward those who are fellow strugglers? How can we build a high fence but retain a wide gate?

A good starting point must be with Jesus and his dealing with sinners. He managed to mix with a fairly undesirable group of people whilst making it abundantly plain that he wanted to see significant change in their lives (Luke 5:29-32; 19:1-10). 'What was attractive about Jesus was not his assimilation to the culture of those he came into close contact with. Rather it was the closeness of one so different that offered sinners a sign of hope. Even if Jesus would have felt at home in a gay bar, it is not so clear that those in the gay bar would have felt so comfortable with what he had to say whilst he was there." [6] R.T.Kendall superbly blends tenderness with straight talk in his book *'Is God for the Homosexual?'* [7], in the course of sermons on which the book was based, one homosexual (at least) became a Christian. Talk of standards in the church could be cold and uncaring, instead such talk should display the tough and tender approach taken by Jesus. For example it has long been realised by groups like Life and Care Trust that saying a firm and decisive "No" to abortion was not enough on its own. The "No" had to be tempered with a support structure which provided women with counselling and if required, a caring environment in which to look after the baby. More recently still these groups have offered post-abortion counselling, which is in part a recognition that we should start where people are rather than where we would like them to be. We need to keep this in view as we wrestle with the complexities of this issue; it must be with a compassionate human touch that we frame our standards.

What then should we be saying about standards in the churches? We will want to look at four main areas: church membership, marriage, service and discipline.

## 1) Church membership

In 1 Corinthians 6:9-11, Paul writes: 'Do you not know that the wicked will not inherit the kingdom of God? Do not be deceived: neither the sexually immoral nor idolaters nor adulterers nor male prostitutes nor homosexual offenders nor thieves nor the greedy nor slanderers nor swindlers will inherit the kingdom of God. And that is what some of you were, but you were washed, you were sanctified, you were justified in the name of the Lord Jesus Christ and by the Spirit of your God'

'And that is what some of you were' are eight of the most exciting words in the Bible. It is good to pause for a while and savour the excitement as Paul rejoices in the liberating power of God's grace. Two things are clear from the passage. First, Paul is talking about behaviour. He is talking about homosexual practice rather than homosexual orientation. Secondly, he implies that their behaviour was a thing of the past. All our church members have a past; by the grace of God they are seeking to leave it behind. They like all new believers have drawn a line under their previous non-Christian behaviour. Yet we all recognize that 100% moral consistency is an impossibility; why then should we be surprised if this is the case for a person converted out of a homosexual lifestyle? The road to holiness often involves three steps forward and two steps back. If this progress were plotted in the form of a graph it would not look like a constantly rising line, but a rather uneven mountain range. There is no instant or complete holiness in the life of any believer this side of heaven. If we have members who formerly had a serious drink problem they may talk in the following terms, 'I am an alcoholic or I have a drink problem, but I am dry at the moment.' We would rightly, applaud their honesty and seek to provide all the help we can to keep dry. Isn't it only reasonable that we exercise the same supportive understanding toward those converted from a homosexual lifestyle?

Martin Hallet the founder of True Freedom Trust, speaks of his own struggles:

'I am still aware of my homosexual feelings at times—there are occasions when my homosexuality could still be an issue in terms of strong temptation—God continues to deal with this in me.' [8] The temptation to slide back can be strong among those who have been involved in a homosexual lifestyle.

Perhaps one of the reasons for the sheer strength of this temptation is to be found in the complex combination of personality, background, experience which influence and shape the homosexual lifestyle. It is one of those clusters of sinful practice which becomes part of a person. Homosexual practice is an expression of what a person perceives him/herself to be, it appears to define their identity. Of course this is not uniquely true of homosexual practice, hence the New Testament teaching on the killing off of sinful practice in our lives (mortification of sin). Paul writing to the church at Colosse says, 'Put to death, therefore, whatever belongs to your earthly nature: sexual immorality, impurity, lust, evil desires and greed. Because of these, the wrath of God is coming. You used to live in these ways, in the life you once lived.' (Colossians 3:5-7). Strangling the life out of long established patterns of behaviour is a painful process. The Puritans used to call some sins 'darling sins' because they recognised that people can become so attached to them that to jettison these sins requires a monumental act of God empowered self-will. Increasingly homosexuals are resenting the idea of their orientation being a condition or still worse an illness; instead they want it viewed as a choice on their part. In that sense there are no homosexuals, only people who choose to engage in homosexual practice. If it is possible to choose to be involved, it must be possible to choose not to be involved.

Whilst homosexuality is not at the top of some league table of sin, sexual sin of all kinds has certain deep and long- term implications. In 1 Corinthians 6:15-20, Paul argues that any illicit sexual encounter has an impact on our life, body and commitments. 'Do you not know that your bodies are members of Christ himself? Shall I then take the members of Christ and unite them with a prostitute? Never! Do you not know that he who unites himself with a prostitute is one with her in body? For it is said, "The two will become one flesh." But he who unites himself with the Lord is one with him in Spirit. Flee from sexual immorality. All other sins a man commits are outside his body, but he who sins sexually sins against his own body. Do you not know that your body is a temple of the Holy Spirit, who is in you, whom you received from God? You are not your own; you were bought with a price. Therefore honour God with your body.' Christians cannot ignore the demands of being 'united to Christ'; it calls for a radical integrity in our sexuality.

As our sexuality is an important part of our identity, it is easy to understand how homosexual practice can come to be viewed as a normal way of life. Paul in this passage wants us to see that it is far from normal: this is not the way that those in God's Kingdom behave. '... a settled and unresisted habit of sins such as these is evidence of the unrighteousness which has no place in the kingdom of God.' 9

We must welcome as members those who have made a decisive break with their previous lifestyle. This is the whole point of this part of 1 Corinthians 6. Paul has argued in verses 1-8 that believers should not take each other to court in an attempt to settle disputes among them for the simple reason that believers are different. A distinctive type of behaviour is to be expected from them. Paul's language reminds us that 'homosexual offenders' (in Greek malakai) refers to behaviour and not merely to an attitude, characteristic or feeling. In the context, the church at Corinth would expect a radical change of behaviour whilst recognizing that feelings continue to exist and that they may return at times with fury and passion. After all Paul went on to write chapter 10:12-13, in which he tells them that they must all take care not to fall and yet that they can be assured of God's enabling as they face temptation.

### 2) Marriage

What are we to say to those new members who are converted from a homosexual lifestyle or who still struggle with a homosexual orientation? While we must not falsely assume that homosexuals are any more obsessed with sexual activity than the average heterosexual, we must not fail to recognize that, where there are strong feelings, acts may not be far behind. The church must say a firm 'No' to same-sex genital acts, partnerships and 'marriage', even if this is in the context of a 'loving' and committed relationship. This firm 'No' must be informed by the biblical understanding of marriage. Marriage is indeed based on a loving and committed relationship, but the context of such a loving commitment is the "one flesh" bond between one man and one woman for life. The definition of marriage given in the Bible firmly excludes same-sex unions and all extra-marital sex.

One can sympathize with those who feel that their 'love' for their partner is so strong that it cannot be wrong. Some talk about God's unconditional love as being like an elastic band which can be stretched to embrace anything we may want to do. Yet the Bible teaches that God's love is conditioned by his total character and his purpose. His character is holy and his purpose is to establish his righteous kingdom in our lives and in the world. And feelings alone are not a reliable guide to moral choices. A paedophile may argue that their 'love' for a child somehow makes their sexual activity legitimate. What about the person who wants a sexual relationship with an animal: is it permissible as long as the animal is loved? Unthinkable and insulting as the last remark may appear to modern ears, it is interesting to observe that the Old Testament book of Leviticus places the prohibition of homosexual practice and of bestiality side by side. In Leviticus 18:22-23 Moses writes, 'Do not lie with a man as one lies with a woman; it is detestable. Do not have sexual relations with an animal and defile yourselves with it. A woman must not present herself to an animal to have sexual relations with it; that is a perversion.' (cf Levitcus 20:13;15.)

Gordon Wenham comments on Chapter 18:23, 'Bestiality ... transgresses the God-given boundaries between man and the animal. Holiness in the Pentateuch is a matter of purity, of keeping apart what God created to be separate.'[10]

No same-sex union, no sexual relations with animals: in both cases God is keeping apart what he created to be separate. This is the point underlined by Paul in Romans 1:26-27 when he talks about departing from what is natural, from what is according to the maker's design. Men are designed to have sexual relations with women, to depart from this creation pattern leads to confusion and a moral climate where anything is possible and any perversion defended or even applauded. That is the ultimate moral nadir anticipated by Paul in Romans 1:32, 'Although they know God's righteous decree that those who do such things deserve death, they not only continue to do these very things but also approve of those who practice them.'

What then are the options for a person converted out of a homosexual lifestyle? They are exactly those which face any other Christian: singleness, or marriage to a person of the opposite sex. Marriage may not be the answer to all a person's problems, it may well produce a few new ones; it is certainly not to be viewed as an infallible way to overcome homosexual urges. Nor must celibacy be viewed as some type of booby prize: both Jesus and Paul commend the state (Matthew 19:10-12; 1Corinthians 7:6-9). The gift of singleness to heterosexual people is one of the ways in which God has enabled certain people so that they can be of maximum usefulness to God's kingdom. During the course of a dialogue with the liberal Anglican David L.Edwards, John Stott makes the following magnificent point, 'Your acceptance or tolerance of a same-sex partnership rests on the assumption that sexual intercourse is "psychologically necessary". That is certainly what our sex-obsessed culture says. But is it true? Christians must surely reply that it is a lie. There is such a thing as a call to singleness, in which authentic human fulfillment is without sexual experience. Our Christian witness is that Jesus himself, though unmarried, was perfect in his humanness. Same-sex friendships should of course be encouraged, which may be close, deep and affectionate. But sexual union, the 'one flesh' mystery, belongs to heterosexual marriage alone.' [11]

If standards are to be maintained we need such role models of celibate singleness. This will combat the inevitable objection that such a state lays an impossible burden on a single person.

### 3) Service
Two extremes need to be avoided on this issue of service within a local church or in any Christian organization: the one too cautious, the other too accepting. In a letter to one of his many correspondents Francis Schaeffer advised 'If you feel homosexual temptations, but do not give in to them, I would see no reason why you should give up your Sunday school class.' [12] If the word 'homosexual', in Schaeffer's letter was replaced by the word 'gossip' we would probably have no

problem with it, but instinctively we have problems with a 'former' homosexual teaching our children. Surely there should be no area of Christian work that is necessarily closed to those who have come out of a homosexual lifestyle.

Lance Pierson is forthright in stating that, "Unrepentant homosexual people (as opposed to celibate homophile) should not be ordained—or in a position of eldership."[13] What, however do we mean by a celibate homophile? Is it permissible for a man who was in an active homosexual relationship, but now converted and going straight to cultivate same sex relationships and even share his home with another man? Would this be acceptable, could we have a homegroup or youthgroup there, could this man be a leader? Given the right circumstances we would want to say a qualified 'Yes' to all those questions; there is an element of trust in all service. Or is this issue the only area where we must take extra precautions? Yet the greater the trust the greater the expectation of progress in the faith. Drifting in and out of a homosexual lifestyle or an adulterous lifestyle undermines the duty of Christian leaders to embody the truth they teach. Paul makes the same point when writing to Titus 2: 6-8, 'Similarly, encourage the young men to be self-controlled. In everything set them an example by doing what is good. In your teaching show integrity; seriousness and soundness of speech that cannot be condemned, so that those who oppose you may be ashamed because they have nothing bad to say about you.' According to Paul in 1 Timothy 3:2 sexual integrity is one of the qualities required to be seen in a church leader, he must be a 'husband of one wife'. In addition the words in verses 6-7 of the same chapter sound a note of caution : 'He must not be a recent convert, or he may become conceited and fall under the same judgement as the devil. He must also have a good reputation with outsiders, so that he will not fall into disgrace and into the devil's trap.' Although this does not speak exclusively to those who have a homosexual orientation; it does remind us that some distance in time must be placed between our conversion and our entering into responsibilities within the church, especially those of leadership—time to establish our new identity in Christ and to work through the areas in our lives where we are struggling. We should not keep from service in the church those who have honestly faced their orientation, and in dependence on God's grace are living a straight life. Indeed such a leader who has faced temptation and stood firm will have a rich store of wisdom and understanding to share with his fellow believers.

A recent biographer reveals that 'don't ask, don't tell' was the policy of Robert Runcie, the former Archbishop of Canterbury, but that cannot be the way the church ought to assess those who serve within it. We may well be at the stage where questions concerning sexuality need to be frankly and routinely asked and satisfactorily answered before people are appointed to responsible positions of trust within the church.

### 4) Discipline
The biblical idea of discipline is a mixture of instruction about moral boundaries and disciplinary action when those boundaries are crossed.

### Informed
Good clear instruction on the moral implications of being a Christian should include a discussion of sexuality. Too few churches have leaders who will deal with these issues in a thoroughly biblical way. If in this area, as in so many moral issues, there is confusion, might it be because Christians lack a renewed mind? If the arguments of the gay movement, including its defenders within the church, appear reasonable and compelling, is it because Christian minds are tainted with the surrounding darkness of our increasingly godless culture? This is the conclusion of Paul in Romans 1:18-32, in which he paints a grim picture of a society living with the consequences of abandoning God. The consequences are increasing moral darkness and escalating self-indulgence especially in the area of same-sex activity. The end result is a darkened mind which accepts the lie of self-regulation over against living according to the design of our maker, and follows a lifestyle which delights in scrapping God's plan for our lives. Such a society is not a reliable guide to morality, its mind is darkened and it is ripe for judgment.

## Tough and tender

However, this tough, uncompromising message must be combined with a tender yet clear presentation of the grace of God in the gospel. We must not lose sight of the carrot of God's work of justifying and cleansing sinners as we wave the stick of the standards of acceptable behaviour and warn of the consequences of ignoring them.

In Galatians 6:1-2 we have a description of how this warning should be carried out, 'Brothers, if someone is caught in a sin, you who are spiritual should restore him gently. But watch yourself or you also may be tempted. Carry each other's burdens, and in this way you will fulfil the law of Christ.'

The aim of all biblical discipline is restoration; we want to reclaim a fellow struggler, not repel an outsider. It requires considerable wisdom to maintain biblical standards on the issue of sexual integrity and yet do so with an attractive biblical compassion. As an example of how to restore others gently the counsel of Christian psychiatrist John White is most helpful, 'So far as your practice of homosexuality is concerned it must stop. Now. And if it has not yet started, then it must never be allowed to. I know what pain this might cause you. Straight friends may find it hard to understand that you may deeply love someone of your own sex and that the break up with your lover will wound you in the same way as the break up of any kind of illicit love wounds those involved. I know too that a period of profound depression may follow the break up. But do not fool yourself. You can do it. And you must. Whatever God may or may not do for you in the way of changing your sexual orientation, he can and will deliver you from any specific homosexual entanglement and from all homosexual activity. Your part is simply to quit. He does not promise freedom from grief and pain. But he does promise strength and consolation.

Flee temptation. Avoid the company of anyone who especially turns you on. Avoid places and circumstances which expose you to sexual arousal. This may cramp your lifestyle, but the price you pay is a bargain price for what you gain in fellowship with God.' [14]

What happens if people do not listen? Exclusion from Christian fellowship must be the next step. If people persistently cross over biblical boundaries they must be disciplined. However, if this is done for homosexual practice, it must also be done for the other sins mentioned in 1Corinthians 5-6. The teaching of Jesus in Matthew 18:15-20 concerning the step by step approach to discipline should be kept in view also. That passage also reminds us that Christians ought to be more careful than they often are in keeping information about the faults of other believers within as small a circle as is necessary. There is something inappropriate about the interest we can have in the sins of others; it is an interest that can feed our pride and stimulate our own sinful desires.

If we must discipline others let it be with the attitude Jesus displayed toward the woman caught in the act of adultery. John 8:10-11 relates the conversation between Jesus and the woman:

"Woman where are they? Has no-one condemned you?"
"No-one sir," she said.
"Then neither do I condemn you," Jesus declared. "Go now and leave your life of sin."

Jesus draws a clear line under the woman's unacceptable behaviour, but he does so without rejecting her as a person. His aim was to retain the person and yet jettison the behaviour. Jesus was building a high wall with a wide gate. He knew that it was not compassionate to tolerate behaviour which repudiates the maker's plans, yet he was able to attract people to himself so that they may hear his call to a new life. It is not an act of Christian compassion to affirm homosexual acts or unions, it is not loving to endorse or encourage any form of behaviour that God forbids. The evangelical church has to take a tough stand on the issue of homosexuality; however this stand must be combined with the tender moral attractiveness of Jesus.

We should follow the example of the one who gained the reputation, 'This man welcomes sinners' (Luke 15:2). Otherwise, however good our standards may be we will seldom need to use them—those struggling with this issue will not come anywhere near us.

## John Woods

John Woods is married with three children. He is an East Anglian, and has spent most of his life there. Until 1997 he was a pastor in Lowestoft for fifteen years. At present he is pastor of Lancing Tabernacle in West Sussex. Since 1993 he has links with the Baltic state of Latvia, where he is involved in teaching the Bible and providing humanitarian aid. John takes a keen interest in most sports, contemporary music and literature. He is also an interested observer of the wider Christian scene, and is at present working on a book about issues that divide believers.

### Chapter 9 notes

1    **Thomas Schmidt,** *Straight and Narrow,* Inter-Varisty Press, 1995.

2    **Rod Beadles,** *Ins and outs of the Church,* Private Circulation, p19.

3    See ref 2, p19

4    **Lance Pierson,** *No-Gay Areas,* Grove Pastoral Series, no 38, 1989, p7.

5    **John Stott,** *Issues Facing Britain Today,* 2nd Edition, Marshalls,1990, p360.

6    **Mark Bonnigton** and **Bob Fyall,** *Homosexuality and the Bible,* Grove Biblical Booklets, 1996, p16.

7    **RT Kendall,** *Is God for the Homosexual?* Marshall-Pickering, 1988.

8    Interview with **Simon Vibert,** *Conduct which honours God?* Orthos, 1995.

9    **David Atkinson,** *Homosexuals in Christian Fellowship,* Latimer House, 1979, p91.

10   **Gordon Wenham,** *The Book of Leviticus,* Hodder and Stoughton 1979 p260.

11   **David L Edwards,** *Essentials,* Hodder and Stoughton, 1988, p272.

12   **Lane T Dennis** (Editor), *The Letters of Francis Schaeffer,* Kingsway, p223.

13   See ref 4, p16.

14   **John White,** *Eros Defiled,* Inter-Varisity Press, 1977, p132-133.

# Responding in the local church

There are homosexual people outside our churches who are open to the gospel. We need to see them and be prepared to love them, as Christ does. **Declan Flanagan** considers the pastoral attitudes and challenges

Picking up the telephone is often an invitation to journey into the unknown. 'I must see you quickly. This is important and cannot be talked about over the telephone.' The sense of anxiety in the voice indicated that there was little time to waste. A meeting was hastily arranged with a young man intending to inform his parents and church that he was homosexual.

In the next few days I was forced to examine what the Bible has to say about homosexuality. I also had the opportunity to learn a great deal about the tensions that a homosexually orientated person faces. The announcement to the church was never made and several years later, the person concerned would declare he has still to combat temptation towards same-sex relationships. However his perspective on himself and on his sexuality are no longer the same. He has a new sense of security in his relationship with Christ. Instead of being tormented by guilt, he shows evidence of personal fulfilment and genuine freedom.

Since then I have had conversations with both men and women seeking guidance about homosexuality, bisexuality and what to do if you are married to a homosexual. Each person is different and there is much to learn from them. To share their struggles has been a privilege and much of what is included in this chapter arises from our conversations and study together of the Bible. You will not find a simple 'five steps to follow' approach: someone seeking help does not want to encounter a formula, but a person with whom they can relate.

## Understanding yourself

My first conversations with someone indicating they were homosexual brought to the surface many inner attitudes and questions that could not be ignored. As a hot blooded man who grew up in a sporting environment I know what it is to struggle with lust for women. No member of the football club I belonged to had ever found an inoculation that made us immune from sexual temptation. We were fiercely heterosexual in orientation and someone declaring themselves as homosexual would be given a very hard time. Among us there was a profound distaste at any suggestion of same-sex activity. We were sure that homosexual men could be expected to display limp wrists, swivel hips, feminine clothing and affected speech. It would have been impossible to think, at that stage, of inviting a known homosexual to play the role of a hard tackling full back. Homosexual women were a little more difficult to spot but short cropped hair, baggy trousers and Dr. Martens boots might give some indication. Certainly we would not have expected a lesbian to be the stunning woman, who would accompany one of the lads for a night out.

Our understanding of homosexuality, conformed to media stereotypes and personal reactions, indicated a lack of any serious consideration of the issue. The notion that outward appearance, or speech, indicate if someone is homosexual is widespread but they are not accurate indicators. The only way to be sure is if someone tells you of their sexual orientation.

My background coupled with some early Christian influences, that suggested anything to do with sex inevitably must be unholy, meant I was not in a good position to help people considering their sexual orientation. Our inner attitudes must be appreciated and examined. All of us can be tempted to use Scripture to confirm our own preferences and prejudices. When we do this, we abuse the Bible and are unable to assist those who may make themselves vulnerable enough to speak to us. If they are met with hostility and anger that comes from our background and prejudices, it is likely that only one conversation will take place. Feelings of rejection can be one of the contributory factors that lead people into a homosexual lifestyle. If we can manage to think ourselves into someone else's situation and realise their vulnerability, we will be aware of the danger of communicating a sense of rejection. It is a privilege to be allowed to share the deepest thoughts and feelings of someone else.

Any human being, regardless of sexual orientation, has the same basic need to love and be loved. Through the grace of God we can find the resources of patience, kindness and a love that is not easily angered, but protects, trusts, hopes and perseveres.

Homosexuality is just one of a whole range of human weaknesses, from which Christians are not immune. If somebody comes to speak to us about alcoholism, drug addiction, gambling, anorexia or other issues, we would be prepared to speak supportively with them. Homosexuality should not be regarded as a special case. Any Pastor after several years of ministry could compile a book detailing particular difficulties that have been considered with Christians. If published it would surely be a bestseller.

### Know and declare the truth

With messages advocating the legitimacy of homosexual relationships being promoted with such regularity, we need to have a clear understanding of what Scripture says about same-sex relationships. The Bible is definite in saying that homosexual practice is a sin. With clarity and compassion we must uphold God's standards.

Specific Bible references are dealt with more fully in other places within this book and it is essential to be well acquainted with them. These passages will probably have been studied, in depth, by a Christian declaring themselves to be homosexual. Rather than entering into a heated debate on particular texts, I have found it helpful to be aware of the whole doctrinal framework which indicates homosexual practice to be wrong. In the three New Testament passages where Paul writes about homosexuality, what is most impressive is his understanding of the character and purposes of God (Romans 1:26-27, 1 Corinthians 6:9-11 and 1 Timothy 1:9-11).

In Romans 1, it is the doctrine of creation that undergirds the argument against homosexual practice. The whole chapter underlines the fact that we are spiritually and morally in rebellion against the creator's design. All homosexual behaviour is wrong, along with lots of other things, including deceit, arrogance, disobedience and that frequently excused sin of gossip.

Paul argues that homosexuality clashes with God's intention for human sexuality, whatever individual homosexuals feel about the 'naturalness' of their orientation. It is not God's plan for the expression of our sexuality. Since the fall, sin has damaged us all. Homosexuality is not a sign of God's order for creation but of fallen disorder. This is contrary to the view advanced by Richard Kirker, secretary of the Lesbian and Gay Christian Movement: 'It would be a very cavalier and capricious God who created people in a certain way and then instructed them that they are forbidden from fulfilling all the potential they have been given.' [1] The potential that Richard Kirker is referring to is the potential for homosexual activity. The lack of understanding of creation and the fall leads to a rejection of both celibacy and chastity.

In 1 Corinthians 6 the attention shifts to what it means to live in God's Kingdom and be subject to the Lord Jesus Christ. Some behaviour, of which homosexuality is referred to as just one example, is incompatible with life under God's rule.

In 1 Timothy 1 Paul highlights the law of God as he gives an updated version of the Ten Commandments. Homosexual intercourse is bracketed with heterosexual adultery: both are 'contrary to the sound doctrine that conforms to the glorious gospel of the blessed God.'

So the arguments against homosexual practice are not found in random texts dealing with cultural issues far removed from life at the end of the twentieth century. There is an impressive biblical chain involving God who reveals himself as Creator, King and Lawgiver. In God's plan for human life, from creation to the coming of his kingdom, homosexual behaviour has no place. This understanding is held by the vast majority of evangelical churches. Ninety-six per cent of churches linked with the Evangelical Alliance believe homosexual sex to be wrong. Clive Calver writes 'the vast numbers of churches stand by 2,000 years of biblical analysis which conclude that homosexual sex is outside the will and purpose of God.' [2]

God has created people with all sorts of potentials, including the potential to disobey his laws. Both heterosexuals and homosexuals have a 'potential' for sexual activity. God declares that the correct place for that potential to be realised is within the context of heterosexual marriage.[3] God's standards are not irrational or cruel burdens; they are for our benefit.

Understanding what the Bible teaches about homosexual behaviour is not an end to the discussion about the way individuals or the church should relate to gay and lesbian people. If I am to love my neighbour, and my neighbour is a practising homosexual, how do I do that? When your child or a close Christian friend declares they are in an active homosexual relationship, what do you do? Being well acquainted with the Bible's teaching is an important starting point, but it is really only a beginning. Simply quoting texts at people is like a police officer's hand indicating "Stop!" without pointing to an alternative, better way.

### Acknowledge the difficulties

Part of the difficulty evangelicals have in ministering effectively to homosexuals is that we may want to find quick and easy solutions to complex issues. The perception is often that the evangelical church has stood with Moses on Mount Sinai hurling down the commandments. While many have received significant help from evangelical churches, others have regrettably encountered anger and rejection.

The homosexually orientated person knows that their feelings are real, they are deep- seated and probably have been unspoken for many years. They are unlikely to have woken up one day and decided to rebel against God and become a homosexual. No exhortation to pray more, to be more Spirit filled, or to be more of anything is likely to imme-diately change the situation.

How many people within our churches are struggling with a tendency towards same-sex relationships? Jeremy Marks, who works with a ministry called Courage, writes: 'Our observations and expe-rience would suggest there are probably five to ten men in any congre-gation of 200 who are struggling with this issue, and another ten who have some personal experience of homosexuality (perhaps less for women).'[4] If these numbers are correct, this is a larger issue than many church leaders appreciate. People are unlikely to wear badges identifying themselves and many are unprepared to speak to another Christian or a church leader. New Christians and many younger people are much more open in sharing their difficulties. They consider that keeping silent on controversial issues is an indicator of failure to address the issues that concern many people.

Where there is a general silence on sexual matters, it leaves those facing same-sex temptation with many questions. Is it better to remain silent? How do you effectively combat temptation and discouragement on your own? Should someone remain in the church and confide in a friend or church leader? Is it better to stay in the church but seek help from elsewhere? Would it be better to move on to another church that is known for its acceptance of homosexuals but does not have the same understanding of the Bible? Does the desire for honesty in relationships mean that significant factors should be disclosed? How does anyone face the potential of rejection and misunderstanding in their lives?

### Challenge the lies

Two of the greatest deceptions that Satan has managed to sow are that 'whatever you feel, you are,' and 'if it feels good, do it.'

Restraint is regarded as repressive today and sexual experimentation is openly encouraged, without any thought of the consequences. Many people, as part of their development, experience an attraction to someone of the same sex. At such points it is not helpful to be told: 'Don't fight it. It's only natural. This is what you really are. Be true to yourself. If you have homosexual feelings it must be that you are homosexual. You can never be anything but what you are.'

The problem with lies is that they appear so plausible, offering freedom not tyranny. They also ignore the fallen state of human nature. We were all born with a corrupt nature that is full of all kinds of evil desires. If we were all to give way to our base instincts, the world would know even greater pain and chaos. Is it being true to oneself to give way to every ungodly lust, however natural it may feel? Is the unmarried person free to become sexually involved with anyone they find attractive? Is the married person free to commit adultery because they are drawn to someone else and they should not deny themselves?

A significant view in our society is that sexual desire should not be restrained in any way. 'Everyone should be free to do as they choose,' is the argument. This is based on a false view that everyone *has to have* a sexual relationship in order to be fulfilled. The Christian way is different. Paul writes that 'the grace of God that brings salvation has appeared to all men. It teaches us to say 'No' to ungodliness and worldly passions, and to live self-controlled, upright and godly lives in this present age' (Titus 2:11-12). A vital part of Christian living is to be aware of what are right and wrong desires. There is a higher authority than our feelings and desires—what God has declared to be right or wrong.

## Understand the varieties of sexual orientations

Labels are dangerous and frequently misleading. Some people believe there are only two types of sexual orientations: heterosexual, where a person is attracted to members of the opposite sex; and homosexual, where a person is sexually attracted to members of the same gender. This is a limited understanding because it ignores other groups. Asexuals are people who feel attracted to neither gender. Bisexuals find themselves attracted to both genders, often in different degrees.

Appreciating the sexual orientation of a person is an important step to understanding the individual and the particular issues they face. Many researchers into human sexuality look upon sexual orientation as a continuum and certainly not as something fixed during adolescence.

## Follow the Lord's example

Should a notorious sinner enter a room, how would you react? What do you really think when you hear for the first time that someone is a homosexual? Would your tendency be to confront or avoid them? Is the issue of their homosexuality so large that you cannot see the person? How do you think Jesus would react?

In an account unique to Luke (7:36-50), a woman living an unspecified immoral life disturbed a well-ordered dinner party at the home of Simon the Pharisee. She is not reported as saying anything, but her actions provoked some strong opinions. Adultery was as big an issue in the time of Jesus as homosexuality is today. People had firm and fixed ideas of what punishment was appropriate. The way in which Jesus handled the situation provides a good model of how to minister to those who know their lives are affected by sin and who seek the Lord's help. Jesus did not dismiss but welcomed her. In the face of opposition he spoke up in her support.

The significance of the actions and words of Jesus were not lost on those attending the dinner. They were aware of the Old Testament expression of abhorrence of prostitution, homosexuality and any form of immorality. Jesus had the power to forgive sins and told the woman to 'go in peace'. In doing so, he stood in stark contrast to the Pharisees. Jesus said to another group who wanted his opinion on whether a woman caught in adultery should be stoned: 'If any one of you is without sin, let him be the first to throw a stone at her' (John 8:7).

I do not find it difficult to identify with the attitudes of the Pharisees. Whether it is adultery or homosexual practice, it is easier to condemn than to have the attitude of Christ and follow his example. Certainly where sin is involved, Jesus is uncompromising. The woman caught in adultery is told to 'go now and leave your life of sin' (John 8:11). Jesus would not agree that anything done in the name of 'love' is acceptable. In the discussion about long-term homosexual relationships, it is quickly forgotten that Jesus said 'If you love me, you will obey what I command' (John 14:15).

In his dealings with people, Jesus conveyed with clarity that sin is wrong, whether in thought or action. However, he always welcomed sinners and was consistently compassionate. This balance is far from easy to maintain. It is the example of our Lord we should seek to imitate, not modern day Pharisees.

### Distinguish between temptation and sin

Is it a sin to feel attracted to someone of the same sex? Does God condemn you for those feelings? Is it all right to fantasise but not become actively involved?

Questions such as these indicate the need for careful thought. There is no getting away from temptation. The devil has greater skill than any advertising agencies. He knows our weak spots and will tempt continuously.

Sexual temptation is part of being human and all Christians have to deal with inappropriate sexual feelings and attractions. Those tempted to homosexual activity are not members of a sub-group within the Christian community. It is helpful to appreciate that the word temptation is neutral. God has no part in directing us towards evil. 'When tempted, no-one should say, "God is tempting me". For God cannot be tempted by evil, nor does he tempt anyone; but each one is tempted when, by his own evil desire, he is dragged away and enticed' (James 1:13, 14).

There is a difference between being tempted and falling. Jesus was 'tempted in every way, just as we are—yet was without sin' (Hebrews 4:15). Temptation is like someone knocking on your door. At times the intensity of the knocking is deafening; other times it is a little quieter. Sin is opening the door and making it possible for the tempter to enter. Being sexually attracted to another person is not the same as 'committing adultery in your heart' (Matthew 5 v 28). It becomes sin when you respond to the temptation in either mind or body. Part of the difficulty in dealing with sexual lust, is that we say 'yes' too quickly and 'no' too slowly.

Temptation gives way to sin, through a process of enticement. There is always a time-gap between conception and birth. An improper desire for heterosexual or homosexual sex, occurring in the mind, can be either killed or nurtured. When, for example, a heterosexual man sees an attractive woman walking down the street, sexual attraction is his likely response. Unless he is to keep his eyes closed (and risk the danger of walking into a lamp post), the situation is largely unavoidable. A choice has to be made either to resist the temptation or to develop fantasies about the woman. The results of that choice determine whether or not he has entered into the sin of lust.

When the person of a homosexual orientation is tempted, the same principles are operative. If every time we experienced hunger we felt a deep-seated guilt, we would be in trouble. Hunger is not gluttony and sexual temptation, in whatever form, is not a specific sin. Sin occurs when we permit our thoughts to grow into lust and when we desire what is not rightfully ours.

Failure to distinguish between temptation and sin leads to unnecessary guilt and a sense of inevitable failure. Every temptation is an opportunity to come closer to God and for his power to be displayed in your life. When the tempter's incessant knocking on the door of your life wears you down to the point of despair, you must know what to do. Do not open the door. Better still, remind the tempter that Jesus Christ has taken up residence and is now in charge.

Michael Saia writes a word of warning about seeing temptation to homosexual sin as the only difficulty. 'Homosexually orientated men often believe that their temptation to homosexual sin is their biggest problem. During counselling they discover there are other weaknesses in their lives that pose far greater challenges than the temptation to homosexuality. Men frequently comment to me that if they are controlling certain other problems, the temptation to homosexuality is easier to resist.' 5 Women attracted to other women are often concerned about loneliness and a lack of friends during adolescence. A sense of inferiority and self-pity may lead to an insatiable desire to find an ideal woman figure. When other significant factors are acknowledged, it helps avoid concentrating solely on homosexuality.

### Develop a carefully considered approach

For many Christians the immediate reaction following disclosure of a homosexual orientation or lifestyle is to pray for healing and seek help from someone with a ministry of deliverance. Some may think that as a result of ministry or counselling the indicator of a changed sexual orientation will be a desire for marriage. While there is much to be gained through prayer and sensitive biblical counselling, any desire for immediate solutions to complex issues should be resisted. Expectations must be in keeping with the overall teaching of the Bible. Not all temptation is put away to the extent that it never has the potential to reappear. It is evident that not all who are physically sick are healed. God's desire for us is not constant personal fulfilment without any difficulties, but holiness. The instruction in 1 Peter 1:15-16 is not specifically for homosexuals, but for all: 'Just as he who called you is holy, so be holy in all you do; for it is written: "Be holy, because I am holy." We aim for wholeness and restoration from the consequences of the fall, which have different manifestations, in order to become like Christ. Any development of a holy life is slow and painful, with many disappointments along the way.

Paul was in no doubt that change is possible in any area of our lives. He wrote that among the Christians at Corinth were those who were 'formerly idolaters, male prostitutes, homosexual offenders, thieves and swindlers. That is what some of you were. But you were washed, you were sanctified, you were justified in the name of the Lord Jesus Christ and by the Spirit of our God' (1 Corinthians 6:10-11).

Immense pressure can be placed on someone if the primary objective of counselling or pastoral care is seen to be a change in sexual orientation. As the life of Christ develops through the work of the Holy Spirit, people cannot remain the same. Where there is a deeply embedded belief that change is impossible, this can give way to a conviction that nothing is impossible with God. His touch has the potential to bring healing to specific areas of our life affected by sin and this can have a profound affect on our whole well being. Where a woman may have experienced sexual abuse, he can bring release from a hatred of men. Forgiveness for those who have caused harm through actions or critical words becomes possible.

There are Christians who indicate that they find little change in their sexual orientation but that the grace of God is sufficient to keep them from sinful actions and relationships. We will have to wait until heaven for absolute wholeness and some aspects of our sinful nature continue to cause all of us problems. We need to be constantly on our guard. Some become aware that their sexuality is not static and either that heterosexual attraction is already present or starts to develop. For those who may be married, Lori Rentzel writes a word of caution. She experienced periods of strong sexual and emotional attraction to women and was aware that 'never again will I view my sexuality as set in stone. Not a year goes by where I do not question, examine and pray about some aspect of what it means to be a woman and uncover some new area of my sexuality that needs healing or redefining. As a mother of three small daughters, I have added motivation for discovering and embracing God's full intent for me as a woman.' [6]

In order to grow in Christ and have the power to resist temptation, it is imperative that we use the means God has provided. The following areas may be helpfully explored by someone with a homosexual orientation or lifestyle and those who seek to befriend them.

### Appreciate the character of God.

Something is wrong with the church in our culture today. Many people want a God of 'love' as they define it. They don't want the biblical God of love, whose love is inseparable from his justice, holiness and righteousness. As we come to know the different aspects of God's character we appreciate his holiness as well as his love. We bow before his majesty and thank him for his faithfulness. Confidence grows as we remember that God is just and that the difficulties we face with living in a fallen world are not what he intended for us. God's mercy and forgiveness are available to those who know they fail. He longs to help in the daily circumstances of life. He shares our pains, rejoices in our victories and delights to answer prayer.

### Find your security in Christ

Wondering about our identity and being over-concerned about who approves or disapproves of us leads to insecurity. Knowledge at a deep personal level that we are very precious earthly children of our heavenly father will take time to develop. We need to learn to think of ourselves the way the Bible describes us. As we see ourselves as God sees us, we become less conscious of how others view us. Trusting God with our past, present and future involves faith in what Christ has done and is able to do for us.

### Grow in honesty

Honesty with God and ourselves is essential. Many are drawn into homosexuality for social or emotional reasons. If the reasons are not predominately sexual, what are they? How can they be met apart from a homosexual relationship? Has an attempt been made to justify what is known to be wrong?

## Deal specifically with sin

In churches with little emphasis on God's character and law, people may be encouraged to come to Christ who have little conviction of sin. Jesus Christ is not seen as the saviour from sin, but the one who is there for our benefit and who will help us in times of difficulty. When old problems do not quickly go away, it is easy to be disappointed and blame Christ for the lack of success. Any lack of conviction of sin in the beginning always leads to weakness as time goes by. It is always important to check what understanding of repentance someone has in order to discern if there is evidence of a relationship with God.

Practising homosexuals often regret their lifestyles and feel sorry for the way they are living but are not prepared to call their actions sinful. Where sin is involved there is no forgiveness without acknowledgment. A loathing of sin needs to develop in order to be free from it. 'If I had cherished sin in my heart, the Lord would not have listened' (Psalm 66:18). Someone is deceived if they think they can have all the benefits of the Christian life while continuing to sin. Breaking known sinful patterns of behaviour and replacing them with new ones will be one of the marks of genuine repentance.

The old sinful nature has an insatiable desire for attention and cries out all the more when it senses any deprivation. Christ provides the power to resist temptation and develop new attitudes. That power is linked to the cross where Christ suffered and died for all our sins. There are times when we do sin, but that does not mean we have to live for ever under condemnation. After repenting of our sin and asking forgiveness, we need to get on with living. Wallowing in self-pity or thinking that there is no hope may well be an indication of preoccupation with self.

## Watch and pray

This command was given by the Lord, to his disciples, shortly before he went to the cross. In the garden of Gethsemane he experienced a long and painful struggle concerning his future. He warned the disciples that if they did not want to be led into temptation, they must watch and pray.

Watching suggests a soldier on guard, alert for the first sign of enemy attack. We watch against temptation by noticing what situations, company and influences are likely to lead us into sin. It was Martin Luther who said 'You can't stop the birds flying over your head, but you can stop them nesting in your hair.' Preventative strategies have to be arranged. There is a battle to engage in and the way Jesus resisted Satan in the desert indicates the necessity of knowing and using the word of God (Luke 4:1-13). Paul writes that we must not 'conform any longer to the pattern of this world, but be transformed by the renewing of your mind' (Romans 12:2). Regular patterns of Bible reading have an impact on our thought patterns and help us resist temptation.

The kind of intensity of prayer that took place in Gethsemane is a good model to help in times of difficulty. We too can pray for strength to do what we know to be right in the face of an inward reluctance to do so. Thanksgiving and praise help put our difficulties into perspective and stop us concentrating on ourselves. Many have found keeping a diary or journal that honestly records successes and failures to be helpful. This can include prayers to God expressing how you really feel.

## Relate to the rest of the Christian family

For many homosexual people this is a particularly difficult area. Regrettably a homosexual person will not find the same love and understanding in the church as they will receive from the heavenly Father. Churches need to consider how they relate to someone tempted by or involved in same-sex relationships. Will they find more understanding in the 'gay community' than among Christ's community? John Stott writes 'At the heart of the homosexual condition is a deep loneliness, the natural human hunger for mutual love, a search for identity and a longing for completeness. If homosexual people cannot find these things in the local church family, we have no business to go on using that expression.' [7]

We all need friends with whom we can share our deepest thoughts. Isolation and inactivity present their own particular difficulties. Bearing each others burdens allows us to talk about difficult issues, without fear, embarrassment or rejection. This may mean trusting a church leader or small group with matters that you agree should remain confidential. It is not necessary or helpful for someone to disclose their sexual temptations to the whole church.

While we all have a need for close, same-sex friendships, it is advisable to have several close friends, of both sexes, in order to avoid damaging emotional and dependent relationships. This is particularly important for lesbians who have been involved in 'all or nothing' relationships that have been very intense. Non-sexual relationships allow love to be given and received, in ways that are enhancing for all involved.

In urging abstinence from sexual relationships, except within marriage, any church must be prepared to actively encourage an environment of love, acceptance and support. A right desire to uphold God's standards must be done in a spirit of humility and gentleness (Galatians 6:1).

### Be strong in the Lord

Before bringing together his teaching on spiritual warfare, Paul has a word of exhortation: 'Finally, be strong in the Lord and in his mighty power' (Ephesians 6:10). He is well aware that our enemy is powerful, clever and experienced. He has a great ally in what the Bible calls the 'flesh'—that conglomeration of ungodly lusts and selfishness which we will have with us until death. In our own strength we will fail constantly. Through the strength of the Lord nothing is impossible.

### When a parent hears their child is homosexual

On being informed that their child is attracted to someone of the same sex, or is homosexually active, parents will face conflicting emotions. These may include shock, guilt, shame and acute disappointment. Fears may arise concerning the potential lack of grandchildren or death through Aids. A surge of emotions and unanswered questions can result in parental love being submerged under a tidal wave of anger and rejection. Condemnation is probably the biggest enemy to someone with a homosexual orientation and has the potential to drive them away.

Your child is still your child and is not so much seeking your approval as your love. God's love still reaches us if we have sinned, and parental love needs to reach out towards the child even if homosexual sin is involved. A child's disclosure concerning their sexuality must not obliterate the many joys you have shared in the past. The decision by a child to speak about deep-seated personal issues is usually a token of trust in parents. No parent can live their life through their children and what they desperately want to know is whether you love them with no strings attached.

Love in the Bible is primarily action and love for a child needs to be demonstrated at every possible opportunity. Parents, brothers and sisters and other relatives all have an important part to play. God's grace is available to those with conflicting emotions. He can give patience and help resist the temptation of sorting this matter out in twenty-four hours.

As parents ask 'Why our child?' and 'Is it our fault?', it is helpful to make contact with others who have faced similar difficulties. A trusted church leader may be able to establish the contact. Hurting parents need support from other Christians and this cannot be received if nobody is told. There is always pain in disclosure, but there is greater pain in bearing burdens alone.

Many parents have very little knowledge of homosexuality and will need to discover from good Christian literature as much as possible in a short time. This will help in understanding the child better and in appreciating the complex issues involved. All children have their needs, dreams, desires, problems, faults, failures and sometimes sins. It can be hard for parents to realise that children are just as human as they are.

### The student scene

Many Christians in the United Kingdom may not be aware that issues openly discussed among students soon surface in wider society. It is often in the University context that ideas are formulated which influence the thinking of future leaders in every aspect of national life. What is a 'hot topic' among Christian student groups usually surfaces some months later in the wider church. Christian students both before and during their courses need help in considering how to exist in a climate where they will face conflicting views on the subject of homosexuality. As well as encountering many new ideas advanced by those who are not

Christians, they will discover a variety of views among Christians and the various Christian groups on a campus. It is necessary for pastors and youth leaders to be well acquainted with some of the issues referred to in this book and explore them with their young people.

As well as the acceptance of homosexuality, there is growing support for bisexuality as a valid alternative. This is a growing trend in society that has interesting implications for the argument that sexual preference is not a matter of choice. Bisexuality must involve both promiscuity and choice. Someone cannot have a permanent, exclusive relationship with more than one person.

Lesbian, gay and bisexual groups meet in the majority of institutions and know how to promote their policies. They will encourage new students to examine their sexuality and openly experiment because there is nothing wrong in expressing your sexuality in whatever way you choose. Groups are politically active and will take steps to have their representatives elected to key positions in the Student Union and the National Association of Students. It may be difficult for a candidate to be elected unless they are actively promoting gay issues and rights. Executive members of a union will often speak of being against sexism, racism and heterosexism. Christian students who decide, as individuals, to become involved in Union activities, face particular pressures to conform. They need to understand the issues involved and be able to carefully articulate their arguments. In doing so they are carrying out Christ's command to be salt and light in the world (Matthew 5:13-16).

Most Student Unions have a position specifically for the representation of homosexuals and some have more than one. Students who are lesbians may consider that no man is capable of representing them. What is evident is that there is a growing move to advocate the legitimacy of homosexual sex and to oppose those who disagree. Christian students who are actively working for the good of all students can gently point out the inconsistency of an argument that urges no discrimination and freedom to choose. Are any students able to challenge the arguments advanced by the lesbian and gay society? Do they have a monopoly on understanding the subject of homosexuality?

Unfortunately I am aware of situations where a minority of Christian students have spoken out with an evident lack of understanding and compassion. Where they have been encouraged by churches to use single texts to justify their hostility to homosexuals, it has been unhelpful to Christian witness. Well reasoned arguments, based on a careful study of the whole Bible, have more potential of being listened to. There will be definite points of disagreement but gentleness and patience in discussion is surely better than provoking confrontation and unnecessary hostility.

## Summary
People are complex: not only is our self-understanding limited, we find it difficult to understand others. Someone will have sacrificed a great deal by sharing their deepest thoughts. We must be careful in listening and avoid the trap of thinking that all homosexual issues and relationships are the same. To commence a conversation with the subject of 'sin' is likely to add to an existing sense of rejection and isolation. What is required is genuine Christian love that appreciates and cares. Immediate support and encouragement for those with a homosexual orientation is required rather than censure. It is in this context that growth towards wholeness in Christ can be furthered and sinful attitudes and actions addressed.

Where churches are unable or unwilling to attempt to minister to homosexual people, contact with specific Christian ministries will be required. Such ministries have a valuable part to play in not only helping individuals but educating the wider church.

There are homosexual people outside of our churches open to the gospel of Christ. We need to see them, and be prepared to love them, as Christ does. Where we have failed to do so, repentance is required. Homosexuality is not an unwelcome issue that is best swept under the carpet. If we do this, Christians seeking guidance and support will be swept right out of the doors of evangelical churches. In preaching and teaching programmes it is time to break any conspiracy of silence that exists concerning human sexuality. Failure to speak clearly and honestly allows secular voices to remain unchallenged. Church leaders need to teach about homosexuality and provide definite suggestions on how to minister to people, inside and outside of the church.

Temptation is something that affects us all in various ways and the Bible tells us how to avoid falling into sin. The way we do that is the same for those tempted to homosexual or heterosexual sin. Sin does not have to master us. The resources to combat sin are powerful: the Holy Spirit within us; the word of God in our hearts and on our lips; the blood of Christ speaking of our justification and cleansing and Christian friends who will stand with us.

At a time when many voices proclaim that we must accept the lifestyle of practising homosexuals, the church needs to understand and declare the truth with compassion and with clarity.

## About the author

**Declan Flanagan** is Senior Pastor of Cheam Baptist Church in Surrey. He has a background in education and youth work. Following a period with the Universities and Colleges Christian Fellowship he has been involved in Christian ministry in Dublin and Cheam. He is the author of *God's Move, Your Move* and *Cohabitation or Marriage?* Declan is a regular speaker at Spring Harvest.

### Chapter 10 notes

1   **Richard Kirker,** Interview with Paul Vallely in the *Independent*, 11 November 1996

2   **Clive Calver,** *Idea Magazine*, Evangelical Alliance, January-March 1997, p.31

3   See the arguments advanced for marriage in *Marriage or Cohabitation*
    by **Declan Flanagan** and **Dr. Ted Williams,** Belmont House 1997

4   **Jeremy Marks,** *The Church that cares for the homosexual person,* Courage, p.4

5   **Michael Saia,** *Counselling the Homosexual,* Bethany House, 1988, p.149

6   **Lori Rentzel** writing in *Striving for gender identity,* German Institute of
    Youth and Society, p.202

7   **John Stott,** *Issues facing Christians today,* Marshalls, 1984, p.231

# AIDS and its care

From his experience as Senior Chaplain at the Mildmay Mission Hospital in East London, **Peter Clarke** leads us though some pastoral and theological considerations when caring for people affected by HIV/AIDS

I have worked in the pastoral care of people with AIDS for nearly a decade and have been inspired and educated by patients and professionals alike. The two most influencing professionals who have helped to shape my understanding of AIDS care have been Ruth Sims and Veronica Moss (the Chief Executive and Medical Director of Mildmay Mission Hospital respectively). In the 1995 revision of their book on palliative care of people with AIDS they describe the twelve common features where people with AIDS differ in their characteristics from other persons with life threatening illness[1]. I have, for convenience, created five clusters of these characteristics and titled them accordingly. To these clusters, I see five key themes that have a direct bearing on pastoral theology and practice. My own work has majored on the care of the dying and bereaved and I have not sought to compound patients' distress by taking an 'if only' line. I have offered to travel with them as they face early terminality with the insights of a gospel of a risen Christ.

My experience at Mildmay is that about two thirds of our patients are gay men, the remainder being intravenous drug users and refugees. A significant number of this latter group are mothers with children. The impression that endures, however, is not individuals with labels of one kind or another, but people. People with personalities, problems and potential. About half of our patients (and many of their carers) voluntarily request spiritual help. There is an open questing, (sometimes for they know not what), for meaning and value and an understanding of life after death.

## Social difficulties

In contrast to other terminal diseases in our country, AIDS is viewed as infectious and so the person who is HIV positive is feared. Added to this underlying dread of contagion is that being HIV positive indicates (if an adult), the person may belong to a group whose behaviour tends not to integrate socially. Becoming HIV positive, if disclosed can and frequently does, result in rejection and stigmatisation of the individual. It is a double blow, one for being 'different' and two for being perceived as a danger and threat to other people's health.

When the HIV carrier's health begins to affect employment, the personal difficulties become heavy indeed. Most people who live with AIDS are in their mid-lives where normally they would be high earners because of acquired skills and experience. Loss of work means an increasing financial problem that can affect family and home. By the time patients come to Mildmay where we specialise in 'end' care, individuals are often on state benefits. A number have tried to be self-sufficient for as long as they can and are often at the point of collapse without housing and appropriate support.

Families of patients suffer too, for many will not share the nature of the diagnosis for fear of being ostracised. This is especially so if their loved one has left the family home which is part of a close-knit community. The emotional strain is very demanding, particularly when the person with AIDS is a gay man and the family have not known or faced the issues. Often, two parties gather around the dying person, where tensions can be stretched to breaking point.

What is the Christian response to this galaxy of difficulties faced by people with AIDS? Perhaps most important is the application of the concept of Christian fellowship or church. One way of understanding church is to see it as the new creation achieved by Christ and made up of those who respond to God's offer of mercy by turning to him in repentance and faith. It is the Spirit who makes church a reality in the experience of the believer. It is an involvement with God in the mystery and majesty of his triune character. Church is the people of God, the body of Christ and the fellowship of the Holy Spirit. It is the application of the concept of the fellowship of the Spirit that begins to answer the challenge of social problems in the person with HIV/AIDS.

The experience and feelings associated with isolation, prejudice and fear, should be cancelled out as Christian fellowships reach out to individuals, not only with the message of acceptance inherent in the gospel, but in a manner that reflects the Christ of that message. Mark 1: 40-45 is a model of identification with suffering humanity where Jesus touches the leper physically, socially and spiritually. Pastors and their congregations will preach and practice the gospel when they fearlessly and compassionately touch hurting and confused humanity. Courageous contact will be encouraged as congregations possess accurate information about the routes of infection. People affected by this virus appreciate others who tend them with understanding, commitment and fearlessness and so do their carers.

In the initial stages of such encounters it is wise to maintain a strict confidentiality. It could well be that pastors and church leaders are the first to be approached and the question of who needs to know, and when, will be one of the first issues to talk through. Pastors and leaders sometimes have to carry in their hearts the secrets of those who need time and space to work through their problems and find the grace and help of God in their time of need. Pastoral support may well be a commitment and could go on for some time as the incubation stage of the virus can be as long as ten years or more. The symptomatic stage can last from two to five years. This is a great challenge to congregations who often look for instant and quick results. The person affected by HIV/AIDS will need time to develop (or redevelop) a relationship with God and so patience and loyal friendship will be required.

Mildmay has proved itself a 'stepping stone' organisation for many who are seeking God. It may be that churches have to explore the nature and scope of such organisations—short and long term—that can provide a safe and caring situation for people with AIDS for whom the intensity of full Christian fellowship is too strong.

### The medical picture

In their book Sims and Moss describe the medical picture for people with HIV/AIDS as a 'misery of co-existing diagnoses' [2]. The progress from first becoming HIV positive to displaying symptoms means that HIV has steadily destroyed the important T4 white blood cells that are crucial to the body's immune response to disease. Opportunistic infections invade the body resulting in one or more distressing symptoms such as blindness, paralysis, skin disorders, severe diarrhoea and chest infections. Most patients will invariably require a range of drug therapies. Some of these combinations are proving very successful at the present time. It is fruitless for those involved in pastoral care to inquire into the origins for either the global or personal cause of where and why infection has occurred—this is best left to the scientists whose specialities can unlock the mysteries which lead to more effective treatment and prevention measures. However, some data is useful for pastoral care.

AIDS is a blood-borne infection—the carrying agent being the specialised white cells that migrate around the body and are especially numerous in body fluids such as semen and vaginal secretions. Hence HIV is mainly spread through sexual intercourse. When patients are first HIV positive they remain healthy but are able to pass the virus on to other sexual partners. Intravenous drug-users who share injection equipment with an HIV positive individual will probably become infected. As many as one in three infants born to HIV positive mothers are infected. There is no evidence that HIV can be passed to other people through normal human contact.

Individuals with HIV will usually begin to display symptoms of disease after about 10 years of being infected, when for some reason, at present unclear, the virus becomes very active. Unless delayed through modern treatments it will kill the person within two years or less. The complete picture is still being investigated and it may well take a considerable time before HIV is fully understood. In my experience I have noticed an increasing number of patients presenting with mental health problems. In response to this phenomenon in April 1997 Mildmay opened a brain impairment unit where specialised care may be offered to patients and carers alike.

Medicine is about healing—and Christian ministry has always been associated with healing. I have heard claims of people healed of AIDS but I have never been able to obtain sufficient data to verify the claim.

AIDS to my understanding, remains a fatal condition. Healing though is more than curing. Healing has to do with being made whole: body, soul and spirit. I do believe that God, in his sovereignty, will display himself in acts of supernatural healing, yet I do not see this activity curing people of AIDS. I do see God at work through compassionate care beginning the restorative miracle of making people whole. The completion of this task may well have to await the bodily resurrection, but through God's grace, the personal and spiritual work can be well on its way this side of death.

Two dangers should be avoided—to give people with AIDS false hope or to give false despair. In the apostolic days, healing was associated with the preaching of the cross. The cross of Christ pre-eminently is about atonement, but it is also about Jesus associating himself with the consequences of our sick world. To explain that Christ has experienced the depth of human suffering and despair is a stepping stone to the place where a person affected by AIDS finds forgiveness in Christ and begins the healing of the inner life. This inner transformation experience can strengthen resolve to face the life that is left.

Because the disease process is so unpredictable, pastoral workers have to avoid two other dangers—one personal, the other presentational. As life could ebb away unexpectedly, the pressure to press the whole counsel of God on an individual all in one moment is great. Very ill people are rapidly slipping down the 'cone of awareness' [3] that makes meaningful contact increasingly difficult. The other danger at this point is the feeling of failure and guilt in the pastoral worker for not having presented Christ to someone before it was too late. One approach to handling unfinished business is to remember that God is sovereign in individual salvation . He reads the heart and fully knows the history and ultimately it is he who will decide a person's eternal destiny. Will not the God of the whole earth judge justly?

### Psychological Factors

Broadly speaking, a person's psychology is the subtle interaction between mental processes or cognition, the range and depth of emotions, and the mechanics of choice that results in behaviour.

Character is the pattern of behaviour that enables others to predict our responses to certain circumstances. Personality is the impression left with others, while the notion of self has to do with subjective awareness of being. These inter-related ideas may help in an understanding of the significant psychological differences between the challenge of AIDS and that of other life-threatening illness. A large number of people with AIDS in our western society are educated and articulate. The group generally is well informed or deeply questioning. Many patients are gifted individuals who are successful, independent and before becoming ill were enjoying a high standard of living. Other individuals who may not be so richly endowed, do suffer deep inner trauma. The gifted group's suffering is compounded by their insight.

HIV/AIDS seriously threatens the psychological inner structures people have built for themselves through life and it is a pitiable experience to witness the collapse of a person's whole meaning and value system. Many are extrovert individuals who are energised by socialising. Most enjoy travel and generally have a zest for life and living. Mobility and hygiene become increasingly difficult and eventually help is required. Self esteem falls and personality can change, almost in proportion to the physical decline seen in the body image. These losses begin to sap vital energies.

The notion of self for the psychologist is approximately equivalent to the biblical concept of soul. In Genesis 3 the soul becomes aware of itself as God creates the body and breathes his life-giving spirit into it. The first human beings are created in the image of God for an eternal relationship that involves worship and work with and for him. Doubt and disobedience brought death but God set his redemptive plan into action that culminated in the achievement of Christ at the cross. In Genesis 3 there was disintegration not only of body soul and spirit but of the soul's constituent parts too. Human beings were intended to function as an integrated whole.

Theologically, evangelism and pastoral care are functions of spiritual integration and begin with the once for all act of reconciliation. Transformation also begins at this moment when faith engages with Christ and then deepens and develops. This deepening and development involves the process of responsive discipleship that can be aided by pastoral counselling.

Pastoral counselling shares some of the insights from the Rogerian humanistic approach, which seems to be the most popular and effective in AIDS care and is described by Roger Hurding in *Roots and Shoots—a guide to Counselling and Psychotherapy* 4. It includes the building of a genuine supportive relationship created through concentrated attention to an individual's story, questions and future plans. This stage, which may take one or more sessions, is subject to changing emotions, and can include black despair or unrealistic hope. Denial of a person's true medical situation and the elaboration of fantasy futures have to be shared without criticism until the fullest picture of the person's inner self is understood. Attentive listening precludes the 'dumping' of the pastoral care worker's own story, questions and problems on the individual, and generates a genuine relationship where true interest is conveyed and trust is formed. This stage is more about 'being' than verbal 'doing'. It may include accepting on behalf of the Christian community rejection and anger.

The fullest picture will be achieved by the pastoral worker listening with prayer and a sensitivity to the Holy Spirit. Once understanding has been achieved then pastoral counsel can move on to the second major stage. This has to do with the replacement of defective thinking about God, about self and about the world. Here Scripture should be used thoughtfully to show how God views the individual and his situation. Having imparted a biblical mind set to the individual, a sense of freedom is often experienced so that new choices can be made about the immediate and mid-term futures. To regain control over one's life with God is to move from a sense of helplessness, which is not far from feelings of hopelessness, to a sense of hope for now and the future.

### Ethical dilemmas

Some of the key ethical dilemmas that surround the care of people with HIV/AIDS include issues of sexuality, euthanasia, personal liberty and privacy and the thorny cost-care equation. A recent cluster is the moral issues that rotate around the refugee and immigrant who develops symptoms while in the UK. Suicide is a challenging ethical issue. Michael Christensen, a Chaplain on the AIDS unit at San Francisco General Hospital, describes suicide as self-deliverance[5].

In Europe and North America, the seat of the epidemic has been amongst the homosexual community. This has caused tension in official circles because of the rise of politically and socially correct concepts and language. Sexual preferences for adults have been seen as a personal and private matter and not as a matter for legislation or prejudicial activity in employment. A complication for those (like myself) who seek to understand moral imperatives from the Bible is that there is a genuine debate between scientists as to the origins of the homosexual orientation.(see chapter 3) The development of a sexual preference is a complex process that involves biology, environment, experience and choice. 'Coming out', for a gay person, is a major event, so life-changing as to be not dissimilar to the confession of faith of a new believer.

A small proportion of individuals with AIDS want to discuss the option of suicide and some actually request euthanasia. The thought of a lengthy period of physical, and maybe mental, decline, is not only frightening but depressing. Life loses all sense of purpose when it begins to be a matter of getting through the day (and often the night as well) and especially as you watch your friends becoming ill and dying.

A high proportion of health resources have been made available to care for people with HIV/AIDS and an enormous volume of work goes into understanding HIV and possible ways of inhibiting the replication of the virus once inside the blood system. The question now being asked is—in the light of all the other health care needs—is AIDS having a disproportionate share? Can we afford the very expensive combination therapies that seem to be so successful at this moment, whilst others with less fashionable conditions, like mental illness and rheumatoid arthritis, have less resources?

Refugees from Africa come to the UK with terrible and pathetic stories of persecution and loss and some with HIV/AIDS. They do not want to return to their own countries, where health care is very much less than here in the UK. But an acute national moral dilemma occurs when refugee status means individuals must be expelled even if they are sick. Should the UK health system become the health provider for increasing numbers of overseas visitors who cannot find adequate care in their own countries? For Christians, as others, ethics is about difficult questions. Mission means involvement and 'neighbourliness' to persons in our mission field. Similar to other missionaries, it means a living with and an understanding of people whose way of life and belief system we do not share. Of course, there will be things we do not wish to associate with, but that is so of other people in all walks of life. It is quite possible to care, without condoning a person's choices. Christians have a special mandate to associate appropriately with those who need the great spiritual physician, not just with those who are whole.

In my experience, most patients who want to discuss suicide want to explore the meaning of their lives. They want to evaluate the past and find some purpose for their shortened futures. People with AIDS feel valueless, taken over by their illness and by their carers. Through attentive listening, pastoral workers can affirm a person's value and eventually lead to the place where control can be regained—and hopefully regained in Christ. Appropriate medication can lessen the effects of debilitating symptoms, allowing more freedom and control for other issues, although as the terminal phase approaches medication has to increase to suppress troublesome and painful conditions. Palliative care in the hospice situation does not hasten or prolong what is inevitable. Death is seen as a 'natural' event and its proper setting is whatever the patient feels is right and comfortable. Ideally it should not be a clinical, cold and lonely experience. Appropriate music, brief prayers and Bible readings can be helpful, but simply to share the experience and so spread the grieving load will build bridges of authentic pastoral care.

As Christians, we need to grasp the challenge of standing with the homeless, the widow and the orphan; to be ready to share sacrificially with the anxious, the sick and the dying without fear or favour. However, Christians should be wise stewards of resources and the person shouting loudest may not always be the most needy.

The basic theme for me in this ethical maze is God's justice. Jesus taught that setting ourselves in the position of the divine Judge is to be avoided, but where discernment is necessary it should be informed, based on God's righteousness and mercy, who is always ready to forgive and restore the repentant. Judgementalism that is an uninformed, gut prejudice is quite inappropriate for those who represent the God who alone, through Jesus, dispenses justice based on his law and the accurate records of heaven.

## Care environment

Not only does HIV/AIDS affect predominantly young age groups (0-5 and 16-49) but it also seems to attract young professional health care givers such as nurses, therapists, social workers and counsellors who are developing themselves professionally and personally. They are full of energy, idealism and imagination and readily take up the various challenges in AIDS care. The mainstream hospice, in contrast, is often made up of established and mature health care givers. In AIDS care the young professional group present two unique issues. The first is that they require more support; the second is that they tend to stay in posts for shorter periods.

One of the demanding aspects of caring for people with AIDS is that there can be sudden, dramatic changes in condition, usually for the worse. The actual onset of the terminal phase is also difficult to pinpoint, and when it does arrive is often extended over many days. This lengthy dying period is enormously exhausting for the family/friendship circle. Repeated deaths with all the surrounding emotions for these family members and friends can compound the inherent sadness for the young professional who is just discovering mechanisms to cope with losses. At Mildmay some of those professional challenges are met together by interdisciplinary team-working.

Christian compassion should be love in action without thought of an emotional response. It is love for love's sake—service in Jesus' name. Christian compassion means a meaningful co-operation with other members of the health-care team and the family-friendship circle. A barrier can be created when pastoral workers and health care givers do not talk to or understand each other. Spiritual, religious and cultural aspects are recognised by health care givers as crucial to good health care practice and as a necessary part of palliative care. This means that most health care givers respect pastoral care.

Pastoral care extends to these professionals and their personal need of support must be recognised. In an unpatronising manner encouragement should be offered in a way that shows how much they are valued. Health care givers want to verbalise their concerns, their frustrations, their sadness and it is helpful to share in an informal way as a fellow health-care giver, as one of the team. This is not counselling but mutual support and it can be beneficial (and humbling) both to give and to receive support as a team member.

A final word about stepping-stone organisations. HIV/AIDS is a specialised area with its own unique blend of hospice care for individuals as diverse as the educated and successful gay men, the disadvantaged intravenous drug user, the HIV positive refugee mother and her children and the families of infected people. Yet all are involved together with a terminal illness that is spread mainly through sexual contact and that strikes at the root of our humanity. While I do not believe God is the author of such a tragedy, he is certainly involved. Specialist stepping-stone organisations supported by the churches could play a significant part in revealing to a frightened world his saving love and power.

### About the author

Peter J. Clarke BA, BSc, qualified as a hospital laboratory technician before joining the Metropolitan Police Force serving for about fifteen years. He trained at Spurgeon's College for the ministry and after ordination first as a pastor at Sidcup Baptist Church and for the past ten years as Chaplain at the Mildmay Mission Hospital, Shoreditch. He is a graduate in Theology and Psychology.

## Chapter 11 notes

1 **Ruth Sims and Veronica Moss,** *Palliative Care for People with AIDS,* Edward Arnold, London. Second edition 1995 p. xvii

2 **Ruth Sims and Veronica Moss,** *Palliative Care for People with AIDS,* Edward Arnold, London. Second edition 1995 p. xvii Table 1 item 3.

3 **Ian Ainsworth-Smith** and **Peter Speck,** *Letting Go -Caring for the dying and the bereaved.* SPCK, London 1982. p 32

4 **Roger Hurding,** *Roots and Shoots- a Guide to Counselling and Psychotherapy.* Hodder and Stoughton, London 1985 pp 109-123.

5 **Michael Christensen,** *The Samaritan's Imperative—Compassionate Ministry for those living with AIDS.* Abingdon Press, Nashville, 1991 pp 142-146.

# Andrew's story

Discrimination, isolation, and despair were all part of the struggle faced by **Andrew James** from Merseyside. Here he tells his story

It is possible to be either a Christian or a homosexual. But is it possible to be both? I am 29 years old and have been a Christian now for 6 years. My family background is one which is non-Christian, although my parents do hold a belief in God. I am currently single, and I have recently graduated from University with a B.A. Combined Honours Degree in English, Information Technology and Psychology. I am also gay and my earliest memory of being different from other boys is from around the age of 5 years old.

The issue of homosexuality alongside biblical Christianity is one which has raged on, it seems for a lifetime. Gay and Lesbian rights groups protest that the way homosexuality is viewed in the Bible is out of date, irrelevant to the times we live in and is something to be ignored or not taken literally. We also have many Gay and Lesbian Christian rights organisations who believe that relevant portions of Scripture have more than one meaning or interpretation, and they view the physical act of homosexuality as something which is not sinful, something that can be united in perfect harmony with an individual's own belief.

Just where does this leave the individual who, like myself, is a Bible-believing Christian and who therefore views the physical act of homosexuality as sinful and against the will of God yet is, at the same time, plagued with homosexual tendencies?

Society in general, whilst becoming more tolerant of alternative lifestyles, still holds a great stigma towards homosexuality and still refuses to accept it as a natural or normal way of life. Gay and Lesbian people are still beaten up for no other reason than that they are homosexual. They are discriminated against in the workplace, and they are often viewed as perverts, child molesters, worthless human beings, second class citizens, the scum of society. How does the church of God's people treat the homosexual? In my own personal experience a small handful of people took time to listen, to understand, to ask questions, to allow themselves to be educated and to show true love just as the Lord Jesus Christ would do. Apart from those few there has been very little difference from the way the world reacts.

It is sad that in today's Christian churches very little encouragement is given to Christians who struggle to come to terms with their affliction of homosexuality. I have met Christians in my own church, old and young alike, who express a great deal of prejudice and disgust at homosexuals in general. There appears to be a total lack of understanding and empathy on the part of these Christians towards their brothers and sisters in Christ. Moreover there is often an air of judgmental supremacy—not the most encouraging surroundings for a fellow believer who wishes to share the burden that he or she is carrying.

I was very much aware of the biblical view on homosexuality before I actually gave my life to the Lord. Even though I knew that becoming a Christian was the right thing to do, I felt that I couldn't make a commitment due to the thoughts and feelings that I had towards other men. It was through the first of many counselling sessions with my Pastor that I began to realise that if I acted upon my thoughts or feelings I was committing sin, but to be plagued by homosexual thoughts was not in itself sin. I became a Christian and put my trust in God that he would take these unwanted desires away from me and give me new desires that were pleasing to Him. I longed to be married and to have children. The difficulties that I experienced did not go away or even ease, if anything they just got harder to deal with. The more I read the Bible, the more confused I became. I found myself continually questioning how the Scripture that I knew to be total truth related to my own situation. If homosexuality was against God's will, and I was made by God, then why did he allow me to continue to experience unwanted, unbiblical urges? Surely if God knew how desperately I wanted to be 'normal' then he would do something about my situation. I couldn't understand why my prayers weren't being answered. I began to confide in a few people concerning my struggle with homosexuality only to be told to pray about it, to read God's word, to get to the prayer meeting, to saturate myself in doing the will of God. I began to do these things yet still nothing changed; it merely became more difficult to deal with. I began to question my salvation, for surely if I was really a Christian then God would listen to me. Perhaps I wasn't praying in the correct manner and that was why God wasn't answering my prayers; so I would pray to God for help to allow me to be able to pray in the correct way.

While all this introspection was going on, I became more and more depressed. Thoughts of suicide dominated my mind. I didn't particularly want to die, but I was torn apart internally between what I knew was the truth and how I felt. If I had not been so certain that the Bible is the Word of God, and that it is literal truth, I might have found a way around my struggle. But I was constantly in conflict with thoughts of not wanting to sin, not wanting to be gay while I knew deep down that I was gay, wanting to fit into society, wanting to be 'normal'. I was uncertain of what I was or who I was. I just wanted all the pain and all the hurt to stop, so suicide became more and more appealing. This however added to the dilemma that I was already having to deal with, if I committed suicide, would God send me to Hell? I had come to believe that Christians can face anything in their lives if they have faith in the Lord Jesus Christ. I would again begin to question why my faith appeared to be very small. Was it because I wasn't really a Christian? I kept going round in circles unable to come to terms with my Christian beliefs and what I was—a gay man.

I scoured Christian bookshops for literature relating to homosexuality. I would read them from cover to cover looking for that glimmer of hope that I might be able to change my desires. Whilst these books allowed me to realise that I wasn't the only Christian suffering with this affliction, they only made me all the more confused.

What made me a homosexual in the first place? Was I born this way? Various reasons were given as the cause of homosexuality in the literature that I had read. These included the following;

The Genetic Theory—that something in the genes of certain humans predisposes them to being attracted to members of the same sex.

Upbringing—that somehow there is something lacking in a child's upbringing which ends up with the child not identifying with members of their own sex.

The Absent Father Syndrome—that small boys lacking the input of a father figure will fail to bond with a correct role model subsequently resulting in them selecting the wrong role model with which to identify.

The Domineering Mother Syndrome—that small boys who have domineering mothers come to view her as a role model thus resulting in a confused sexuality in later life.

A Personal Choice—that a person actually chooses for themselves whether or not they will be homosexual.

Although I could actually identify with a few of the reasons that were given, I didn't think any of them applicable on a general scale. For example, why would only one of a number of siblings from the same set of parents turn out to be homosexual while the rest were heterosexual?

The main reason why I didn't engage in homosexual activity was my fear of God. I do not believe that God is an ogre, I believe him to be a loving and caring Father. However, I had a great fear of being judged by God for deliberately going against his will when I had been enlightened enough to know the truth.

Although my homosexual feelings have remained, there have been times when during great temptation to give into my desires, the Lord has given me enormous strength to resist. These have not only been times of great joy and celebration in doing the will of God and honouring him, but also of sadness because despite the feelings of self-hate for being a homosexual, I still have natural longings and desires to be able to express love to another individual and to be in a relationship with another person.

It is at these times that I am at my lowest. I long and yearn so much to do the will of God, yet I feel completely constrained by my situation. I believe that all human beings should be allowed to have the opportunity to give and receive love and to express that love in a sexual way, yet no matter how hard I try, I cannot make myself have these types of feelings for women. I have them for men, and because of my knowledge of the truth, I am not allowed to act upon them.

Life for the Christian with a homosexual orientation can be an extremely isolated lonely struggle. Instead of being criticised and ridiculed we should be encouraged, prayed for and loved. It is an extremely sensitive and delicate area. Whilst we need support and prayer, it is only possible to receive them by being open to other people within the church. However, in order to be open with the people in the church, the church needs to become a lot more aware and understanding and a lot less rejecting of the Christian who struggles with homosexuality.

Christians with a homosexual orientation constantly see themselves as failures: a failure as a human being, a failure to man or womankind, a failure as a Christian. We also take on board the guilt for failing to produce grandchildren for our parents and for all the shame it brings upon our families. Society is so geared up to people being in couples that such a Christian often withdraws from social gatherings for fear that they don't fit in. In fact, the only niche society has for us to belong to is the gay scene. Therefore he faces a hard struggle to restrain himself from being around people that he can relate to.

Many television documentaries have been made regarding the Christian's struggle with homosexuality. One in particular had a great affect on me personally: it was called 'Better Dead Than Gay'. This documentary detailed the enormous struggle a young Christian man had with homosexuality. His family and friends knew nothing of his predicament. He felt himself forced to live a double life, one in the homosexual community, the other as an upstanding member of his local Christian church. However, the guilt that he felt regarding this double life became too much for him. He was unable to unite his Christian beliefs with his own sexuality. He knew the Word of God to be true—he also knew just how strong and deep rooted his desires and feelings were towards other men. The young man in question killed himself because he could no longer deal with the pain and the anguish that his affliction caused him, and with the guilt of being a homosexual whilst at the same time being a committed Christian. The young man's family only found out about his dual lifestyle in a letter that he wrote to them prior to taking his own life. He was buried in a small part of the grounds of the church that he used to attend every Sunday and because he had committed suicide, he was buried in an unmarked grave.

Christians who are ignorant of the homosexual Christian's plight, and who are totally judgmental in their views, opinions and attitudes, often fail to acknowledge individuals such as the young man mentioned above as 'real' or 'true' Christians. Allow me therefore, to say on behalf of many that this is a totally incorrect accusation. We do have a personal relationship with the Lord Jesus Christ. We are secure in the knowledge of the promise of salvation. We too have been forgiven of all our sins, washed clean by the precious blood of our Saviour. Therefore, we do not need to be looked down on or viewed as someone who is playing around with their spiritual life. We have enough negativity, abuse, suppression and prejudice to contend with without being laden down further with the ignorant and uneducated opinions of Christians who should know better.

This particular documentary really upset me because that young man could so easily have been me. I know the constant struggle, the guilt, the feelings of self-hate, the wanting to ends one's life, the rejection from others, the feelings of not being a whole person. There are many various emotions and feelings that we go through as Christian men and women who are struggling with homosexuality. If the young man in the television documentary had belonged to a church that offered help, support, prayers, love and understanding then he could well have been alive today. How many more people have to go through the turmoil of this unbearable situation only to end up buried in an unmarked grave?

To anyone reading this who struggles with their Christian beliefs and their homosexual tendencies, let me say God is good. There will be times in your life, as there have been in mine, when you think God is far away, that he is not listening to your prayers and your cries for help. The answer we get from God may well not be the answer we'd like; however, I firmly believe all things have a purpose. We have to hold onto the truth, grasp firmly the promises of God and cling onto our faith with all our might. This can be helped enormously by the

Christian church demonstrating God's love for all his children through their actions to their fellow Christian brothers and sisters.

There are also many practical things that Christians struggling with their homosexual tendencies can do. These include the removal of any homosexual literature or magazines that they may own, as continual reading of such magazines or literature merely leads to the individual being drawn away from things of a spiritual nature and focuses all their attention on things of a sexual nature. To have such magazines available to the individual also stunts their growth, preventing them from becoming a whole person. All temptation must be removed in order for them to be able to progress with their lives. It is extremely difficult for them to accept themselves as they are, without having guilt and feelings of worthlessness. The owning and the reading of such homosexual literature and magazines only serves to perpetuate the enormous sense of failure.

It is also vital that we form correct, spiritual, loving friendships with people whom we can trust. In my own situation, these friendships have included people taking on parental roles, allowing me to identify correctly with members of the same sex. I have also found great encouragement in their wisdom, guidance, sincerity, acceptance of me as I am and their overall love, support and many prayers. It is extremely important to find acceptance from others, for without it we are unable to accept ourselves.

We must also make sure our Christian walk is a continual process. We must take each day as it comes and not allow ourselves to become bogged down with thoughts of tomorrow. That may sound easy, but I know personally how difficult it is to put into practice. However, it is the only way that we are going to be able to get on with our lives—we must take things one day at a time.

We can also become totally engaged in our own difficult situation, whilst disregarding the many positive things that we have. Personally, I would much rather struggle on each day for the rest of my life knowing that I have Jesus as my Saviour and that I have the promise of Heaven when I die, rather than being in spiritual darkness, without Jesus as my Saviour, though without the affliction of homosexuality. As Christians, we have a glorious God, a wonderful Saviour, and the promise of ever-lasting life in Heaven when we die.

One final remark. I sometimes describe myself as a 'Christian homo-sexual'—that may need a little explanation. Many people define a homosexual as someone who engages in sexual acts with a member of the same sex. As a Christian, I believe such activity to be sinful. But I call myself a 'Christian homosexual' because that is my orientation; that is the affliction with which I, as a Christian, struggle. Unfortunately, society does not make this distinction: it fails to differentiate between men who are attracted to other men, yet who abstain from sexual activity, and men who engage in sexual acts with other men. In the eyes of society they are all the same. The ignorance and prejudice people like me have to face daily adds to our difficulty, but with the strength of the Lord we can rise above it all.

**Andrew James**

Andrew James is 29 years of age and has been a Christian for nearly 7 years. He comes from a non-Christian family. He is single and has a B.A. Honours Degree in English, Information Technology and Psychology. Currently working for a major telecommunications network, Andrew has participated in various children's work at his local church. He is influential in seeking to provide more understanding for Christians afflicted with homosexual orientation, and has worked closely with Pastor Bill Bygroves on raising this issue.

# Jeremy's story

**Jeremy Marks,** Founder and Director of *The Courage Trust,* describes his own experiences and offers counsel to those who face similar battles

Today, Jesus Christ is not only my Lord; he is my dearest friend. My greatest desire is to learn to do what pleases him. This is what God has accomplished in my life; I can take no credit. However, in 2 Corinthians 4:4-7, Paul wrote:

'The god of this age has blinded the minds of unbelievers, so that they cannot see the light of the gospel of the glory of Christ, who is the image of God. For we do not preach ourselves, but Jesus Christ as Lord, and ourselves as your servants for Jesus' sake. For God, who said, "Let light shine out of darkness," made his light shine in our hearts to give us the light of the knowledge of the glory of God in the face of Christ. But we have this treasure in jars of clay to show that this all-surpassing power is from God and not from us.'

### From a worldly perspective...

As a married man of almost six years now, it seems strange to recall that twenty years ago I was concluding a rather fruitless year of psychotherapy. Diagnosed as having a classic background for a homosexual man, my therapist could not understand why I was unable to come to terms with being 'gay' and get on with living a 'gay' life—like many others in this day and age! He was a good therapist, but ideologically he saw things very differently from me. I could not in all good conscience continue with the course of psychotherapy knowing he was committed to encouraging me to embrace the 'gay' life. Concluding my time of therapy, his opinion was that my biggest problem was my religion! (I subsequently found that this therapist's pro-gay opinion would not necessarily have been typical among psychiatrists and do not wish to sound in any way dismissive of the good work of many.)

My therapist discerned accurately that I was full of guilt and fear, which I attributed to my homosexual orientation and desires. His conclusion posed quite a challenge for me. For several years I had attended a very well-taught church, where the preaching and pastoral care had always been life-giving—never intended to burden a person with guilt or shame, especially anyone who struggled with a sensitive issue like this. Indeed when I first shared the matter with my pastor, he responded with great sensitivity; he was sincerely concerned for my well-being and, above all, my spiritual development. There was no trace of judgement or homophobia in his attitude. As I prayed about my therapist's comment, I began to realise that my oppressive feelings had their roots much further back than my new and enlightening Christian experience, although I had not yet recognised how to apply the liberating message of the cross of Jesus Christ to my own situation.

## The battle of the sexes

I first noticed an attraction to men around the age of thirteen, when my school-mates began talking about their growing interest in girls. I did not share their enthusiasm. Although I had grown up with two lovely sisters, I had otherwise been surrounded by women all my life, many of whom were strong, discontented, controlling personalities, inclined to be very critical of men. My parents were unhappily married (they divorced when I was 16) and none of the marriages around me seemed happy. I was amused by popular songs from 'My Fair Lady', such as 'I will never let a woman in my life!' I concluded that the possibility of marriage was only for the naïve or romantically-inclined. I became very cynical in my teens!

My child-like belief in God and acceptance of Christian principles soon gave way under the pressures of my teenage years. When my parents' marriage broke up, I reasoned, 'What use is a religion that imposes laws that just make people miserable and are impossible for anyone to live up to?'

## Society's homophobia

Meanwhile, the subject of homosexuality was increasingly being discussed in the media because of the change in the law that came in 1967 when homosexual acts were decriminalised. In popular conversation, the subject was spoken of only with scorn and derision; I intuitively recognised that you must **never** divulge an erotic interest in men. No-one must have the remotest suspicion! I had little enough confidence in myself as a teenager anyway, but to face the ridicule of my school-friends would have been more than I could bear. However, these feelings of erotic attraction towards men persisted, in fact strengthened, in spite of every effort I made to drive them away.

## Detestable behaviour (Leviticus 20:13)

The first Christian literature I read which specifically mentioned homosexuality was a little book by John Eddison that my godmother had sent me for a birthday. The author explained the topic briefly and with compassion, then quoted the main Bible passages that prohibit homosexuality. Reading Leviticus 18:22 (& 20:13), Romans 1:26,27 and 1 Corinthians 6:9,10 filled me with fear of God's unequivocal rejection of homosexuality. The Bible seemed only to confirm that, if God existed at all, he was a heartless tyrant who accepted people only if they complied with his oppressive demands! Jesus was no comfort either—condemning those who even **thought** with impurity; his words in Matthew 5:28-30 seemed to me to imply condemnation of masturbation too!

When someone enlightened me as to the real nature of homosexual acts, my initial reaction was one of revulsion. By this time however, I associated the thought of any kind of intimacy between men so strongly with homosexuality (as I had understood it) that God's disapproval of all same-sex intimacy seemed absolute. Consequently I felt totally rejected by him and certain to be shunned by anyone who found out my guilty secret. With plenty of 'knowledgeable-looking' people around me who openly dismissed God as irrelevant, it was more comforting for me to believe God did not exist!

## Born again!

When an old school-friend became a Christian I was impressed to see that his life changed radically over a couple of years. Although I would not have admitted it, I was desperately hungry for answers to my misery and isolation. In spite of my previously cynical frame of mind, because of his testimony I accepted Christ personally at the age of 21.

I began my Christian life full of expectancy, assuming that turning to Christ would in itself be enough to rid me of my homosexual attractions for ever and prepare me for normal married life. The discovery, about a year later, that my erotic attraction to men was re-emerging, brought a resurgence of the guilt and fear that had ruled my life as a teenager. 'Perhaps I never repented enough!', I reasoned; or 'perhaps this was the unforgivable sin and I could never truly be redeemed?'; or 'perhaps I was an incurable hypocrite—masquerading as a Christian, whose destiny was to be a vessel of God's wrath and a tool of the devil liable to corrupt others around me!' I was stuck in a double bind where, if I told others my secret they might confirm my worst fears, but if I did not, then I probably faced exposure when the Holy Spirit blew my cover to other discerning Christians. This only cultivated my paranoia!

## Spiritual battle

The intense spiritual battle into which I was plunged was new to me. As a non-Christian I had experienced a raging internal battle over my sexual orientation, but that came more out of fear of the opinions of others than godly conviction. Now I faced a new battle as to whether or not I could ever be truly accepted by God with such an orientation. I had not learned to recognise that such paralysing and fearful thoughts were part of the spiritual battle we all face. Deep-felt shame reinforced by selective Christian teaching and mixed messages from well-meaning people, who felt very uncomfortable with this subject, all robbed me of the hope of the gospel—a hopelessness that I would now attribute to demonic oppression.

For the next ten years of my Christian life, I became preoccupied with a frustrating search for some answers. Surely if God had any compassion he would not leave me feeling so miserable; forced to maintain the appearance of being a good Christian, while secretly fighting an inner longing for intimate same-sex friendship that relentlessly became more attractive to me right into my thirties?

## Taking matters into my own hands

A dismissive remark from someone insinuating that my homosexuality was 'all in the mind' exasperated me. I decided to investigate the 'gay' life for myself: I reasoned that if my inclinations were really 'just in the mind', the real thing would bring me to my senses! Alternatively, I might discover this was truly for me. Since it appeared that God was not prepared to lift a finger to help, either to relieve my unbearable frustration or enable me to fulfil the requirements of his law, I felt the time had come to take action! Prayer seemed too passive an approach and brought no answers, in my view. I had absolutely no confidence that I could make it in the 'gay scene' with any more success than I could manage to be a Christian, so it was only with enormous trepidation that I began to seek out other gays.

## God's love for a sinner

Eventually I met a young man with whom I became physically involved for a short time. God's response was entirely unexpected: for the first time I almost tangibly felt his love as never before. Clearly he understood me perfectly. Paradoxically, I was still perfectly aware that his love and approval for me did NOT convey approval of my activity. Perhaps, like the woman caught in adultery, I did not feel condemned in the presence of God (John 8:11). For the first time, I realised that his love for me was truly unconditional. The tenderness of his response melted my anger. This encouraged me once again to resume my search to find God's way rather than taking matters into my own hands. Truly God's kindness leads us to repentance (Romans 2:4 & 11:22).

Reassured of God's love, though puzzled to discover it in this context, I confessed my sinful adventure to one of my church leaders. This pastor responded with great wisdom: he confirmed that I was free to choose the way I wanted to go; that God's character was such that he could not love me less if I chose to go against him, although he would be deeply disappointed. He suggested that perhaps letting down my barriers for the first time had been God's opportunity to reveal his love to me. This pastor kindly offered his commitment to stand by me and give all the help he could to work this through, if that was what I wanted. His offer came as a complete surprise and I gratefully accepted.

## The search for deliverance

Following that time, I received much excellent counselling within my church against a background of superb biblical teaching; the leadership team gave a great many hours to helping me for which I shall always be grateful. As an embittered and cynical young man I was not easy to deal with; but their patience, time and commitment taught me much about what it means to become a disciple of Christ.

In spite of enjoying a promising-looking friendship with a beautiful Christian girl for a while, to our mutual disappointment the potential romance never took off: I was not ready for marriage. No amount of counselling brought about any change in my homosexual orientation.

I sought 'deliverance' ministers who tried to cast out the 'demon of homosexuality' (along with all the other demons they imagined were there too!) to no avail. Inner healing prayer proffered another answer. One of the supposed keys to homosexuality, according to them, was the existence of early traumas. It was expected that these would be dissolved away by a manifestation of the presence of Jesus, but in my case there was no lasting effect. My disillusionment over the whole question as to whether God would or even could provide any constructive answer to my struggles grew deeper all the time.

I should add here that I do believe there is a right and proper place for deliverance ministry and healing prayer, but these can only be used effectively where there is God-given discernment and must not be applied indiscriminately as a 'cure-all' for every problem. There is no substitute for dependence on God's Spirit in biblical ministry, exercised in the context of true Christian love.

## Gay christians?

Perhaps it was inevitable that sooner or later I would come across some Christians who had come to terms with their homosexuality in a different way—they 'realised' that God intended them to be 'gay' and was 'pleased to bless' committed homosexual relationships. Like me, these men had spent years of fruitless searching for answers which had never materialised. I met two homosexual couples who had been together for some years: the quality of their relationships would put some marriages to shame! Although this is not common among gays, years later I learned that to argue against homosexual relationships on the basis of whether or not they work is irrelevant: the essential question is whether or not they are part of God's order and loving purpose for our lives (see Genesis 2:23-25; Matthew 19:4-6; Romans 1:25).

The 'gay Christian' interpretation of Scripture did not convince me, but to my surprise their advocates were not dogmatic. Acceptance of their homosexuality had ended years of trauma (including attempted suicide) and gay relationships had opened the way to more settled and peaceful lives. People who had known them well throughout those difficult years of struggle could witness to their apparent change for the better, since their struggle against their homosexuality had been 'resolved'. No-one likes to see someone struggle endlessly in pain; the relief the individual feels at giving up the struggle may be shared by their friends and families too. (However, an emotional or rational response to this scenario can never be a guide to the truth.) I eventually realised that because these gay partnerships fulfilled such deep needs, the participants had settled the moral question in their minds from a purely pragmatic viewpoint, even concluding that '...God led us into these relationships!'

### Christians can be deceived too

'Not everyone who says to me, "Lord, Lord," will enter the kingdom of heaven, but only he who does the will of my Father who is in heaven.'
Matthew 7:21

Once again, I was offered a free choice, to seek the homosexual partner I desired, or to continue to seek God, accepting the likelihood that I would have to be celibate for the rest of my life—and miserable! The pro-gay view was very tempting and I wrestled with the options. One verse of Scripture in particular came to mind during this time of struggle: 'Do not be deceived…', Paul wrote in 1 Corinthians 6:9. These words indicated to me that the possibility of deception exists. I did not want to be deceived, only to find out later to my cost. Somewhat reluctantly, I prayed that God would help me live according to his Word, whatever the cost. This was a turning point in my Christian life and I found a measure of peace in making this decision.

Several years later, incidentally, I noted that one of these gay men who had gone into ordained Christian ministry was quite unable to use Scripture to help his parishioners make discriminating choices in other circumstances requiring moral judgement. I saw that once you manipulate the Scriptures to suit yourself, the floodgates are opened to every other perversion. Ironically such people are often forced to resort to an unbelievably convoluted legalism, to try to explain how exactly one kind of perversion can be 'right' while another is wrong!

As time went on, I discovered that God primarily seeks to win our hearts; he is not merely interested in modifying our behaviour. I have come to realise that Jesus desires relationship much more than simply to save us from sin, essential though that is. He wants to restore us to a loving intimacy with the Father that has a romantic theme of its own. Our true identity as human beings is only to be found in oneness of heart with our creator and is fulfilled in a sacred covenant. The following promise was a liberating revelation to me:

"This is the covenant I will make with them after that time, says the Lord. I will put my laws in their hearts, and I will write them on their minds. Their sins and lawless acts I will remember no more." Hebrews 10:16,17

### A Christian psychologists view

At the turn of the 1980's, the requirements of my job necessitated moving to Watford, where I bought a home of my own. This brought an end to the counselling period, from which I had benefitted so much. However, as we were finishing, my counsellors and I discovered a helpful book by Elizabeth Moberley, a Christian psychologist, called *Homosexuality—A New Christian Ethic*. The title is misleading since it has nothing to do with proposing a new ethic, but rather a fresh pastoral approach from a biblical point of view. Her basic thesis is that homosexuality is caused by a deficit in same-sex relationships in the critical growing years of a person's life; therefore close same-sex relationships are not the problem (provided sexual intimacy is recognised as being inappropriate), on the contrary they are the solution. Her work was backed by many years of research and came as very good news, forming the basis for a positive way forward.

### The solution: intimate (non erotic) same sex friendships

Over the next couple of years, as I prayed for new friends, the Lord brought several significant men into my life who remain the best of friends to this day. None were married at that time, nor were they homosexual. We met through a rapidly growing house church which fostered a tremendous sense of expectancy in God. With great trepidation, I began to open up to these friends. They were not perturbed; they believed that no challenge was too difficult for the Lord Jesus Christ. God created a small community immediately around me. One man bought a flat next door which he shared with a second friend while a third rented a bed-sit nearby before coming to share my flat. We regularly met for prayer-breakfasts and other meals. Gone were the awful days that so many single people face, returning from meetings alone to an empty house. The openness and vulnerability of our sharing fostered the development of an exceptionally close level of fellowship between us. At this point I should stress that it is so important we do not allow same-sex relationships to be slurred with the notion that they are all intrinsically 'gay', bowing to the pressure of the pro-gay agenda in today's society; the Scriptures are clear that there **can** be deep, fulfilling non-sexual relationships between men that are pure.

As my new flat-mate began to trust me and realised I was not seeking to exploit the situation for my own satisfaction, he became aware that I was really locked-up, when it came to any expression of my feelings. My fears of losing control, in the event of same-sex attractions developing, compounded the matter. An unusually secure man in his sexuality, he decided, with the assent of the others to whom we were totally transparent and accountable, to commit himself to a deeper involvement with me. If it were not for the fact that we really **were** all seeking the will and mind of the Lord, not our own solutions, this would have been extremely risky. As he encouraged me to talk about my feelings and express my need for physical intimacy, he assured me, as often as necessary, that he was NOT going to have a homosexual relationship with me—however much I might want it! He was able to respond to my acute but child-like need for affection and reassurance, recognising the importance of building my self-respect as an adult man.

### Christ centred friendships

I knew nothing in those days about the perils of emotional dependency. Fortunately God had warned me in advance, that close friendships could only last as long as I remembered they were a gift from him; I had no rights over them. This enabled me to let go of the intimate level of friendship with my flatmate when he got married and also, when similar circumstances required, relinquish other friends who I had grown to love very deeply. These friendships were real; we had no falseness or hidden agendas. As we sought God together, we learned how to face all kinds of challenges in life.

Now, after ten years experience of ministry to the homosexual, although I know of a few instances where people have experienced something similar, it is uncommon to find this depth of involvement working well. This is either because the focus of the individuals tends to be more on their needs and problems than the Lord or because accountability is only superficial. I am not therefore suggesting that people regard my story as a pattern or method that can be easily imitated but only recommend that people should be honest and carefully follow the Lord's prompting, within a setting of accountability to others. Moreover, it should be noted that this was simply an expression of my needs; homosexual people are not all the same; their needs are as varied as the individuals themselves. It is vital that we seek the mind of the Lord to discern how to appropriately help each person who is seeking him.

**The fruit of Spirit is love... and self control (Galatians 5:22,23)**
For me, the provision of these new relationships not only demonstrated God's understanding but also his care: God can meet these human needs for nurturing contact if he has people available who will respond out of a genuine compassion and concern, prompted by his Spirit. The fact that we were totally accountable, with no secrets from others around us, committing every stage to God in prayer as a group, meant that I no longer had to carry the burden of responsibility for my own growth alone.

We also discovered that true friendships, of the kind that seek the best for one another, are the most reliable insurance against impurity in relationships. The great pull of illicit romance is the sense of mystery and clandestine adventure. When you take responsibility for your feelings and share them honestly, with vulnerability, this potentially draws out a responsible and honest reaction from others rather than an exploitative one. The importance of love and compassion is easy to talk about, but it must be demonstrated too. God will not answer our prayers in ways that let us opt out of loving one another as he commanded (John 13:34)!

**Jesus' relationships are our model**
Our view of male relationships in the modern Western world bears almost no resemblance to a scriptural model. In biblical times, indeed in other cultures around the world today, it would not have seemed at all strange for two men or two women to relate much more intimately than would be acceptable in the West, because suggestion of homosexual involvement would have been unthinkable. Such is the obsession with sex in our day and age that unless our sexual interest falls unequivocally into heterosexual or homosexual stereotypes, we are under suspicion! I have learned that we need to follow Jesus' example, our true guide in all things.

God provided this healing community situation for nearly four years. However, one by one, each of my closest friends got married. As Best Man at my flatmate's wedding, I was so grateful to God that we had never done anything to be ashamed of that could undermine either their marriage or our continued friendship.

Having reached a more secure place in my relationship with God, I hoped that my turn had come to find a wife! However, I still needed my same-sex friends and had not yet developed a secure heterosexual orientation. Several false starts in attempting to develop relationships with girls came to nothing. Well-meant 'words of prophecy' given to me proved to be no more than wishful thinking! After several near disasters, I asked God how anyone could be sure of prophetic words? He replied, "I will **never** tell you who you are to marry. But when you find a girl you love who you **want** to marry, then come and talk to me about it." Several years were still to pass before I was ready for marriage.

## Suffering is part of God's purpose too

In 1986 I moved to another church, led by Frank Gamble—a remarkable man who suffers from the excruciatingly painful, crippling condition called ankylosing spondylitis. He is one of those rare people who is always ready to encourage others, usually with great humour and a face that shines, yet never has a word of complaint to say for himself! He knows only too well what it means to suffer acute pain, yet has learned to respond graciously to those who pray for his healing and then blame him for his lack of faith when it does not happen! He was so open and receptive to me with the background of my own struggles. Frank has a great ability to recognise and encourage people in their gifts. Later on, his confidence in me and his friendship encouraged me to consider starting my own ministry.

## Comforting others with the comfort we have received (2 Corinthians 1:3,4)

At this time I joined a weekly meeting in central London run by the True Freedom Trust. This group was my first introduction to a fellowship of men and women who struggled with homosexuality but were committed to focusing on a Christ-centred way forward. There I made many friends and this proved to be an important new step for my life.

I had been attending this group for about a year, when one night a young man from California gave an amazing testimony of how God had brought him out of a life of male prostitution and to the point where he had a leadership role in a ministry called Love in Action. In concluding, he appealed to us that some should consider offering ourselves to be used by God in this kind of ministry as the need is so great and the number of people willing to be involved so few. On a subsequent occasion, I asked him to say more about his closing words. To cut a long story short, he invited me out to California to see the ministry. Within three weeks, he had arranged for me to attend a leaders' retreat and meet a wide number of people. This opportunity necessitated an immediate decision on my part to go, agreement with my employers to take the time off, and raised the question of covering costs. It was a new experience for me to see God rapidly move into action; everything fell into place with astonishing speed including provision of a generous financial gift that covered all the costs.

## A new vision and opportunity

The ten days I spent there were among the most exciting days of my life. The Love in Action ministry runs a live-in community discipleship programme for men and women committed to leaving the homosexual lifestyle. To me, this was like seeing a dream come true. The clear biblical emphasis that ran through the course reassured me. Frank and Anita Worthen welcomed me with such warmth; they are among my closest friends today. Their commitment to the Lord was clear and wonderful to see, although they have always had to struggle against extraordinary challenges. Frank Worthen, who often seems able to sense intuitively who God is calling into ministry, invited me to return to California for training.

I returned to England after these ten days eager to resign from my job at once. My church leaders advised me to wait for three months before making any decision to ensure it was in God's timing. That was hard enough! But as a director of a small publishing company, for whom I had worked for the past 11 years, I was also required to give three months notice of my decision to resign. Those six months were the longest of my life! In the meantime, however, a number of opportunities opened up for me to speak in churches and share God's compassionate response towards Christians who struggle with homosexuality. As I shared about my plans to return to the USA for training, gifts came in which covered all the costs of my extended trip. To cap it all, a friend who worked for an American airline arranged for me to fly first class to San Francisco—for just £70!

I loved every moment of the four months I spent with Love in Action, returning to England early in 1988. Before coming home, Frank Worthen encouraged me to consider starting my own ministry based at my local church, rather than move to join another ministry. I came back equipped with boxes of excellent resource materials that he had given me. When I discussed his suggestion with Frank Gamble and the eldership of my church, they agreed and gave me every encouragement to begin a locally-based work.

### Courage: faith in action

I chose the name "Courage" for this ministry because that is what it takes to face and work through something as deep-rooted as homosexuality. I wanted to avoid a name that might imply quick and easy results. Within a year God gave me an excellent team and a larger house that enabled me to begin a small residential programme modelled along the lines of Love in Action.

A year or so later, the friend who brought me to Christ asked me if I still hoped to get married. I replied casually that I had burned my boats, sinking all my resources into a community house, so I hardly expected that any woman in her right mind would give me a second thought! He admonished me for my negative attitude, reassuring me that God can do anything he wants.

### Nothing is impossible for God

Soon afterwards I happened to renew contact with Brenda Robson, whom I had known and liked for 15 years or more. She had a lively sparkle and was very attractive. However, not seeing myself as her equal, I'd never had the confidence to hope for a deeper relationship with her. Our renewed contact was prompted by a ministry referral. Over lunch, Bren asked what my future goals were. I felt I had nothing to lose, so I replied that I would like to get married. I learned soon after that She was intrigued, to say the least! She began thinking back over the past couple of years and realised that I had dropped hints of my interest in her on a number of occasions. My lack of confidence had meant that I was easily discouraged when she did not respond. Knowing my background and ministry, Bren had resisted any thought of personal involvement with me; it is hardly an attractive story! However, after my bold statement she began to pray seriously and felt that perhaps God was gently prompting her to think about it now. It did not take long before she realised that her own feelings were reciprocal. We began going out together a few weeks later.

## Courtship and marriage

Once again, events started to move quickly and in some remarkable ways. Someone kindly paid for us to visit California together, so that Bren could meet Frank and Anita and visit the ministry that had been such an inspiration for me. Bren had been a pioneer in ministry and had many years of leadership experience behind her. Her attractiveness had struck me years before this. Through our courtship, we discussed everything in detail, even my fears about the physical side of marriage. There was absolutely no question for us of any sexual experimentation before marriage. God gave Bren, especially, a deep assurance that all would be well. We became engaged in February 1991 and married the following October. God has been faithful; we have been able to enjoy a full heterosexual marriage! In caring for my wife, I have discovered that aspect of manhood which had been my unrealised potential from the beginning, though I had not been ready for it any sooner.

## God alone knows when all things are ready

Looking back I also realise that when we struggle with problems like homosexuality, it is so important for God to take us through a healing work, **before** we marry. We need to be secure in God first to be properly prepared for the full responsibilities of a marriage commitment. We should never seek marriage as the answer to our problems, nor should we presume that our spouses are somehow going to be the catalyst for our healing. Only security in the Lord can truly heal. If we marry too soon, we only burden our partners intolerably: tragically many such marriages are short-lived.

## How did my orientation change?

People often ask me how my orientation changed. This is a difficult question to answer because rather than there being a conscious change, I simply experienced more of a growing awareness of heterosexual potential. In taking hold of my God-given responsibilities in marriage my homosexual orientation has gradually been displaced. An essential part of this process, however, required a clear decision on my part to acknowledge how God has ordained these things to be and work with him, rather than allowing my feelings to be the judge of truth, which is so often the last major stumbling block for 'ex-gay' men to overcome. A key scripture for me over the years has been Paul's words in Romans 12:1:

'Therefore, I urge you, brothers, in view of God's mercy, to offer your bodies as living sacrifices, holy and pleasing to God—this is your spiritual act of worship. Do not conform any longer to the pattern of this world, but be transformed by the renewing of your mind. Then you will be able to test and approve what God's will is—his good, pleasing and perfect will.'

## Embracing God's natural order

Over twenty years or more, I had come a long way from the hardened cynical attitude I had as a teenager. God's grace at work in my life had borne much fruit, but the process is imperceptibly slow when you are going through it yourself, day by day. Gone was my perception of a legalistic and unsympathetic God and my negative attitude towards women and marriage. I could begin to appreciate the wonders of a relationship with a woman as God intended and marvel at the possibility of my reaching out to her, and see her want to make a commitment to me too. At one time the idea of physical intimacy with a woman had been repugnant to me, not because I was truly 'gay' but because emotionally I was like a child and not at all ready for marriage. However, now there is a naturalness and sense of normality for me about developing a relationship with a woman, that I had never experienced before. Through my twenties and thirties, in God's timing and with the help of others I had grown up without realising it and left behind my child-like need for male intimacy and reassurance.

Those in our society who rebel against God's word may find they become personified by their chosen path, in this case taking on the label 'gay' with all its implications and associated lifestyle. For those who seek God, however, I believe that the whole 'gay' identity and political agenda is a demonically-inspired fantasy: there are no true homosexuals. There are just lonely, insecure, disenfranchised people who have never properly grown up and are in need of same-sex role models to show them how to become what God truly meant them to be from the beginning.

### Am I totally free from homosexual temptations

Sometimes people ask me today if homosexuality is still ever a problem, only too aware that many people unfortunately seem to revert to the homosexual lifestyle. While I still notice good-looking men and feel the need for close male friendship, I do no longer believe that this is the exclusive preserve of the 'gay' community. On the contrary I think it is quite normal. Though I do notice the attractive women as well now! Without wishing to be presumptuous in any way, I can thank God for the fact that I have not been at all tempted to look back, or seek any homosexual contact. However, the scriptures are clear in warning us that, *'If you think you are standing firm, be careful that you do not fall.'* (1 Corinthians 10:12). When people go through difficult times, it is all too easy to gravitate back to something we found comforting in the past; although this has not so far been my experience in six years of marriage. However, I dare not presume that I could not fall in that way, but always hold firmly to the grace of God. At the same time, I do believe that motivation for homosexual involvement is rooted in immature childlike needs that we try to address in a sinful way. Having been provided with good same-sex friendships of a godly kind, there is little inducement to seek ungodly relationships. Satan is able to tempt us most severely when he can exploit a deep unmet need; I do not have that kind of need now. More important than that, I have an enjoyable and fulfilling marriage relationship with Bren that carries with it new challenges and responsibilities that are stimulating and fruitful.

Jesus told a parable of a merchant who sold everything he had (see Matthew 13:45,46) to buy a fine pearl of great price. This shows that when you see the very best, you lose interest in anything second-rate and never bother with something that is counterfeit. So as a fallen human being, although I can always be tempted to sinful thoughts and actions, I trust that God's work in this area of my life will have permanent effect.

Those stuck in the 'gay' lifestyle and persuaded by their 'gay' agenda often see all same-sex relationships as being homosexual in some degree or another. They would no doubt accuse me of being in denial, and tell me that I am simply sublimating my 'true' homosexual nature in non-sexual friendships. I disagree, but in the end only God is able to search the depths of a man's heart. My priority now is to prepare myself for the day when I shall meet with my Lord face to face; really it is only his opinion I need concern myself with.

### The problem of unanswered prayer

Many ask me why it is that people seem to pray and pray for years that God would take away their homosexuality, and he never seems to answer? This seemed to be my own experience for so long. However, now I believe that it is not in any sense God's unwillingness to answer; it is more our unwillingness as Christians to be committed to showing love for one another as Jesus taught us. We are too afraid of the opinions of others, and overly concerned to keep up good appearances. Instead we need to fear the Lord and be obedient to what he has taught us. If we loved one another as Jesus commanded, many people would surely flock to our churches, because their hearts long for the real thing.

### Obedience: the essence of change

The greatest lesson I have learned through the long years of struggle with homosexuality is that if growth and discovery of our potential in God is to be realised, we must relinquish our own plans for sorting out our lives and learn to live by faith in whatever ways the Lord challenges us. We all need the healing love and care of others; locked in an immature phase of my personality development, I could never have reached my potential through any method, programme or therapy alone. Over the years, the love and commitment of a number of Christian brothers and sisters helped me grow out of my neurosis about homosexuality.

To fully realise the good of all that he has for us, we must believe God—and be prepared to walk on water if Jesus requires it!

## Postscript: the walk of courage

The years of my own struggles have not been wasted. God has been working his purpose out. Now I have the experience to help others find release from bondage to homosexuality through following Christ, if they want it. The main aims of my work are twofold: first to help those who seek it, when they struggle with homosexuality and their families and friends who are also greatly affected. Secondly to help equip the Church to respond in a biblical and compassionate way to the issue.

## Conclusion

We cannot avoid the challenge of the pro-gay agenda that threatens to divide our churches today. However, I believe our emphasis must be on proclaiming and being a demonstration of the gospel that transforms lives. If we allow ourselves to get drawn into the debate, arguing over the subtle points of bogus theology, we appear to collude with the belief that Christians are homophobic and anti-gay, thereby discrediting the gospel. Many 'gay' people I have met are not at all strident or confident of the 'gay' life at all; their honest question, after years of suffering pain, is to appeal, 'show me something better!' We surely owe it to them to share the good news of Jesus Christ and make sure they can see the reality as it transforms our own hearts and lives. Ordinary people recognise the love of Christ when they see it and are drawn to him as a result. Fuelled by anger, frustration and disappointment, those who pursue deceptive doctrines end up being more interested in their own agendas than the truth, so we must leave them to God's mercy. The writer to the Hebrews warned us:

'See to it that no-one misses the grace of God and that no bitter root grows up to cause trouble and defile many.' Hebrews 12:15

# From a pastor's heart

How would you respond to a member of your congregation who tells you that he or she would love to become a Christian, but is homosexual? From his pastoral experience, **Bill Bygroves** shares his response to a young man who faced that very dilema

### Roger's letter:

*Dear Bill*

My name is Roger and I've been coming along to your church for a few weeks now. Your series on facing temptations has been a help. I am not a Christian, at least I don't think I am. I believe in God but I am fairly sure that He would not be interested in me.

You see I am a homosexual. I don't like the fact that I am, but I am. I fantasise about men, I use the late night chat lines a lot. I frequent gay bars and have had some casual homosexual encounters.

I would like to be a Christian but, to be honest, I don't think I could change. I suppose one of the things that puts me off a lot is that I have been in churches before and sometimes it is worse than being at work. 'We don't want perverts like you here'. 'Stay away from my children, weirdo'. 'You people are sick'. 'Are you an Aids carrier?'.

I'm tired of the discrimination. I want you to know that there are some really nice, genuine, intelligent, successful, caring people who frequent gay bars.

However, the purpose for my writing to you is that something you said the other Sunday really struck a chord. You quoted Woody Allen saying 'I only have one regret, that is that I wasn't born somebody else'. That's me. I don't like being me. I hate being a homosexual. I just want to be normal. I want to have a family.

I would like to be a Christian, a real Christian, but being what I am I suppose, that can never be, can it? Every time I think about myself and God I feel dirty and ashamed. Do you think you could do something in your Sunday night series (without mentioning my name) on how someone like me could be helped?

*Thank you —Roger*

**My response:**

*Dear Roger,*

Thank you for your openness, honesty and courage in sharing your pain with me. May I take this opportunity to apologise for the hurt caused to you by the attitudes of many who should have known better.

'Homophobia' is not only a problem in our society, it is a real problem in the church. However, homosexuals are just one group of hurting people in a very broken society. We *all* need to play our part in learning to understand each other better, whatever our suffering may be.

May I also say that *the* place for acceptance, understanding, tolerance, growth and love ought to be the church of the 'friend of sinners'. I would like to share one or two things which I believe will help you.

First **there is hope**, for you Roger. This hope is found in the unconditional love, the undeserved grace and the mighty transforming power of Jesus Christ the Son of God. He loves you Roger! He loves you more than anyone you have ever known and will ever know. He loves you as you are, in all of your sin and shame, in all of your fear and pain. But he loves you too much to leave you as you are! He alone has the grace to forgive you and the power to change you.

In the New Testament, in 1 Corinthians 6: 9,10, we read these words, 'Do you not know that the wicked will not inherit the kingdom of God? Do not be deceived: Neither the sexually immoral nor idolaters nor adulterers nor male prostitutes nor homosexual offenders nor thieves nor the greedy nor drunkards nor slanderers nor swindlers will inherit the kingdom of God. And that is what some of you were. But you were washed, you were sanctified, you were justified in the name of the Lord Jesus Christ and by the Spirit of our God.'

This verse gives us wonderful hope concerning our sin. It tells us that sinners, all sorts of sinners, can be washed (made clean through the forgiveness Jesus has secured for sinners like you and me on the cross), sanctified (made different, with a change of heart, a change of desires, a change of will, and a change of behaviour) and justified (with a new record in heaven and the covering of our sinfulness with the righteousness of Jesus). All this can take place through the name of Jesus and the power of his Holy Spirit.

Corinth was sin city. It was a seaman's paradise, a drunkard's haven, a den of homosexual activity and a virtuous woman's hell. Yet there were men and women in the city immersed in that culture and lifestyle who were radically and permanently changed through the name of Jesus and the irresistible power of the Holy Spirit. Roger, as I think of this verse and think of your plight it reminds me of two old Christian songs. One says:

'He breaks the power of cancelled sin,
He sets the prisoner free.
His blood can make the foulest clean,
His blood availed for me.'

The other says:

'It is no secret what God can do,
what He's done for others He'll do for you.
With arms wide open He beckons you.
It is no secret what God can do.'

Come to Christ, Roger, right now. Find a secret place, pour out all your sins, all your guilt and all your pain and shame. Ask for his forgiveness. Cry out 'God be merciful to me a sinner', from the very depths of your being. Tell him you want to change. Invite the Lord Jesus

Christ to be the Lord of your life. Ask Jesus to take complete control of your whole being by his Holy Spirit. Tell him that you are sorry for all the things that have hurt him. Tell him you are willing to do anything he says in his Word with his help and power. But please don't just say it, mean it! Because I tell you, Roger, in coming with a broken and contrite heart to Jesus there is hope!

The second thing that I want to say is that there is healing. And how is this to be found?

### Get to know your Saviour

Jesus told his disciples a story of a man who found treasure in a field and sold all he had to buy that field; also another story of a pearl merchant who found an especially precious pearl and sold his entire collection to buy the best. This shows us what Jesus is like; that he is the most wonderful friend, Saviour and Lord we could possibly have and that it is worth giving *everything* up just to follow him. He knows exactly what he is taking on when he calls us to follow him, Roger. There are no hidden surprises for him that will put him off you later on. So we can be completely secure in his love. The number one priority therefore is to get to know Jesus in a deeply personal way. You will find that reading the scriptures regularly, perhaps getting some good teaching and worship tapes also, will be a good start to a practice that will enrich your whole life. As you grow more confident in his love for you, an important step is to be baptised; this is not only an important step of obedience to take, it will also help reinforce your sense of being separate and cleansed from your old lifestyle.

### Be discriminating about the company you keep

To grow in your relationship with Jesus you will need the company of other believers, so find a good church that teaches the Bible and encourages you to belong to your new family in Christ. The company you keep will determine the way you go forward, so if you stay with your old acquaintances in the gay life, with their value system, their literature and ideology, it will be impossible to separate yourself from the old life, which will undermine your Christian commitment. It may seem strange at first to change your familiar circle of friends, but your decision to do so is the only way to leave the old lifestyle behind.

## We all need the love and support of others

You will not survive long outside the gay life unless you find a few close male friends who will love and care for you in the way God intended. So ask God to show you who can be your new friends. Having two or three friends is better than one friendship which can get rather intense anyway. We still have much to learn about the roots of homosexuality, but we do know for certain that a significant root is the lack of wholesome same-sex friendships that provide secure loving relationships and good role models so that we can learn who God intended for us to be. Unfortunately, many men *are* cautious about the whole homosexual issue, but if you approach them just as an ordinary person who appreciates them, rather than a problem person who *needs* them, people will be less threatened and more open to develop the kind of friendships you need. As you gradually feel confident to become more open with them, they in turn can help encourage you to grow and help you break unhealthy habits. This is called accountability. They will soon come to appreciate your openness and honesty and then they can share their problems so that you can pray for them. After a while, you will realise that your problems and struggles have pretty common roots and really you are not the outcast you think.

## What about the future?

There is no limit to what God can do in the life of a man who is completely surrendered to Him. If it is your heart's desire to marry one day, Roger, then what is impossible for man is entirely possible for God. However, right now, it is important to pray for God's grace to live a celibate life. Nobody finds this easy, especially if we have become accustomed to gratifying our sexual desires in ungodly ways. However, you are not alone in this; every unmarried Christian faces the same challenge. When you have built a good foundation for your Christian life and have become confident that you are ready for marriage, then it is time to seek the Lord for a wife.

## We are in a battle

Before we come to Christ, we never realise the enormity of the spiritual battle that exists. As well as a loving God who wants to restore us to a relationship with Him, there is a devil who is hell-bent on trying to defile and destroy everything that brings honour and glory to God. The devil hates people coming out of homosexuality, which has been a useful tool to destroy people down the centuries. So, if he can persuade you to believe the lie that change is impossible or that the way of Christ is too hard, you can be sure he will do all he can to undermine you. But in reality, God is infinitely greater.

Suffering is a normal part of life for Christians, Roger, but if we persevere in following Christ, the rewards are great - beyond our imagination. Once you accept Christ, you have a new identity that is neither homosexual nor heterosexual, these are just labels; you are a son of the most High God. A man of God learns to become like Jesus, whose Spirit teaches us what true and unselfish love really means. You will have your times of discouragement and failure, just as we all do, but if you press on to follow Jesus and let nothing else distract you, *God is able to work all things* together for good, including our failures and mistakes.

It is best for us to learn to live one day at a time, as Jesus said. That way, we will not be overwhelmed by the enormity of the challenges that lie ahead. Jesus has promised that *He* will complete the work He has begun in us; our role is to walk with him in simple trust and obedience, remembering that the best decision we will ever make for our lives is to follow the Lord Jesus with all of our hearts.

Finally, Roger, I want to tell you that **There Is Heaven**. The Christian life certainly is not a playground, it is a battle ground. You will have to face the world, the flesh and the devil. I wish I could tell you that you will never struggle with temptation again. But I can't. I wish I could tell you that all your wrong desires will leave you and never bother you again. But I can't. I wish I could tell you that you will meet Miss Wonderful, fall madly in love and live happily ever after. But I can't. All I can promise you is wet eyes, a broken heart and a joy that comes through walking with Jesus. But there is one thing that I want to remind you of and that is that this life with all its struggles and woes is not all.

Heaven is for real, Roger. Count on it. One day we who believe in our Lord Jesus Christ will be rid of our sinful bodies, we will be given a brand new body and will live in a brand new world. We will be free from all sin, all frustrations, all restrictions, all limitations and corruption. One thing is for certain. The moment we enter into Heaven we will know for sure that 'All the sufferings of this present time will not be worthy to be compared with the glory that will be revealed in us.' All our sufferings - physical, mental, emotional, psychological, sexual, relational and spiritual - will be over for ever.

As J. C. Ryle, an evangelical bishop wrote; 'One breath of heaven's air will be enough to extinguish all the foul smells of earth.' It may be, Roger, that you will be tempted for the rest of your life with this particular affliction. But you do not have to give in to it. In fact you can experience victory over it in the mighty name of Jesus!

**Let me close this letter by reminding you of just three things:**
❯ Sinful homosexual behaviour can be stopped and changed by the grace and power of the Lord Jesus Christ.
❯ Innate homosexual pre-dispositions can be changed with the help of our God. This comes by his Word and Spirit being applied to your life and by the total restructuring of your daily habits and lifestyle.
❯ Even your sexual orientation can be lived with and life can still be fulfilling living for Jesus until we get to heaven.

Commit yourself wholeheartedly to Jesus. Live one day at a time with your eyes fixed on Jesus only. Love him, trust him, serve him, obey him, praise him and follow him all the days of your life.

*Yours in the battle—Bill*

### About the author
**Bill Bygroves** is the Pastor of 'The Bridge Chapel' in Liverpool. It is a growing congregation in a very needy area of the city. The work began from scratch 17 years ago as a Church Plant and has under God grown considerably. Bill is married with 4 children.

# Christian organisations that can help

**Peter Glover**

Once we are clear in our underlying theology, that God *has* declared the practice of homosexuality outside his design for humankind, we immediately have to face the consequences of this understanding. To continue practising a homosexual lifestyle would be to remain in our sin. As a true Christian, we would need to turn from it. But where could we find help? And where can Christians seek to find the right kind of help on behalf of others?

While help does exist for Bible-believing Christians, it needs to be understood that great care should be taken if further hurt is not to be inflicted on an individual genuinely struggling with homosexual feelings. The same applies to any deep psychological problem. In our day evangelicalism has broadened into a neo-evangelical belief that has unfortunately adopted many distinctly non-evangelical practices. This appendix will therefore identify some Christian organisations where help can be found and will also briefly highlight some issues to be aware of in the search for the right kind of help.

Increasingly cultures and societies are 'affirming' the right to be (a practising) homosexual. Any different view is branded 'bigoted' and 'small-minded'. This should come as no surprise to us. More and more Christians have also bowed to the spirit of the age by holding increasingly subjective beliefs that find objective truth difficult to accept. Liberals (social and theological) have always, in reality, been among the most illiberal and dogmatic individuals. Consequently, those involved in a ministry to 'help' or 'change' the sexual beliefs and practices of self-confessed homosexuals (male or female) or wishing to help re-orientate their sexual tendencies, are increasingly viewed in Western society as judgemental and offensive.

What those who take this view fail to realise is that it is perfectly possible to love someone without agreeing with them. The classic example of this is a passage I have preached on many occasions (in my work with a national Christian AIDS charity): John 8:1-11. In the story of the woman taken in adultery Jesus is shown to identify the sin *and* refuse to judge the sinner, declaring: "Neither do I condemn you, go and sin no more"(NKJV). If the Son of God had no mandate to judge (NB 'judge' as in condemn and *not* critically assess) then what right do the rest of us possess? But does that mean we should always affirm and/or accept the practice or belief of another? Clearly, when it comes to truth, the Bible does not allow us to do so.

Lists of Christian organisations set up specifically to help those struggling with their sexual orientation and lifestyle are available in the UK Christian Handbook. It is not at all my purpose to list and critique all of those organisations in-depth here - that would require a magnum opus given the various backgrounds, denominational perspectives, counselling techniques, qualifications and training and (highly significant this) the biblical/psychological understanding of the counsellors. I will instead confine myself primarily to identifying a handful of specific groups *where God's Word is considered central to the process of change.* First, however, a much-needed word of caution needs to be injected. Many organisations set themselves up as 'professional' and some would call themselves evangelical. The fact that they may hold the labels 'Christian', 'evangelical' and 'professional' does not mean that our own spiritual discernment, and that of our own church, should not be brought to bear on the techniques used and the psychological approach adopted when we involve outside agencies in treating 'psychological problems' like homosexual belief and practice.

Too many churches today are inclined to take the view that such problems are not a matter for those in the church. Consequently, individuals in great spiritual need are too often handed over for non-Christian help. Others take the view that 'professional' Christians are the only ones who can help and again pass on responsibility outside the local church. We do this far too easily. What people suffering with psychological problems need all too often is love, care and best of all the loving and caring offered by a biblically-grounded local church and Christians—as well as professional—Christian help. Christian belief and practice especially in many evangelical churches has today become heavily tainted with psychological worldly wisdom. As one writer puts it, 'Psychology deals with the very same areas of concern already dealt with in Scripture.'[1] Even the philosopher Carl Jung recognised that psychoanalysis far from belonging to the world of science (the popular-science view) more appropriately belonged to the sphere of religion.

We need then to beware the philosophies of men no less in helping those who find the passions of the flesh (heterosexual or homosexual) a difficult battleground. Paul's words are a stark reminder to us in all areas of thinking, belief and personal behaviour: 'Beware lest anyone cheat you through philosophy and empty deceit, according to the tradition of men, according to the basic principles of the world, and not according to Christ' (Colossians 2:8 NKJV).

Where can we usefully turn for outside (the local church), biblically-based help? Fortunately, the few evangelical groups who specialise in the issue of homosexuality do have contact with a larger number of individual and appropriate biblical counsellors etc. to whom they are able to refer us. In this way the problems of the proximity of a group can be overcome. It is only possible to provide details of the groups themselves and not the individuals to whom that group may refer. The groups are not listed in any particular order.

**Note:**

1  Martin and Deidre Bobgan, *Psychoheresy: The Psychological Seduction of Christianity*, Eastgate, 1987, p11

**THE COURAGE TRUST**
**PO Box 338, Watford, Hertfordshire**
**WD1 4BQ**
☎ 0181 420 1066  **Fax:** 0181 421 1692
**Founder & Director**: Jeremy Marks
**Founded**: 1988
**Affiliated to**:
The Association of Christian Counsellors,
Exodus International Europe,
The Evangelical Alliance.

Courage's literature makes it explicitly clear
that it is *not* a counselling organisation. The
introductory leaflet sums up its provision:
*'Courage offers support to those who wish
to follow Christ, yet need encouragement
and understanding because of the inner
conflict between their homosexual
orientation (or related issues) and Christian
faith. We also seek to make help available
for families, friends and anyone else in close
contact with 'gay' people.'*

This above is reflected in the provision of
the following services:

▶ **Discipleship Group Meetings** –
Courage facilitates local church group
fellowship in the home church designed to
complement rather than replace other
church group meetings.
▶ **Befriending** - again no counselling *per se*
is offered.
▶ **Seminars** (for churches and conferences)
▶ **Literature** - for a variety of readership

including those struggling with
homosexuality, friends, families, pastors.
▶ **Newsletters** (quarterly) containing
relevant news and teaching information.

Excerpts from their material include:
*'...one of the principal origins of a same-sex
orientation is a strong need for affirmation
and unconditional love.'*

*'It takes time for the Holy Spirit to clear
away the rubble of our past experiences
and rebuild our lives upon a godly
foundation; it is not realistic to expect
instant deliverance.'*

*'We believe the Bible forbids all sexual
relationships (including homosexual) outside
a lifelong commitment of marriage between
a man and a woman.'*

**Observations**
The Courage Trust is a Christian evangelical
agency which appears to have been built
on a solidly Scriptural foundation. I am
impressed with the literature of the
organisation which is amongst the most
extensive I have come across. Much of the
literature, generally in helpful small
leaflet/booklet form, is written by others
outside the organisation itself and is freely
available. Courage even sent me materials
relating to other groups around the
country and even abroad that it itself
recommends.

**Jeremy Marks** has come from a homosexual background himself and has the insight which goes with personal experience and knowledge. Two things jumped out at me in reading Courage's introductory leaflet: 1. the challenge of the Cross (ie the gospel message and scriptural teachings) which provided the initial barrier that prevented Jeremy uncritically sinking into the homosexual lifestyle. 2. the provision of open and demonstrative relationships in the church (love for the person without agreeing with a wrong lifestyle) which drew him to Jesus. These two things helpfully provide a rich insight into a proper approach to the whole issue before us.

Courage's reading and teaching materials list is extensive and includes many names that crop up in the lists of other Christian agencies. They are also involved in co-sponsoring Christian conferences from time to time.

Above all else what comes through all of Courage's materials is a compassion for others borne out of personal experience. It is additionally beneficial for Christians to be aware that though some material speculates on the issues surrounding homosexuality (are we born with homosexual genes? etc.) the biblical basis of every aspect of Courage's work is unequivocal. Courage's starting point as regards why men and women become homosexual is 'that homosexuality is **learned** behaviour, not inborn.' (excerpt

from 'Is Homosexuality Inborn or Learned?')

Courage's literature also contains a hint that more formal counselling may well become a feature of their work at some stage. I think any church or Christian would be in good hands with the Watford-based Courage Trust. But do bear in mind that Courage is *not* a counselling organisation per se.

**TRUE FREEDOM TRUST**
**PO Box 3, Upton, Wirral,**
**Merseyside L49 6NY.**
☎ 0151 653 0773  **Fax:** 0151 653 7036

**Founders**: Martin Hallett (Director) and Canon L. Roy Barker
**Founded**: 1972
**Affiliated to**:
Association of Christian Counsellors,
Exodus International Europe,
The Evangelical Alliance.

True Freedom Trust (TFT) offers support for those struggling with homosexuality and for their families. The very first principle of TFT's basis confirms that 'Our teaching and counselling work seeks to be in accordance with Scriptural principles.' The second makes it clear that 'homosexual genital conduct falls short of God's plan for His creation.' In contrast to Courage Trust, counselling is very much at the heart of TFT's work.

## TFT offers:

▶ **Counselling** - within a 'regular contracted counselling relationship'. If TFT is unable to take referrals they do undertake to refer people to other qualified counsellors and therapists outside TFT.

▶ **Help & Advice** - pastoral support for relatives, spouses and friends.

▶ **Pastoral Support Workers** - men and women trained to meet with clients to decide with them the most appropriate type of support or therapy.

▶ **Befrienders** - carefully selected and offered to people near their own homes.

▶ **Barnabas Groups** - support groups where Christians can meet for encouragement, to learn and to pray. The group is designed to complement other church groups—not replace them.

▶ **Correspondence** - a letter and telephone ministry for those unable to visit personally.

▶ **Teaching** - speakers available for Christian Unions, Theological Colleges, Churches etc.

A membership scheme for supporters is also in operation. TFT produces a newsletter, literature, cassettes and videos. The reading list includes material from Martin Hallett and from a number of other writers generic to Christian groups in this ministry. Martin Hallett states, *'An essential part of our ministry involves sharing with churches and fellowships what we have learned and are learning about the complex issues of sexuality and especially homosexuality.'*

## Observations

While True Freedom Trust does work with Courage Trust and other Christian organisations, it has been established longer than most. It specifically does provide counselling help and has one or two other unique aspects to its work. As with Jeremy Marks, **Martin Hallett** came from a homosexual background. For all those in doubt about biblical counselling, preferring instead psychological techniques, Martin reveals that *'My lifestyle changed quite dramatically, and I became convinced* **through Scripture,** *that homosexual sex was wrong. I was given a strong determination to turn away from sexual temptation.'* (excerpt from *'With God Anything Is Possible'*).

There is also a very helpful leaflet entitled, *The Bible, Sexuality and Homosexuality* by Martin Hallett. TFT's ministry is meaningfully biblically-based and would be a useful partner for most churches seeking appropriate guidance and counselling.

## U-TURN ANGLIA TRUST
**PO Box 138, Ipswich, IP4 4RY**
☎ (Counselling) 01473 785129
☎ (Family Support) 01440 820594
**Founder & Director**: George A. Harvey
**Founded**: 1988
**Affiliated to**:
Association of Christian Counsellors.

U-Turn Anglia offers counselling to those who are struggling with homosexuality and support to the families of those so struggling. Director George Harvey's involvement in this ministry had a very different beginning from that of Jeremy Marks or Martin Hallett. It was the trauma of his son's suicide—a son he did not know to be a practising homosexual. It transformed his judgemental attitude into one of understanding and wanting to help those struggling with the homosexual problems. Mr Harvey is the minister of a local church.

An interesting aspect of U-Turn's ministry is the goal of helping individuals to seek '..freedom through change from their sexual *orientation*.' Many Christians, of course, believe that orientation is okay and that it is practice which presents the problem.

The material is clearly biblical and U-Turn is well-placed as a local Christian presence in East Anglia.

**G.H.O.B.E MINISTRIES**
**(God's Healing Of Broken Emotions)**
**PO Box 5511, Inverness,**
**Scotland IV1 2ZH**
☎ No telephone number
**Directors**: Dolina Geddes & Joyce MacLeod.

No further details of organisation from their introductory leaflet but included in the

Courage Trust mailing and therefore recommended by them.

GHOBE offers ' a professional and Christian response to those whose lives have been affected by sexual and emotional brokenness' (taken from GHOBE Ministries leaflet).

GHOBE provides professional counselling. As well as homosexuality further material available helps with other areas of 'sexual brokeness' (sic) such as sexual abuse, emotional abuse, transvestism and sexual addiction.

**EXODUS INTERNATIONAL EUROPE**
**PO Box 407, Watford,**
**England WD1 5DU**
☎ +44 (181) 420 1066  **Fax:** +44 (181) 421 1692
**Founded**: Netherlands 1982
**Affiliated to**:
Exodus International North America.

Exodus International Europe (EIE) was founded by its American counterpart as the result of a conference in the Netherlands in 1982. EIE is made up of member organisations from a number of European countries including: Denmark, France, Britain, The Netherlands and Switzerland. Addresses and contact points for each of these European member agents are contained in the organisation's leaflets. Courage Trust and True Freedom Trust are both UK member agencies.

Exodus International unions of Christian counselling services, seeking to help people out of homosexual lifestyles, now exist for USA and Canada, Latin America and the South Pacific regions of the world. Addresses are as follows-

For agencies in USA & Canada:
**Exodus International North America**
PO Box 2121, San Rafael CA 94912 USA
☎ + 1-415-454 1017

For agencies in Latin America:
**Exodus International Latinamerica**
PO Box 26202, Colorado Springs CO 80936 USA
☎ no telephone number.
**Fax**: + 1-719-637 3481

For agencies in South Pacific:
**Exodus International South Pacific**
PO Box 308, Fortitude Valley, QLD 4006 Australia
☎ +61-7-371 4705

**NB.** All of the above are non-denominational agencies specialising in helping those wishing to come out of a homosexual lifestyle in accordance with the gospel and the teaching of the Bible. THIS LIST IS NOT DEFINITIVE. There are, of course, many other counselling organisations who do not specialise but who also deal with many issues including homosexuality. Specialist counsellors may well be denominationally-based or in local churches or church groups.

For further guidance in finding the right help you can contact:

**ASSOCIATION OF BIBLICAL COUNSELLORS**
Townsend Chambers, Amherst Hill, Sevenoaks,
Kent TN13 2EL
☎ 01732 460625 **Fax**: 01732 742733

**Other useful contacts**

HIV/AIDS in Britain is an illness which is closely linked to the homosexual community. Certainly most infections in this country are among the homosexual community. However, the global picture is very different. Worldwide 75% of all existing infection was heterosexually transmitted and 90% of all new infection, with three years to go to the new millennium, is among heterosexuals. Our churches are certainly going to see an increase of HIV positive infected people in attendance in coming years. This itself may provide a motivating factor (ie believing one has a death sentence) in driving individuals to seek God.

The agencies already mentioned may be among those to whom churches and Christians may turn for help. Often, however, practical love in the form of help during the sickness may be an additional benefit. There are unfortunately very few agencies to which one may refer someone ill or dying with HIV or AIDS. Many are either from homosexual self-help agencies such as the well-known Terrence Higgins Trust. Others refer to themselves as 'Gay' Christian help agencies. These include CARA, based at the London Lighthouse, in central London, and a number of similar groups.

As evangelicals, the very last help and support individuals struggling with a new found Christian faith, (as well as the debilitating illnesses that go with AIDS), need is the help of 'gay Christians' who will simply further confuse them. There are, however, one or two Christian HIV/AIDS agencies to whom one can turn. These include the one for whom I myself have worked for a number of years:

**ACET (AIDS Care Education & Training)**
**PO Box 3693,**
**London SW15 2BQ**
☎ 0181 780 0455 **Fax**: 0181 780 0450
**Founder:** Dr Patrick Dixon
**Chief Executive**: Patricia Macaulay
**Founded**: 1988
**Affiliated to**: The Evangelical Alliance

National & International Christian agency providing care in the home for those ill and dying with HIV/AIDS. ACET operates care services in many urban centres of England and Scotland.

ACET provides home care provision using local church volunteers around the country. It also works overseas in Uganda, Thailand and a number of other countries. While not pro-actively evangelical, ACET's home care work and its sexual health education in schools *is* based on Christian teaching and principles. At the time of writing most of ACET's staff and home visitors would describe themselves as evangelical.

**MILDMAY HOSPITAL**
(formerly Mildmay Mission Hospital)
**Hackney Road, Shoreditch**
**London E2 7NA**
☎ 0171 739 2331   **Fax**: 0171 729 5361
**Director**: Ruth Sims
**Founded**: 1985

Mildmay is a specialist AIDS hospital in London's East End. It has excellent hospital/hospice facilities and has a high-profile through its pioneering work in London. In recent years Mildmay has also partnered a hospice initiative in Uganda.

Mildmay, like ACET, has Christians roots and maintains its Christian ethos. As a Christian social work it could not be said to be pro-actively evangelical (indeed, in common with ACET, local Council contract regulations would preclude it from being so). Many of the staff, senior and otherwise, would describe themselves as evangelical.

**FOOTNOTE**

It is quite clear that we are living in an age when biblical Christianity is becoming viewed as an anachronism. It is only a short step to viewing it as unacceptable in practice and legislating against evangelical Christian groups or belief. The issue of homosexuality has forced itself on to the political agenda. It is almost impossible to air publicly views that do not affirm homosexuality as an acceptable lifestyle. To do so almost always attracts the accusation of homophobia and brings verbal abuse. That is why we are seeing so many parts of the church (not least the Anglican hierarchy) giving way and giving tacit, if not pro-active, approval promoting homosexuality as a socially acceptable lifestyle.

In this hostile climate those who hold to biblical views on this subject will find the heat being increasingly turned up. The words 'bigots' 'small-minded' and 'un-Christian' will be the words ringing in our ears over this and other issues - unless, in common with many of our brothers and sisters in the faith, we adopt the ways of the world and submit to the spirit of the age. Those who are currently working in this area - the very groups and individuals I have mentioned above - and those churches and Christians who will seek to help people out of both homosexual and heterosexual lifestyles, are going to need our love, support and our prayers.

For people wishing to come out of homosexual lifestyles as well as for those helping them in this course, contemporary society will only make the process harder. Over this issue of homosexuality, in particular, all Bible-believing Christians in the years ahead are going to have to 'contend earnestly for the faith which was once for all entrusted to the saints' (Jude 3). The organisations listed here and Bible-believing churches and Christians are going to need the sustaining Word of life in the difficult days ahead.

**About the author**

**Peter Glover** is Director and co-founder of the Christian Research Network (CRN) a Christian educational organisation which researches beliefs and practices in the contemporary church. He is co-author and editor of the best-selling *The Signs & Wonders Movement—Exposed*. He has led an Anglican Evangelical church-plant for six years while working as a freelance Public Relations Consultant for a number of Christian and other charities.

Peter is married to Sara and lives in South London.

# Book reviews

## Reviewed by Alan Gibson

These recently published books will be of interest. This is by no means a complete bibliography of a subject which has become a growth area in contemporary publishing.

### Straight and Narrow?

Thomas E Schmidt, IVP, 1995, 240 pp, £8.99

Sub-titled 'Compassion and clarity in the homosexual debate', this is a British edition of an American work and can now be commended as the best evangelical treatment of the subject. Schmidt's writing is earthed in his experience of pastoral relationships with individuals who '..seek love with members of their own sex' and he is aware of them looking over his shoulder as he writes. As well as handling the Bible in a truly masterly way, his work is also remarkably informative on medical and behavioural aspects of the issue and, as one reviewer says, 'This is a book which deploys accessible scholarship with prophetic power'.

Schmidt is crystal clear about his approach to the Bible. He begins with the primacy and finality of the Bible's authority. 'I choose the words **primacy** and **finality** carefully. They mean that Scripture is the first place to look and the last place of appeal for guidance' [p 18]. 'While tradition, reason, experience and Scripture are all involved in the process of interpretation, only Scripture has the place of revelation among these conversation partners. The Bible, therefore, is not an equal partner but the teacher in the conversation. We cannot overrule its message without great risk of inconsistency and arbitrariness, which are evident in many revisionist proposals concerning homosexuality' [p 161].

Furthermore, Schmidt reiterates what is a basic tenet of evangelical interpretation. He insists that 'the primary task of Bible study is to seek the intended meaning of its authors'. While he acknowledges that we all bring a certain amount of baggage to complicate the task of reading, it is also true that 'the original writers meant something by their words' [p 19]. This principle is not sustained in many of those who, claiming to be evangelicals, yet challenge what has been for centuries the accepted morality of Bible-believing Christians.

Four well-packed chapters are devoted to a detailed consideration of the biblical material, with careful exegesis and close scrutiny of alternative interpretations. Schmidt begins by insisting that *'a biblical view of sexuality does not depend on a list of prohibited activities but on the pervasiveness and reasonableness of an affirmed activity: heterosexual marriage'* [p 39].

He works from the positive affirmations of the creation narrative and constructs a case for the exclusivity of heterosexual monogamy. Introducing the concept of 'responsibility' into the discussion of personal sexual conduct may not be popular today but Schmidt rightly shows that it is a necessary consequence of the biblical concept of community. However frightening, his conclusion of chapter 3 is incontrovertible, *'There is ultimately no argument against pedophilia or any departure from heterosexual monogamy if Scripture is taught by individual experience'* [pp 62-63].

A full chapter is given to considering of Romans 1:26-27 in its context. The background and Greek terms used by the apostle Paul are carefully scrutinised and set alongside the thesis proposed by Boswell, and later Countryman, that Paul regards homosexuality as impure but not sinful. Schmidt uses a striking play on words to express his own conclusion. *'Homosexual behaviour is "revolting" not*

*because heterosexuals find it so - they have their own dirt to deal with (2:22) - but because it epitomizes in sexual terms the revolt against God. It is sinful because it violates the plan of God, present from creation, for the union of male and female in marriage'* [p 85].

Chapter 6 is given to a painful and yet realistic survey of the health issues associated with homosexual conduct and it is not pleasant reading, Here he depends heavily on secular and respected survey research, both from sociological and medical sources, concluding that *'If there were no specific biblical principles to guide sexual behaviour, these considerations alone would constitute a compelling argument against homosexual practice'* [p 130]. Richard Wilkins, General Secretary of the Association of Christian Teachers, uses this chapter to challenge school teachers to include such hard evidence in their health education lessons that those engaging in homosexual practices are harming themselves. To withold important health information in order to conform to our society's pagan reverence for the sex urge, Wilkins insists, would be irresponsible to the children and would constitute a highly personal censoring of these proven facts [ACT Now, Spring 1997, pp 22-23].

The book closes with Schmidt's own modest advice to evangelicals concerned to *'find avenues of ministry consistent with* our moral stance', by which he means periodically to make it clear that the church represents forgiveness and power to change, as well as redemptive discipline in all cases of sexual disobedience, including homosexual acts. There is solid advice here about the challenge of cross-cultural communication to those as far removed from most evangelicals as you will find on a mission trip up the Amazon. And, by the way, don't fail to read his Postscript, *'A letter to a friend'*.

**Homosexuality and the Bible**
Mark Bonnington & Bob Fyall,
Grove, 1996, 28 pp, £1.95

This booklet, the first in the new Grove Biblical Series, offers a clear presentation of the 'traditional' over against the 'revisionist' approach. It is all the more interesting that the two authors are both tutors at Cranmer Hall, St John's College Durham, where they are colleagues of Michael Vasey, whose controversial book, *Strangers and Friends,* they directly oppose throughout.

It is offered as a contribution to the current debate in the Church of England and in wider evangelicalism. Chapter 1, Being Biblical, recognises the role of hermeneutics but insists that, *'the biblical texts are not infinitely flexible'.* [p 5] and relates homosexuality to the major themes of Scripture: creation, incarnation and final redemption, further linking all these to the theme of *the body.*

Being Human, chapter 2, properly begins with a consideration of creation principles in Genesis 1 & 2, tracing the divine image to male and female realities in humanity. *'They are not social constructs, subject to the mores of changing societies'* [p 8]. Turning to the NT they conclude that only the marriage relationship reflects the actual nature of God himself and of humans who are his image. *'For the revisionist case to stand, there would need to be demonstrated a similar positive affirmation of homosexuality as a controlling model for God's relationship with the universe and humankind'* [ p 10].

Chapter 3, Being Holy, gives a good outline of the Leviticus material, answering the revisionists' abuse of these texts and concluding that *'The acceptance of sinful people by God is not a licence to continue in ungodliness but a call to holiness'* [p 14]. Vasey is again challenged in their treatment of Being Open, chapter 4, where they deny that the genuine church is open to homosexual conduct. *'The task of Christian openness is to keep the church in the world and to keep the world out of the church'* [p 17]

The key New Testament texts are explained in chapter 5, Being Honest, and the three revisionist interpretative strategies are exposed, i.e. to marginalize the texts, to 'fuzzify' the texts and to distance the texts from the contemporary debate. They quote Schmidt with approval that *'homosexual acts are quite literally 'revolting', in that they represent a revolt against the created order'* [p 20]. It is honesty to Scripture which compels them to conclude that *'all forms of homosexual behaviour are ... to be regarded as sinful'* [p 23].

The final chapter, Being Practical, addresses some current questions about caring for and reaching out to those engaged in homosexual activity. They warn against the interpretative approach which *'can reduce the authority of the text to the self-interested power- play of the interpreter'* [p 27]. Altogether this booklet is a brief but valuable statement of a consistently evangelical approach.

**The Christian Faith and Homosexuality**
David F Wright, Rutherford House, revised ed. 1997, 33 pp, £1.95

David Wright is Senior Lecturer in Ecclesiastical History at New College, Edinburgh and elsewhere he has written several scholarly articles on the biblical and theological aspects of the subject. This small booklet is probably the best short treatment of the issues for the non-specialist from a genuinely evangelical perspective.

Wright is concerned to set the debate in the current social context so he asks why there is such sexual confusion in most Western societies. He recognises that Christian convictions are under pressure yet he is anxious to avoid unnecessary prejudice against his biblical arguments. For example, he rightly shows that predominantly heterosexual populations have produced plenty of child-abuse and sexually transmitted disease. *'Yet rampant sexual licence of itself does not discredit all expressions of heterosexuality.'* Consequently he suggests we avoid the use of the term 'sodomy' since the behaviour of the Sodomites had more to it than homosexuality—it was also gang-rape and a grave breach of the sacred duty of hospitality [p 7].

The biblical material is handled competently, even to the extent of tracing the word *arsenokoites* [males who lie with males], which Paul himself seems to have coined, back to the Greek translation of Leviticus 20:13. At the very least this proves that *'this part of the Levitical Holiness Code was not viewed as superseded by the early Christians'* [p 16]. By using the parallel of Jesus' treatment of the adulterous wife in John 8, Wright shows that *'although the Israelite penalty for male homosexuality has lapsed, the practice itself remains unacceptable to God'* [p 17]. In a longer passage he demonstrates the futility of suggesting that the love of God can safely be used to condone what Scripture clearly identifies as sin.

The Bible nowhere recognises the right of every innate disposition to express itself in outward behaviour and Wright uses this fact to answer those who claim the biblical material is today irrelevant, because the writers knew nothing of the distinction between homosexual orientation and homosexual acts. His concluding section quotes a Christian who can gratefully say with Peter, *'his divine power has given us everything we need for life and godliness'* (1 Peter 1:3).

Although written primarily to address the current discussions within the Church of Scotland this booklet will be valued more widely for its unambiguous approach and the accessibility of its material.

### Strangers and Friends

Michael Vasey, Hodder & Stoughton, 1995, 276 pp, £9.99

The author is Tutor in Liturgy at St John's College with Cranmer Hall at the University of Durham, preparing candidates for Anglican ordination. Three features of his approach to the Bible characterise his book.

Firstly, Vasey strongly urges that the work of hermeneutics cannot be done in a vacuum. Consequently, he claims that traditional evangelicals have been unable to read Scripture without being blinded by their own prejudices, formed not by Scripture itself but by *'concepts of homosexuality framed in the nineteenth century and often wedded to a cultural allegiance to the scientific or economic assumptions of modern society'* [p 72]. The book cries with the personal pain of the individuals who struggle with problems their peers do not understand and who are even driven to suicide by the rejection of an uncaring church. As a result of this emphasis on the homosexual subject's sympathies he finds in Scripture meaning which is entirely unwarranted, such as sexual implications in the friendship of David and Jonathan while Jesus' intimacy with the Apostle John is said to sound *'a natural echo with the love gay people share'* [p 123].

Secondly, Vasey writes seven substantial chapters before he comes to consider *'What does the Bible say?'*. The longest of these chapters is entitled *'Culture, Creation and Grace'* and its opening sentence sets the tone. *'If bodily and sexual acts have to be understood in the light of the social structures and symbolic systems that give them meaning, then Christians cannot simply read off rules of sexual behaviour either from the text of scripture or from the 'facts' of human biology'* [p 48]. In a major critique of contemporary culture Vasey traces all human desire back to the desire for God found in Psalm 63. By insisting that all desire has a physical aspect he seeks to broaden all human attraction, including same-sex desire, seeing this too as being biblically valid.

Thirdly, two chapters of *Strangers and Friends* are devoted to a consideration of the history of same-sex love. Graeco-Roman literature is scoured for innocent, indeed laudable, examples of such relationships and an example from the monastic period, St Aelred of Rievaulx, is said to reflect '*a Christian culture at ease with sexual feeling and imagery*' in which there was '*widespread liturgical celebration of permanent non-monastic same-sex unions*' [p 84]. The legislation against sodomy in the Tudor period was largely political in purpose and Vasey links this with the Nazi concentration camps of the Second World War as '*a horrifying testimony to the continuing vitality of the cultural myths created in the late medieval period*' [p 88]. The nineteenth century comes in for particular treatment as Vasey believes that the era of science brought in categories which described and 'medicalised' homosexuals as a distinct personality type, the actual term 'homosexual' only being coined as late as 1869. His interpretation of history is aimed to disarm Bible interpreters of their own cultural prejudices and to predispose them towards the needs of those now portrayed as the innocent victims of an unnecessarily hostile church.

The treatment this book gives to particular texts is covered elsewhere in the present work and need not be repeated here [cf. chapter 6].

In summary, we must reluctantly conclude that Vasey does not hold an orthodox view of the **sufficiency** of Scripture, '*truth is not to be found in scripture alone*' [p 52], nor of the **harmony** of Scripture, as he quotes Colossians 2:16-7 to claim that the NT abrogates the Sabbath commandment [p 53], nor of the **perspicuity** of Scripture, since he proposes that the Bible consists of '*... sixty-six extremely heterogeneous, strange and difficult books. As an exercise in divine communication God's use of scripture is almost as bizarre as his... entrusting a saving message to a corrupt and fallible church*' [p 12].

This book amply demonstrates how the writer's own cultural assumptions have pre-determined his approach to the hermeneutical task. He accepts a sanitised and unrealistic picture of homo-sexuality. He filters out of his reckoning biblical principles and sociological realities which are unwelcome to his position. His horizon ignores whatever contradicts it. Alan Storkey's review is right in insisting that the prohibition involved in the biblical norm of marriage '*is different from adultery and premarital sex ... for its focus is the man-woman nature of marital union.*'

This significant book shows that the

focus of evangelical divergence has today moved from issues of the authority of Scripture to debate over its interpretation. The moral repercussions of these differences are now obvious.

**Not for Turning**
Tony Green, Brenda Harrison & Jeremy Innes, privately published, 1996, 96 x A4 pp, £5

The three authors combine to present this 'Enquiry into the ex-gay movement', which is their term for the ministries seeking to help Christians desiring to be free from homosexuality. Tony says that he had *'an evangelical conversion experience at the age of 14'*, Brenda describes herself as *'a lesbian feminist post-evangelical Christian'*, while Jeremy *'recognises his conservative-evangelical upbringing as the most significant factor which inhibited his coming-out process'*. They welcome the *'number of significant evangelical contributions to the debate in recent times which argue for a positive assessment of lesbian and gay sexuality'*. The Foreword is written by Michael Vasey.

Their approach to the Bible is that we all *'bring assumptions and life experiences through which we filter what we find there'*. They hold that those taking a traditional approach should be careful to lay aside their homophobia. *'An honest attempt at understanding the Bible's*

*teaching can only take place within the context of its cultural limitations and we cannot find all the answers to our questions about sexuality in the Bible'*.

They make no attempt at all, either to specify or to expound particular verses. Instead they warn, *'Evangelicals committed to the authority of the Bible should ... allow the broader themes of grace, justice and relatedness to inform their perceptions of the Bible's witness to human sexuality'*.

The book is useful in helping the general reader to understand the concern of serious people struggling to integrate their sexuality and their Christian profession. Its primary purpose is to highlight the problems facing evangelical organisations seeking to minister to such people. In so doing it also illustrates the impossible dilemma of those who profess both a confidence in the authority of the Bible and a confidence in the validity of their own sexual preferences.

**The Way Forward?**
Editor, Tim Bradshaw, Hodder & Stoughton, 1997, 229 pages, £8.99

Twelve authors, mostly Anglican academic theologians, here present essays in response to the St Andrew's Day Statement, published in November 1995. The context of that Statement was the conflict in the Church of England over calls for 'homosexual marriage' to be given legitimacy and the ordination of practising homosexuals.

That the Statement has drawn out these very different reactions and enabled the writers to engage over the meaning of its theology, exegesis and applications will make it useful beyond its immediate Anglican origin. It goes without saying that the contributions are uneven in approach, one being from a psychiatrist (Dr Tom M Brown) and another from a counsellor (Martin Hallett).

The specialist theologians, too, vary enormously in their presuppositions. Not all the contributors are evangelicals. For example, Dr Jeffrey John makes no bones about asserting that, ' ... we know that this fundamental assumption on Paul's part is false. His belief that homosexual acts are committed by naturally heterosexual people is untrue' p 50. As we would expect, Professor Anthony Thistleton's essay [the longest] majors on strictly hermeneutical issues and warns the revisionists that, 'It is ... misleading to appeal to theories of social construction to disengage Romans 1 from today on the ground of "hermeneutics"' p 186. On the other hand, Dr Elizabeth Stuart, writing as a Roman Catholic lesbian who lectures in theology at Swansea, submits 'that in the modern lesbian and gay liberation movement we see the seismic activity of the Spirit unfolding something of the revelation promised by Christ ...' p 84.

From what he has written elsewhere we are not surprised to read Michael Vasey contradicting Bishop Wallace Benn's assertion that 'the acceptance of 'homosexual practice' should be treated (along with the uniqueness of Christ) as a defining point for authentic evangelical Christianity' p 63. It is left to the editor, Dr Tim Bradshaw, to respond to these essays in a concluding chapter which includes a neat summary of Divine grace amid human perplexity, 'God provides the fig leaf for his fallen creatures, as in confusion they scrabble about in the dust after losing their place of confident well-being' p 225.

In itself this paperback will clarify but not resolve the growing anxiety posed by homosexual issues in the Church of England. Perhaps its chief value will be to indicate to conservative readers the level of sophistication employed by those arguing for the liberalisation of sexual policies in the traditional churches. In the face of such philosophical, philological and exegetical scrutiny it will not be easy for church lawyers to frame legislation which will succeed as an adequate disciplinary instrument. Even if they have a mind to.

**Reviewed by Alan Gibson**